BLOOD, SWEAT AND CHEERS:
GREAT FOOTBALL RIVALRIES OF THE
BIG TEN

TODD MISHLER

TRAILS BOOKS
A Division of Big Earth Publishing
Madison, WI

Library of Congress Control Number: 2007932370
ISBN 13: 978-1-931599-95-5

Cover Photos: top, center, and bottom center, University of Iowa Athletics;
bottom left, Purdue Sports; bottom right, Northwestern University Athletics.

Editor: Mark Knickelbine
Design: Colin Harrington

Printed in the United States of America

12 11 10 09 08 07   6 5 4 3 2 1

Trails Books, a division of Big Earth Publishing
923 Williamson Street • Madison, WI 53703
(800) 258-5830 • www.trailsbooks.com

DEDICATION

To my late father, John, who passed away in February 2007 but long ago fostered my love for sports, especially the great game of football. And to Tim, who was always ready to play catch, dive into snow banks, or serve as a tackling dummy for his older brother.

TABLE OF CONTENTS

ACKNOWLEDGMENTS

To Mark Knickelbine and Eva Šolcová, and all of the staff members at Trails Books/Prairie Oak Press and Big Earth Publishing who've given me this wonderful opportunity and helped, often behind the scenes, to see that the job got done.

To the media relations/sports information staffs at the Big Ten Conference schools for their cooperation, especially for providing me with media guides, information, and photographs.

To the library personnel throughout the Midwest who dug up information, provided names of prospective interview sources, and got the ball rolling early in the process.

And to the former players, coaches, and fans who took the time to reminisce and share their perspectives about Big Ten football; without their input, this book project wouldn't have been possible.

POMP AND CIRCUMSTANCE:
THE BIG TEN TAKES A BACK SEAT TO NOBODY

Venerable broadcaster Keith Jackson described college football like no other announcer.

He understood the nuances of the game well, but more importantly the originator of such wonderful phrases as "Whoa, Nellie" put his finger on the sport's pulse. When asked in 2005 what its soul was, he simply said "tradition."

No other game at any level captures the pageantry, passion, and nostalgia of athletic competition better, and that's what sets it apart, especially from its big brother, the National Football League. And a big part of that tradition is the classic rivalry, the intercollegiate blood-feud passed from generation to generation.

The closest thing to the passionate rivalries of college football to be found in the NFL is when the Green Bay Packers and Chicago Bears, who have met 172 times since 1921, tangle in their storied series. In more recent times, say the last 45 years, such donnybrooks as Dallas vs. Washington or Kansas City against Oakland evoke many of the same emotional highs.

However, none of those professional showdowns galvanize a region or state like the annual feuds that pit Auburn and Alabama in the Iron Bowl or Texas and Oklahoma during the Texas State Fair in Dallas.

These are but two of the nastier battles for bragging rights that repeat themselves at locales in almost every state in the union. And the great thing about them is that the legendary players, coaches, and games are only part of the story.

Division I-AA foes Lafayette and Lehigh have played an amazing 142 times. Princeton, which tangled with Rutgers in the first collegiate contest only four years after the Civil War ended, has played Yale 129 times since 1876. Meanwhile, Yale and Harvard have danced on 123 occasions.

Nothing compares with the electricity, the adrenaline, and, yes, the romance. And much of what makes college football so grand is what happens before the

1

whistle blows and after the clock stops: the myriad festival-like, off-field customs and rituals that occur at universities across the country.

No campus can claim a richer gridiron tradition than Notre Dame: the Golden Dome, Touchdown Jesus, the famous fight song, the leprechaun mascot, and the list of legendary football heroes that includes the Four Horsemen, Knute Rockne, George Gipp, Frank Leahy, Paul Hornung, and Ara Parseghian.

And don't forget the Friday night pep rallies before every home game that feature the Irish band marching through campus en route to the Joyce Center, where a packed house listens to coaches' and players' speeches.

That kind of camaraderie and allegiance for one's alma mater is played out every week. And whether you find these celebrations venerable or hokey, most true fans must admit that they are pieces of the wonderfully woven tapestry that help make college football so colorful.

A quick list of a few such rites of college fandom will suffice to suggest the whole giddy, surreal picture:

- Oklahoma introduced its Conestoga covered wagon, the Sooner Schooner, in 1964. White ponies named Sooner and Boomer pull the contraption, which resembles the wagons used by the pioneers to settle the state.

- However, Oklahoma supporters weren't kicking up their heels in the 1985 Orange Bowl. The Sooners received a 15-yard unsportsmanlike conduct penalty when the schooner raced onto the field after an apparent OU field goal. The kick was called off because of a penalty, and the happy driver hadn't been given permission to take his fourth-quarter jaunt. The subsequent three-point attempt was blocked and helped change the game's momentum as Washington claimed a 28-17 victory.

- One of college football's most endearing settings is the Army-Navy game, which was first played in 1890 and has taken place in Philadelphia 80 times. Traditions surrounding the game include cadets from both academies marching into the stadium, members of the winning branch throwing their hats into the air, and cadets doing push-ups after their team scores.

- Texas A&M could be considered the Notre Dame of the South, and its most well-known ritual concerns the 12th man, which started in

1922 when E. King Gill, who was a basketball player, was told to suit up because coach Dana X. Bible's gridders had suffered several injuries. Gill grabbed a sidelined player's uniform but never entered the Aggies' 22-14 victory against Centre College in the Dixie Classic. The A&M students stand throughout the game to show their support and are thus known collectively as the 12th man.

Other activities include a midnight yell practice that often draws 20,000 noisy backers to Kyle Field the night before home games, and the bonfire that students ignite on the eve of their team's annual grudge match against Texas.

• Florida State showcases one of the more intimidating pregame displays as Osceola, a student wearing a Native American costume, rides an Appaloosa horse named Renegade onto the field and stabs a flaming spear into the turf at the 50-yard line. This tradition at Doak Campbell Stadium began in 1978. Foes, no doubt irritated by the performance, have tried to prevent the rider from reaching his destination several times, but to no avail.

• Another equestrian tradition involves Southern Cal's Traveler. Bob Jani, USC's director of special events, saw Richard Saukko riding a white horse during the Tournament of Roses parade in 1961. He and another student talked Saukko into becoming the Trojans' mascot, riding his Arabian-Tennessee Walker around the Los Angeles Coliseum during home games. Saukko also periodically wore Charlton Heston's helmet from the Academy Award-winning movie "Ben Hur."

• One of the most difficult places to play is Clemson, South Carolina, where Memorial Stadium is known as Death Valley. Coach Lonnie McMillan of tiny Presbyterian College tagged it with that nickname after one of his team's many beatings in one of the hottest and rowdiest stadiums in the country. Tigers players rub Howard's Rock before running down the hill to the field. The rock, which sits atop a hill overlooking the stadium, was given to coach Frank Howard in 1966 after a Clemson alum reportedly found it in California's Death Valley.

• And don't forget about Ralphie, the 1,300-pound buffalo who thunders around Folsom Field in Boulder, Colorado.

These and dozens of other wonderful tributes show how college football has captured the nation's collective imagination, and the Big Ten Conference's combination of history, big-time players and coaches, tradition, success, and/or atmosphere are second to none.

Some of the game's most recognizable names showed off their skills throughout the Midwest, including Harold "Red" Grange of Illinois (also nicknamed "the Galloping Ghost"), Ralph "Moon" Baker and Otto Graham of Northwestern, Elroy "Crazy Legs" Hirsch of Wisconsin and Michigan, Howard "Hopalong" Cassady of Ohio State, Alan "the Horse" Ameche of Wisconsin, Charles "Bubba" Smith of Michigan State, and Jack "the Assassin" Tatum of Ohio State.

And don't forget Hall of Fame coaches such as Fielding "Hurry Up" Yost, Fritz Crisler and Glenn "Bo" Schembechler of Michigan, Bob "the Little Dutchman" Zuppke of Illinois, Hugh "Duffy" Daugherty and Clarence "Biggie" Munn of Michigan State, Forest Evashevski and Hayden Fry of Iowa, Wayne "Woody" Hayes of Ohio State, and Jack Mollenkopf of Purdue.

Through the 2005 season, Big Ten schools had won or shared 28 NCAA Division I-A national championships (31 counting Penn State), and fans have celebrated—and imbibed—with the best of them.

Attendance figures attest to that: the Big Ten is rivaled only by the Southeastern Conference in setting national attendance records since league average figures were first tabulated in 1978. Michigan or Ohio State topped the country every year from 1949 through 2005, except for the time Tennessee held that honor in 1997.

Illinois was one of the first schools to conduct homecoming festivities, starting the tradition in Champaign from October 14 to 16, 1910, during the team's 7-0 campaign in which the Illini outscored their opponents, 89-0.

The land hasn't seen any better marching bands than those hailing from Columbus, Ohio, and Madison, Wisconsin.

Trumpet player John Brungart stood at the dot in the "i" at the OSU band's first performance in 1933, and Script Ohio was born. A major change occurred in 1937: A sousaphone player named Glen Johnson switched places in the formation. Now, every year the 225-member band selects a fourth- or fifth-year sousaphone player to do the honors. Hayes and Bob Hope are among the dignitaries who've occasionally filled that role.

And if tailgating were not enough, Badgers faithful take things to another level with help from their musical brethren. The contingent is best known for its "Fifth Quarter" postgame performances that last nearly an hour and entertain upwards of 40,000 rabid fans near Camp Randall Stadium. Those who stick around enjoy renditions of such classics as "You've Said It All," the band's take on the old Budweiser jingle, the "Beer Barrel Polka," and "Dance Little Bird," or as most call it, the Chicken Dance.

Although understandably biased, former players and longtime followers say that Big Ten teams and fans are special, a breed apart in many ways.

Scott Nelson, who patrolled the Wisconsin secondary as a safety from 1990 to 1993 and helped lift the Badgers from basement dwellers to the school's first Rose Bowl trophy, still recalls the impression playing in the Big Ten left on him.

"Some of these places are hallowed ground, especially when you consider some of the biggest names from the NFL or the business world played in the Big Ten," Nelson said. "Playing at Wisconsin was a way to showcase how good you were because you were always going up against the best players in the country. Every week somebody was on national TV.

"Michigan was an awesome venue, but it wasn't as imposing for a visiting player as, say, Kinnick Stadium, where the fans are only three feet behind your bench," Nelson added in reference to the home of the Hawkeyes in Iowa City. "All of these places have tradition, but I would say that Iowa and Ohio State were the most challenging. But then you take Camp Randall, and the student section was going so nuts that you were nervous being in your own stadium. Part of the experience about playing at Wisconsin was driving down Regent Street and seeing all of the people throwing balls around and firing up their grills. We didn't have what they do now with the 'jump' thing. I've been at games and you can just see opposing players' heads snap around because they don't know what's going on. Those kinds of things are what made playing here and in the Big Ten so neat."

Charlie Sampson lives in Indiana but is a longtime Hawkeyes fan who started following the league in the early 1950s.

"That's when Wisconsin, Iowa, and Minnesota were like Ohio State and Michigan are now," Sampson said. "They were tough, and those battles were important and determined who won the title depending on who knocked off the others. TV was emerging in the '50s, and the Big Ten was the preeminent conference. The teams had tremendous fan bases and filled up monstrous stadiums like at Michigan and Ohio State. And Big Ten teams dominated the Rose Bowl."

That they did, winning nine of 10 contests during the decade. The only loss was Wisconsin's 7-0 setback to USC after the 1952 season. Five league schools claimed victories, including two apiece from Iowa, Ohio State, and Michigan State.

Bud Sueppel, another diehard Iowa fan, has attended home and away games for nearly 50 years, so he knows his way around.

"I'd rank Wisconsin as the No. 1 place to go, Ohio State second, and Penn State third," said Sueppel, whose floral business in Iowa City has decorated the Rose Bowl and many other environs around the country for special occasions.

"There's nothing like a Big Ten game in Madison. It's the same way I feel about Iowa City. I throw big tailgate parties and more Wisconsin fans show up, and they treat us the same way. As for Minnesota, it's hard to tailgate up there, but it'll be a lot better when they get a new stadium. College football wasn't meant to be played inside domes."

Paul Janus, an Edgerton, Wisconsin, native who helped resurrect the Northwestern program as an offensive lineman in the mid-1990s, cherished his time in the trenches.

"Oh my God, to have watched games on TV and then being a part of it every week was awesome," Janus said. "The Big Ten wasn't always on top, but it was the classic blood, sweat, and tears. I mean, the traditions like Michigan's Big House and the Horseshoe at Ohio State. You grew up on the Big Ten, when you'd smell the leaves every fall. Going to Illinois and all the people tailgating and booing or cheering you would get the juices flowing. I lived in Carolina while playing in the NFL, so I got a taste of Florida State and Clemson, and those schools. It was wine, cheese, and crackers. It just wasn't the same as having brats and beer. That's when Saturdays in October or November are special."

Joey Eloms didn't enjoy much success as a four-year letterman at Indiana from 1994 to 1997, but he said his experience meant everything. "It was phenomenal to play in the Big Ten," Eloms said. "You don't find more tradition than playing at Ann Arbor, Madison, or Happy Valley. Even as a freshman or sophomore, you realized what hallowed ground some of those places were. Big Ten football is the closest thing to Friday nights under the lights."

No truer statement has been made. And colleges have carried on those customs longer than the high school and professional ranks. But which rivalry inspires the most passion, offers the best games, features the most unusual customs, and creates the most bad blood?

Little did officials from Illinois, Chicago, Michigan, Wisconsin, Purdue, and Northwestern realize that their schools were creating an athletic dynasty when they gathered in the Windy City in 1895. They agreed to form the Intercollegiate Conference of Faculty Representatives, which became known as the Western Athletic Conference and ultimately the Big Ten.

The students and teams picked up interesting hardware along the way, symbols to spice up the games and add even more incentive to contests against their geographical neighbors, or enemies, the preferred description in most parts. Fifteen of the 66 so-called trophy games, contests that in many cases are treated like the Super Bowl, involve Big Ten schools.

Almost every trophy has unusual twists and turns behind it, complete with fraternity and dormitory hijinks and pranks. Politicians have often grabbed onto these symbols, especially in election years. Governors started four cups and mayors three.

Teams and players in the Midwest inherited an unquestioned work ethic from their European ancestors, so they're used to a harsh, rugged style of play and unfazed by Mother Nature's extremes. As a result, their emotions are as raw as the weather, especially when they're fighting for pieces of metal and wood that look more like they should be sitting at a garage sale.

Not only do most of the decades-old donnybrooks involve bragging rights and trophies, but many are filled with bowl game and national championship ramifications.

Yet even in the rare instance when the Buckeyes and Wolverines—who don't even strap it up for a trophy—aren't contending for the league crown, their bitter, intense meetings create memories that last for another 365 days and beyond. That goes for many other skirmishes among Big Ten combatants.

Indiana hasn't been at the top of the league standings since 1967, when it shared the title and participated in the school's first and only Rose Bowl on January 1, 1968. Nevertheless, the Hoosiers continue to show up every Saturday and display as much school pride as anybody else, even though that's all they've had to show for their efforts during many long seasons.

One such example is the Hoosiers' series against Michigan State, a grudge match after which the winner gains the Old Brass Spittoon, a prized possession they've wrestled over since 1950. The battered spittoon comes from a Michigan trading post and is more than 100 years old. The junior and senior classes, and student council at Michigan State initiated the award.

The intrigue and gamesmanship boost the interest and add to the excitement, especially for the squad that hasn't tasted victory in a while. After Indiana's 37-28 triumph at East Lansing, Michigan, in 2001, the Hoosiers refused to leave the field until Michigan State surrendered the spittoon, a situation that had rankled Indiana ever since the visitors failed to bring it to Bloomington for their 1991 tussle. Bill Mallory summoned an assistant to retrieve the treasured item, but the Hoosiers found out that their spoils had been mistakenly shipped to Iowa instead.

The Spartans hold a 38-12-1 lead in trophy games and are 38-15-2 overall in the series that began in 1922.

Indiana also has faced Southeastern Conference foe Kentucky for the Bourbon Barrel, which started in 1967 but was retired in '99, even though coaches and players still recognize the tradition. Indiana leads, 18-17-1.

Meanwhile, Michigan State fills one of Notre Dame's Big Ten slots, a series that the Irish lead, 44-25-1, after their stunning win in 2006, a 40-37 decision in which the Spartans were ahead by 16 points until the final 8:18.

Regardless of those misfortunes, the Spartans trail, 30-23-1, since 1949, the year that the teams started squaring off for the Megaphone Trophy, sponsored by the Detroit alumni clubs of both universities. It is printed half blue with a gold ND monogram and half white with a green MSU.

The Irish also have re-established a fierce series against Michigan the past 30 years, which has become one of the early highlights every fall even though they don't play for a trophy. The Wolverines hold a 19-14-1 advantage.

Down the road a spell, Purdue and Illinois hook up to see which team gets to haul the Purdue Cannon home, a task that's been carried out most seasons since 1943.

The real artillery piece dates back to a covert operation in 1905, when students took the weapon to Champaign, Illinois, to help celebrate an expected victory. But by the time Purdue rendered its 29-0 verdict, Illini fans had confiscated the cannon, which had been hidden in a nearby culvert. They moved it to a farmhouse in tiny Milford, situated about 45 minutes northeast and near the Indiana state line. It survived a fire among other things, before being proposed to serve as a trophy.

Illinois leads, 41-37-6, but since the cannon took center stage Purdue has had the upper hand by a 29-26-2 margin.

Penn State boasts a magnificent gridiron history and tradition, and it got into the trophy business upon joining the Big Ten in 1993.

The Nittany Lions and Minnesota created the Governor's Victory Bell to mark Penn State's first league contest and the teams' initial meeting. Penn State leads, 6-4. Meanwhile, Joe Paterno's program faces Michigan State for the Land Grant Trophy, which commemorates the universities' place in history as the first two land grant schools in the nation. They were established 10 days apart in 1855. The Nittany Lions lead, 11-3.

Penn State has won 768 games from the program's inception in 1892, the last 363 victories having occurred since Paterno took over in 1966. Nearly 90 first-team all-America players have made Beaver Stadium their home, including Dave Robinson, Jack Ham, John Cappelletti, and Larry Johnson.

Still, although the Nittany Lions have fit in well academically and competitively with the Big Ten, they don't warrant a chapter among the league's best rivalries simply because they're in their infancy by comparison with other intraconference rivalries. There's a long history there, no doubt: Penn State first hooked up against the Buckeyes in 1912, the Spartans in 1914, and Iowa in 1930, and initially tangled with Illinois, Wisconsin, and Purdue during the early 1950s. It's just that the number of encounters is lacking; they've played MSU on 24 occasions and Ohio State 22 times, the most against any Big Ten schools. Penn

State's great rivalries are truly with non-conference teams, such as its 59 games against West Virginia, its 68-game series with Syracuse, and its venerable 96 games against home state rival Pittsburgh.

And then there's the inter-conference, intra-state showdown between Iowa and Big 12 member Iowa State, whose tug-of-war for the Cy-Hawk Trophy has been waged since the schools renewed their rivalry and made it an annual affair in 1977. The Hawkeyes hold a 36-18 advantage.

So, even though the aforementioned series are special in their own right, they lack the longevity that the 10 greatest rivalries involving Big Ten schools have attained. The schools in each of these showdowns have met at least 78 times (the number of contests between Notre Dame and Purdue). Minnesota-Wisconsin, Indiana-Purdue, Michigan-Ohio State, Illinois-Northwestern, and Iowa-Minnesota have played 100 or more times, and Michigan-Michigan State joined the illustrious century club in the 2007 season.

Sure, school spirit has been tarnished in recent years by incidents of trash-talking and in-your-face bravado, some of which have erupted into ugly mob scenes like the Miami-Florida International affair in October 2006. Then, too, the plethora of post-season bowl games now gives teams more opportunities for high-profile victories, and the trophy rivalries have lost their importance as a result. Sadly, the value, significance, and even awareness of these classic rivalries have diminished, as have so many things in our era of technology-induced attention and memory deficits.

Nevertheless, the traditions live on, if only as reminders of what the games used to be, and should be, about. There's no better example than the lovable antics of Ohio State fans Orlas King and Jerry Marlowe.

King died at age 62 in October 2004, but people around Columbus won't forget the gentleman nicknamed the "Neutron Man." The native of New Albany owned a restaurant and sports bar in Newark called The End Zone, but he was better known for his gyrating moves in the stands, which started in 1973. Ohio State marching band director Jon Woods introduced the "Neutron Dance" song in 1984, giving King a name to go with the craze.

Marlowe made his reputation by crashing Ohio State-Michigan games disguised as everything from a pizza delivery man, nun, concessionaire, parachutist, referee, cheerleader, scoutmaster, band director, and TV crew member. The Dover native and 1961 graduate of the school's college of pharmacy "bought" his way into the contest without a ticket nearly 20 times, although he always made handsome donations to the school that more than compensated for any embarrassment to stadium security.

These are just two of the small but entertaining pieces that add to November's rivalry week, which culminates with some of the year's biggest and best games and usually features four of the Big Ten's most storied series. Rivalry games determine the final standings, of course, but they often also dictate who qualifies for what bowl games and cause friction in many households.

And today's landscape would be much different had a seemingly innocent incident involving a Little Brown Jug not occurred.

TROPHY GAMES STARTED WITH A JUG:
MINNESOTA vs.
MICHIGAN

Tommy Roberts and Henry Hatch didn't score a touchdown or make a tackle. They didn't even wear the proper costumes that Halloween Day in 1903 as their team, Michigan, visited Minnesota. The Gophers' Oscar Munson had a similar, apparently undistinguished day.

But the three equipment managers played integral roles in what would eventually become one of the most unusual series of events in college football history.

The game brought together two unbeaten teams. Fielding Yost's "point-a-minute" Michigan squad entered with a 7-0 record, while the Gophers had won their first 10 contests.

Willie Heston scored first, to give Michigan a 6-0 first-half advantage at Northrop Field in Minneapolis. Egil Boeckman finally registered the equalizer with two minutes left in the fourth quarter; the 20,000 fans, some of whom had been perched in nearby trees and atop telephone poles, exuberantly rushed onto the field, forcing officials to call the game.

Given Michigan's reputation as an unstoppable juggernaut, it's no wonder a tie created such a hullabaloo in the Minnesota stands. The Wolverines had ripped off 27 shutouts in the course of winning 29 straight games, including the 1901 Rose Bowl. Minnesota's performance seemed all the more amazing as time went by: Michigan went on to win its next 26 outings to stretch its unbeaten string to 56 games.

The rough-and-tumble action created enough excitement, but what happened before and after the heated battle would become the stuff of legend. As the story goes, Coach Yost was unsure whether Minnesota would provide adequate drinking water for his team, so he summoned Roberts to run an errand: go buy something to hold the Wolverines' own water. Roberts paid 30 cents for a gray, five-gallon jug at a local variety store. Because of Michigan's haste to avoid the pandemonium and catch its train back to Ann Arbor, the jug was left near the Wolverines' bench after the game.

Munson found the receptacle the next morning and delivered it to Minnesota athletic director L.J. Cooke's office. He decided to keep the jug and painted "Michigan Jug: Captured by Oscar, October 31, 1903" on it, along with the score of the game, to commemorate the unexpected deadlock. Yost eventually wrote the Minnesota athletic department a letter, requesting the return of his hardware. Cooke's defiant response was along the lines of "If you want it, you'll have to come up and win it."

Oscar Munson, who stumbled on the famous Jug

Michigan accomplished just that with a 15-6 decision the next time they played, but that was not until 1909. The Gophers then suggested that the jug become a trophy. Michigan agreed, the jug was painted brown and M's for both schools were added, together with the scores of the two contests. In the process, they created the famous Little Brown Jug, a full 16 years before the invention of such trophies as the Illibuck (Illinois-Ohio State), the Old Oaken Bucket (Indiana-Purdue), and the Beer Barrel (Kentucky-Tennessee).

Meanwhile, the Wolverines defended the jug at home in 1910, but because Michigan had withdrawn from the Big Ten, the trophy didn't go up for grabs again until 1919. That's when Arnie Oss and underdog Minnesota posted a 24-7 win at Ferry Field in Ann Arbor. The Gophers, naturally, wanted the piece of crockery back, but no one at Michigan could find it until Hatch tracked it down.

"I'm the one who left the jug on the field [in 1903]," Hatch said years later. "When Minnesota made such a fuss about getting it back, I started looking around and found it behind a clump of shrubbery near the gym. I shined it up and shipped it to Doc Cooke."

The case of the mysterious jug didn't end there. The trophy disappeared from the building that housed the Michigan athletic department in 1930. A replica of the prized piece was displayed in the Wolverines' trophy case until four years later, at which time an Ann Arbor gas station attendant found the jug sitting behind a clump of bushes. The original's authenticity was confirmed because of a flaw unlikely to be duplicated.

"I never expected anything like this to come of it," said Munson, then 74 years old, on the 50th anniversary of the jug's initial abandonment in Minnesota. "A little can sure go a long way, can't it?"

Needless to say, officials on both sides have protected the Little Brown Jug much better ever since.

The Wolverines and Gophers met every year from 1929 until 1998, when the league's new unbalanced schedule forced them to skip two seasons before playing again in 2001. Minnesota reeled off nine consecutive wins from 1934 to 1942, cutting Michigan's lead to 14-11-1. However, since the Gophers' 20-15 win in 1967, the Wolverines have pulled away to a huge advantage, registering strings of 9, 8, and 16 consecutive victories to take a 68-24-3 overall lead in the series.

Although the Wolverines have dominated the past four decades, they continue to fight to keep the trophy at home. Jim Brandstatter and the Wolverines whipped Minnesota by 26 points twice and by 28 points a third time from 1969 to 1971, but the former offensive lineman said that the fear of losing the jug—not to mention the wrath of coach Bo Schembechler—helped motivate him and his teammates against the Gophers.

"They always put the jug out in the locker room, so we were always walking past it and it was a constant reminder," said Brandstatter, a longtime broadcaster in Detroit. "They told us about how Fielding Yost had left it up there and that it was part of college football history, so it did have an impact. We viewed it as a game that we had to win in helping us earn the Big Ten championship.

"Michigan has kept the jug a lot more, so Minnesota definitely wants it," Brandstatter added. "You never realize what that little piece of crockery means until it's gone. It's like something in your house and somebody comes in and takes it. You may never use it, but you're not happy until you get it back."

Ex-Gophers know how special the series and jug are because they've tasted victory so rarely during the past 40 years. Darrell Thompson, the Gophers' all-time touchdown leader with 43, played for Green Bay and Chicago in the NFL from 1990-1995. He was a true freshman in 1986 when Minnesota ended a 1-17 run against Michigan with a shocking 20-17 defeat of the No. 2 Wolverines at Michigan Stadium. Place-kicker Chip Lohmiller's heart-stopping 30-yard field goal with no time showing on the clock cemented the upset.

"Michigan had such a storied history, but I was 19 and just having fun," said Thompson, now a Minnesota broadcaster. "And I'm worn out and in pain from running and returning kickoffs, and other guys are crying and everything. Minnesota hadn't beaten them in so long. Michigan had Jim Harbaugh and other guys who went on to the NFL. We had a few talented guys like Rickey Foggie and Chip Lohmiller, but we were a solid defensive team with a bunch of tough guys, guys who beat the crap out of me during the week. I mean, people met us at the airport when we got back and were talking about it all week."

Tom Luckemeyer played in what may have been Minnesota's biggest upset against Michigan, the Gophers' 16-0 stunner in 1977. Marion Barber ran for a score, and Paul Rogind kicked three field goals for the Gophers. Minnesota's triumph ended Michigan's streak of 112 straight games without being shut out, a run that started midway through the 1967 season.

Assistant Coach Butch Nash hugs the jug after a Gopher win.

Luckemeyer said that he, like many Gophers, welcomed a history lesson to reinforce the significance of playing against Michigan. "The Little Brown Jug had been well documented, but assistant coach [George] Butch Nash, who had played under Bernie Bierman back in the late '30s, got up and gave a speech," Luckemeyer said. "He ended up being with the program for more than half a century, so that really fired us up. It was big because Bo [Schembechler] had never been shut out at Michigan before, and they were ranked No. 1."

Bill Dufek starred as a strong-side offensive tackle on that Michigan team, so he knows what it feels like to have the jug taken away unexpectedly.

"The Jug wasn't that big of a deal unless they had it and we needed to get it back," said Dufek, whose brother, Don Jr., and father, Don Sr., also earned all-Big Ten honors for the Wolverines. "Minnesota didn't have a top-notch team at the time but pulled off a victory or two. But they always had big teams that would hit you."

Michigan has won an astounding 34 of the last 37 meetings, but the Wolverines have had to rally several times to persevere, including back-to-back three-point thrillers in 2003 and 2004.

Greg Hudson, then the Gophers' defensive coordinator who had enjoyed plenty of big games as a player at Notre Dame, said the experience was hard to describe but that nothing can match the feeling.

"There's a mystique that goes with college football, and there's a mystique that goes with playing certain opponents," Hudson said. "It's something you can't explain. It's only something you feel as a player and a coach. There's just something different when you play against a program with that tradition. It's the excitement of it."

Minnesota entered the 2004 contest ranked No. 13, while Michigan held the 14th spot in the polls. The Gophers were looking to reach the top 10 for the first time in 42 years, but Michigan ruined that bid when quarterback Chad Henne hit tight end Tyler Ecker for a 31-yard score with 1:57 left to finish off the 27-24 verdict. That capped a six-play, 87-yard march that lasted only 1:07.

Michael Hart set Michigan freshman marks with 35 carries and 160 yards rushing, adding 53 yards receiving on six catches. Henne, also a freshman, completed 33-of-49 passes for 328 yards. Laurence Maroney, also a first-year player, gained 145 yards rushing for Minnesota.

It was yet another frustrating afternoon for the Gophers, but that wasn't always the case in this series. The schools were among the best in the country during the first 60 years of the twentieth century as Michigan won national championships in 1932, 1933, 1947, and 1948, while Minnesota earned titles in 1936, 1940, 1941, and 1960.

The Gophers compiled a 4-3-1 mark in those key matchups, and seven of the eight games were decided by 13 points or less, including a scoreless tie in '33.

Pete Elliott, who later coached at Illinois, played quarterback and corner-back for the Wolverines from 1945 to 1948, a span that saw Michigan sweep the Gophers. Elliot says it was one of the best rivalries in the land.

"It was almost equal to or bigger than Ohio State," said Elliott, who served as director of the Pro Football Hall of Fame for 17 years after leaving the coaching profession. "[Herbert] 'Fritz' Crisler coached at Michigan and had coached at Minnesota [1930–31]. Tom Harmon and Michigan always had trouble with Minnesota, and it was 'the' game back then."

Jack Mulvena, a Delaware prep standout, initially didn't know where half of the Big Ten schools were located and understood the significance of the Little Brown Jug even less. But he and other teammates from distant states learned in a hurry.

"I didn't know anything about jugs, axes, and that other stuff," said Mulvena, who lettered at offensive guard and linebacker for the Gophers from 1959 to 1961, when they finished 2-1 against Michigan. "We were the lunch-pail guys that the coaches counted on to be steady and stabilize things because we hadn't had fathers who played there or whatever. But we certainly wanted to win, and the trophy meant more in those days because you only had one bowl game to go to and it gave you bragging rights over another state."

David Lothner was his teammate those last two seasons and finished 3-0 versus the Wolverines from 1960 to 1962, but he knew how imposing it was to play against such a storied program, especially at Michigan Stadium, where he and the Gophers won 10-0 and 17-0.

"Michigan is certainly the longest standing rivalry and we were fortunate to win all three times," Lothner said. "Michigan Stadium was always an intimidating place to play and had well over 80,000 seats at the time. They have that long corridor that leads to the field and the visitors have to walk the farthest, and just when you start coming out of the tunnel and get ready, the Michigan players would rush out and get on the field first and make you go around them."

MORE SERIES HIGHLIGHTS

1920: Frank Steketee scored the game's only points on a 30-yard field goal in the second quarter to give Michigan a victory.

1932: The teams squared off with the national championship on the line as the temperature started at 6 degrees above zero and fell to 6-below by game's end. The host Gophers were held to negative yardage and never crossed midfield.

Minnesota fumbled at its 30, and Harry Newman booted a field goal in the second period for a 3-0 Michigan win.

1934: Francis "Pug" Lund, despite two broken ribs, helped Minnesota erase a scoreless halftime tie as the Gophers tallied 34 points after the break for a 34-0 triumph.

1938–41: Crisler's Wolverines lost only five games during this four-year span, but four of the defeats came against Minnesota, including two by 7-6 scores. Crisler coached at Michigan for 10 seasons, with a 71-16-3 record. His 1947 team finished 10-0 after a 49-0 defeat of Southern Califor-

Minnesota's legendary Bronko Nagurski

nia in the Rose Bowl. Tom Harmon never scored against the Gophers during his final three seasons, 1938 to 1940.

1940: The Wolverines took 15 train cars of fans to this contest. Both teams entered 5-0, with Michigan ranked third and Minnesota second in the polls. The Gophers pulled out a 7-6 decision on Bruce Smith's 80-yard touchdown run. All-American Harmon scored the Wolverines' only touchdown but missed the extra point in a quagmire. Michigan marched down to the Minnesota goal line one other time, but Harmon slipped and was stopped short.

1951: Paul Giel churned for 104 yards rushing for Minnesota, but Michigan doubled up the Gophers, 54-27, which included Lowell Perry's 75-yard score on a punt return with more than 83,000 attending.

1953: In the 50th anniversary of the Little Brown Jug, Giel rushed for 112 yards on 35 carries and two scores for Minnesota. A fine passer, too, Giel completed 13-of-18 for 169 yards and a touchdown, averaged 59 yards on four punts, and intercepted two passes as the Gophers whipped the fifth-ranked Wolverines, 22-0. Jim Soltau had 102 yards receiving for host Minnesota.

1957: Michigan reclaimed the Jug, throttling the Gophers 24-7 in Minneapolis. The visitors were up, 24-0, at the half, with a rushing advantage of 276 yards to 47 and 14-1 in first downs. Quarterback Jim Van Pelt tossed one touchdown pass, and kicked a field goal and three extra points. Minnesota slipped to 2-2 in the conference race with its second straight setback, while Michigan improved to 2-1 in Big Ten action.

1958: Minnesota had lost its first four games and trailed Michigan, 20-7, early in the second half. Gophers quarterback Jim Reese scored, but the visitors missed the point after, leaving their deficit at seven, 20-13. Minnesota got the ball back at its 38 with three minutes remaining and moved to a fourth-and-goal call from the Wolverines' 2 with time for just one more play. Reese kept it on the option and scored to make it 20-19. Minnesota coach Murray Warmath called for a two-point conversion attempt, and under intense pressure, Reese threw a pass that went off the fingertips of 6' 4" Dick Johnson in the back of the end zone, allowing Michigan to escape.

1959: Darrell Harper's 83-yard punt return for a score was crucial during the Wolverines' 14-6 decision in Minneapolis.

1961: Quarterback Sandy Stephens broke loose for 160 yards on the ground as Minnesota edged the Wolverines, 23-20, with nearly 64,000 fans watching.

1967: George Hoey set a Michigan standard with 140 yards in punt returns, but the Gophers prevailed, 20-15.

1969: Wayne King recorded 25 tackles for Minnesota, and he had to do a lot of chasing in the Gophers' 35-9 setback in Minneapolis. The Gophers fell to 0-5-1 for the season but rebounded to win their final four contests.

1970: Fritz Seyferth rushed for four touchdowns to lead fifth-ranked Michigan's 39-13 romp in the Wolverines' homecoming contest in front of 83,496 fans.

1972: Ed Shuttlesworth reached the end zone four times on the ground as the No. 5 Wolverines whitewashed the Gophers 42-0. David Brown also returned an interception 68 yards for a score.

1974: Rob Lytle carried 20 times for 158 yards, and Gordon Bell chipped in 134 yards on 17 attempts as third-ranked Michigan roared by a 49-0 margin.

1976: Lytle gained 129 yards, and quarterback Rick Leach scooted for 114 more during Michigan's easy 45-0 win, its third shutout in the teams' last five meetings.

1979: No. 11 Michigan got the upper hand, 31-21, although the Gophers' signal caller, Mark Carlson, completed 27-of-51 attempts for 339 yards. Glenn Bourquin hauled in 12 catches for 123 yards for the Gophers. The Wolverines' vaunted running game featured 194 yards from Butch Woolfolk and 179 from Lawrence Reid in front of 104,677 at The Big House.

1982: Lawrence Ricks rushed for 184 yards, and Kerry Smith added 113 during Michigan's 52-14 triumph, the most points the winner had scored since the Wolverines hung 54 on the Gophers in 1951.

Minnesota's Rickey Foggie

1984: Michigan handled the Gophers easily, 31-7, despite Rickey Foggie's 101 yards running at Michigan Stadium.

1985: Gilvanni Johnson's 84-yard punt return TD was one of the highlights in eighth-ranked Michigan's 48-7 win.

1987: Darrell Thompson rumbled 98 yards for a score, the second-longest running TD in Minnesota history behind O.C. Nelson's 100-yard burst against Carleton in 1898. Thompson finished with 201 yards, but the Gophers still lost, 30-20 at home.

1988: Mike Gillette established a team mark with five field goals in lifting No. 14

Michigan to a 22-7 victory. Mark Messner, the Wolverines' career leader in sacks, recorded four tackles for loss, another category in which he tops the charts.

1989: Thompson again shattered the century mark with 125 yards, but No. 3 Michigan won a 49-15 laugher in front of only 35,013 fans at the Metrodome as Michael Taylor passed for four touchdowns and Greg McMurtry caught three of them.

1992: Marquel Fleetwood connected with John Lewis on a 94-yard scoring pass for Minnesota, however, the third-ranked Wolverines went the distance. Registering the highest scoring output in the series, they handed the Gophers a 63-13 shellacking that featured Elvis Grbac's four scoring tosses. Derrick Alexander caught four TDs.

1994: Michigan scored 28 points in the second half to win, 38-22. Todd Collins passed for 352 yards and three scores for the victors. The 23-point underdog Gophers had led 15-10 at the break. Tim Schade was 30-of-50 for 394 yards passing for Minnesota, while Aaron Osterman set a team record with 13 receptions, accumulating 187 yards.

1995: Brian Griese accounted for four aerial touchdowns in Michigan's 52-17 decision. William Carr spearheaded the defense with six tackles for loss, including three sacks for the No. 9 Wolverines.

1998: Michigan, ranked No. 22, gained a lackluster 15-10 decision for its 12th consecutive triumph in the rivalry. Tai Streets hauled in six receptions for 192 yards and one touchdown for Michigan.

2002: John Navarre passed for 225 yards and two scores, and B.J. Askew ran for 126 yards on only 11 tries to propel No. 13 Michigan to a 41-24 win, breaking away from a 17-all tie in the second half.

2003: No. 20 Michigan allowed 424 yards rushing but rallied from a 28-7 fourth-quarter hole to win, 38-35. Navarre passed for 356 yards and Chris Perry added 122 receiving and 85 rushing as the Wolverines mounted their largest comeback in school history. Garrett Rivas' 33-yard field goal provided the difference with 47 seconds left. Marion Barber gained 197 yards rushing and Asad Abdul-Khaliq added 106 in a losing effort for the No. 17 hosts.

2005: Jason Giannini kicked a 30-yarder from almost the same spot as Lohmiller did in 1986, the Gophers' last win in the series, to give Minnesota a 23-20 win over No. 21 Michigan. It was the first time the Gophers led the entire game. Gary Russell ripped off a 61-yard run on a third-down call after Minnesota had taken over at its 13 with 2:49 showing. Russell's burst put the Gophers at the Michigan 13, and after two runs to center the ball, Giannini made the winning boot with six seconds left.

ALL-TIME SERIES RESULTS

MICHIGAN LEADS, 68-24-3

October 17, 1892—Minnesota 14, Michigan 6
October 28, 1893—Minnesota 34, Michigan 20
November 23, 1895—Michigan 20, Minnesota 0
November 7, 1896—Michigan 6, Minnesota 4
November 13, 1897—Michigan 14, Minnesota 0
November 27, 1902—Michigan 23, Minnesota 6
October 31, 1903—Michigan 6, Minnesota 6 (T)
November 20, 1909—Michigan 15, Minnesota 6
November 19, 1910—Michigan 6, Minnesota 0
November 22, 1919—Minnesota 34, Michigan 7
November 20, 1920—Michigan 3, Minnesota 0
November 19, 1921—Michigan 38, Minnesota 0
November 25, 1922—Michigan 16, Minnesota 7
November 24, 1923—Michigan 10, Minnesota 0
November 1, 1924—Michigan 13, Minnesota 0
November 21, 1925—Michigan 35, Minnesota 0
October 16, 1926—Michigan 20, Minnesota 0
November 20, 1926—Michigan 7, Minnesota 6
November 19, 1927—Minnesota 13, Michigan 7
November 16, 1929—Michigan 7, Minnesota 6
November 15, 1930—Michigan 7, Minnesota 0
November 21, 1931—Michigan 6, Minnesota 0
November 19, 1932—Michigan 3, Minnesota 0
November 18, 1933—Michigan 0, Minnesota 0 (T)
November 3, 1934—Minnesota 34, Michigan 0
November 16, 1935—Minnesota 40, Michigan 0
October 17, 1936—Minnesota 26, Michigan 0
October 16, 1937—Minnesota 39, Michigan 6
October 15, 1938—Minnesota 7, Michigan 6
November 11, 1939—Minnesota 20, Michigan 7
November 9, 1940—Minnesota 7, Michigan 6
October 25, 1941—Minnesota 7, Michigan 0
October 24, 1942—Minnesota 16, Michigan 14
October 23, 1943—Michigan 49, Minnesota 6
October 7, 1944—Michigan 28, Minnesota 13
November 3, 1945—Michigan 26, Minnesota 0

November 2, 1946—Michigan 21, Minnesota 0
October 25, 1947—Michigan 13, Minnesota 6
October 23, 1948—Michigan 27, Minnesota 14
October 22, 1949—Michigan 14, Minnesota 7
October 28, 1950—Michigan 7, Minnesota 7 (T)
October 27, 1951—Michigan 54, Minnesota 27
October 25, 1952—Michigan 21, Minnesota 0
October 24, 1953—Minnesota 22, Michigan 0
October 23, 1954—Michigan 34, Minnesota 0
October 22, 1955—Michigan 14, Minnesota 13
October 27, 1956—Minnesota 20, Michigan 7
October 26, 1957—Michigan 24, Minnesota 7
October 25, 1958—Michigan 20, Minnesota 19
October 24, 1959—Michigan 14, Minnesota 6
October 22, 1960—Minnesota 10, Michigan 0
October 28, 1961—Minnesota 23, Michigan 20
October 27, 1962—Minnesota 17, Michigan 0
October 26, 1963—Minnesota 6, Michigan 0
October 24, 1964—Michigan 19, Minnesota 12
October 23, 1965—Minnesota 14, Michigan 13
October 22, 1966—Michigan 49, Minnesota 0
October 28, 1967—Minnesota 20, Michigan 15
October 26, 1968—Michigan 33, Minnesota 20
October 25, 1969—Michigan 35, Minnesota 9
October 24, 1970—Michigan 39, Minnesota 13
October 23, 1971—Michigan 35, Minnesota 7
October 28, 1972—Michigan 42, Minnesota 0
October 27, 1973—Michigan 34, Minnesota 7
October 26, 1974—Michigan 49, Minnesota 0
November 1, 1975—Michigan 28, Minnesota 21
October 30, 1976—Michigan 45, Minnesota 0
October 22, 1977—Minnesota 16, Michigan 0
October 28, 1978—Michigan 42, Minnesota 10
October 13, 1979—Michigan 31, Minnesota 21
October 18, 1980—Michigan 37, Minnesota 14
October 31, 1981—Michigan 34, Minnesota 13
October 30, 1982—Michigan 52, Minnesota 14

November 12, 1983—Michigan 58, Minnesota 10
November 10, 1984—Michigan 31, Minnesota 7
November 16, 1985—Michigan 48, Minnesota 7
November 15, 1986—Minnesota 20, Michigan 17
November 7, 1987—Michigan 30, Minnesota 20
November 5, 1988—Michigan 22, Minnesota 7
November 18, 1989—Michigan 49, Minnesota 15
November 17, 1990—Michigan 35, Minnesota 18
October 25, 1991—Michigan 52, Minnesota 6
October 24, 1992—Michigan 63, Minnesota 13
November 13, 1993—Michigan 58, Minnesota 7

November 12, 1994—Michigan 38, Minnesota 22
October 28, 1995—Michigan 52, Minnesota 17
October 26, 1996—Michigan 44, Minnesota 10
November 1, 1997—Michigan 24, Minnesota 3
October 31, 1998—Michigan 15, Minnesota 10
November 10, 2001—Michigan 31, Minnesota 10
November 9, 2002—Michigan 41, Minnesota 24
October 10, 2003—Michigan 38, Minnesota 35
October 9, 2004—Michigan 27, Minnesota 24
October 8, 2005—Minnesota 23, Michigan 20
September 30, 2006—Michigan 28, Minnesota 14

AN AXE TO GRIND:
WISCONSIN vs.
MINNESOTA

No game typifies the Wisconsin-Minnesota series more than the 1962 showdown in Madison. It was perhaps the most hotly contested, as late-game temper tantrums erupted, and no other meeting had as much riding on the outcome.

It pitted the third-ranked Badgers against the fifth-ranked Gophers, both of whom sported 5-1 marks and shared the Big Ten lead. A trip to the Rose Bowl was on the line at a time when the pageant in Pasadena was the only post-season opportunity for Big Ten teams.

A then-record crowd of more than 65,000 packed Camp Randall Stadium to watch Wisconsin chase its second outright league title in four years. The Badgers faced a Minnesota squad that had disposed of Iowa and Purdue, Nos. 10 and 8 in the polls, respectively, in successive weeks. They also had limited five straight conference opponents to single-digit scoring.

Pat Richter was an All-America end for UW that season and won't forget the weird circumstances that helped the Badgers reach the Rose Bowl with a comeback 14-9 victory.

"It was special in the sense that it determined who went to the Rose Bowl, and it turned out a little more unusual than people anticipated because of the penalties and the way things unfolded," said Richter, who as athletic director oversaw his alma mater's resurgence 30 years later. "Bobby Bell was called for hitting Ron Vander Kelen late, and Minnesota coach Murray Warmath got all excited and threw a tantrum, and got another unsportsmanlike conduct penalty on top of that. We went on to score and they came down, but Jim Nettles intercepted in the end zone to clinch it. It was highly controversial, and everybody from Minnesota thought they got screwed. From our perspective, we thought it was a game that shouldn't have been that close."

But it was just one of 50 outings in the illustrious series that have been decided by seven points or less, and it unfolded like this:

Quarterback Duane Blaska connected with halfback Jim Cairns for a 15-yard score, but Collin Versich's extra-point attempt failed, keeping Minnesota's lead at 6-0. Wisconsin moved ahead on Vander Kelen's 13-yard pass to end Ron Leafblad and Gary Kroner's kick with 10:15 left in first half. Versich nailed a 32-yard field goal for a 9-7 Minnesota cushion with 4:49 showing in the third quarter. Wisconsin fumbled on its next two drives, including a lost punt return at its own 36, but the Gophers were stopped on Billy Smith's interception three plays later.

UNIVERSITY OF WISCONSIN ATHLETICS

Ron Vander Kelen was Wisconsin's QB in the early 1960's.

Wisconsin started the deciding drive with 3:54 remaining at its own 20. Carl Eller, like Bell a future Pro Football Hall of Fame defensive performer, registered a sack for Minnesota; however, 18- and 12-yard completions to Richter gave the hosts a first down at the Gophers' 43. Jack Perkovich picked off Vander

Kelen, but the flag against Bell changed the drive and turned the game around. It left the Badgers with a first down at the 13 at the 2:25 mark, and fullback Ralph Kurek scored the go-ahead touchdown three plays later on a 2-yard run.

Minnesota, thanks to two pass interference calls and a 15-yard piling on penalty against the Badgers, quickly traveled to the Wisconsin 14. But Nettles stole Blaska's toss into the end zone with 59 seconds left and batted down another pass at the Wisconsin 5 to end the game.

The Badgers moved up one spot to No. 2, setting up their date with Southern Cal, the first time in history that a bowl game featured the top two teams. Wisconsin already had crushed then-No. 1 Northwestern two weeks before its season finale against the Gophers.

Richter caught six passes for 82 yards in a contest that saw Minnesota win the first-down battle, 21-14, and outgained Wisconsin by 353-219. Warmath and the Gophers, who had split the previous two Rose Bowls, finished with 14 penalties for 130 yards, while the Badgers were whistled for eight infractions for 88 yards.

Badger All-American Pat Richter

Tom Butler covered the Badgers for the *Wisconsin State Journal* from 1953 to 1987 and recalled the chaos that ensued during those final dizzying moments. "I remember the week before, writing a column the same time as the Cuban missile crisis was going on, about Minnesota having defensive weapons, not offensive weapons," Butler said. "Minnesota was ahead and they intercepted Vander Kelen, but it was called off because of a penalty. Minnesota people went crazy. Twin Cities sports writer Sid Hartman was sitting next to me in the old press box, but I turned around and he was already down on the field next to Warmath and arguing with the officials."

Warmath naturally said that the outcome shouldn't have been in doubt. "I think the facts were evident," he told reporters after the disheartening loss. "You interpret it any way you want. There's no doubt about which team is better. Not one bit."

David Lothner was a two-way end for the Gophers from 1960 to 1962 and agreed with his former coach after ending his career with that frustrating defeat.

"That was controversial because it kept us from going to the Rose Bowl for three years in a row," said Lothner, who hails from Red Wing, Minnesota, but lives in Duluth. "The penalties turned the game around, so it was a hard one to take. But we had beaten them to close out my sophomore season and that put us over the top. I had a lot of respect for guys like Pat Richter."

Jack Mulvena lettered for the Gophers from 1959 to 1961 and remembers the difficulties they faced when tangling with the Badgers. "Wisconsin, unlike most other teams, was a pass-first, run-second team," Mulvena said. "It was no easy task covering guys like Richter. They won three out of the four years I was there, but they showed great sportsmanship.

"We had beaten Iowa but then lost to Purdue, so we figured it was all over as far as the Rose Bowl and winning a national championship, and we were playing for pride," Mulvena said of the 26-7 win at Camp Randall in 1960. "We had little or no pressure and won handily in front of a national TV audience, which helped us with voters, and the fact that Wisconsin had been to the Rose Bowl the year before. And Mississippi, which had been unbeaten, tied its last game. So that's what won the national title for us."

Both foes struggled mightily to reach that pinnacle again. Minnesota shared the Big Ten crown with Purdue and Indiana in 1967. That was the only time since then that the Gophers have finished in the top two in the Big Ten standings. Meanwhile, Wisconsin suffered through 11 campaigns in which it won three or fewer games before smelling roses again in January 1994.

Minnesota leads the overall series, 59-49-8. That's 116 games, the most of any rivalry in NCAA Division I-A history and one more than Big 12 combatants

Missouri and Kansas. The Gophers and Badgers have tangoed every year since 1890, except for 1906, when the match up was one of the contests that President Teddy Roosevelt canceled because of its viciousness and the fear of injuries or even deaths.

Such a storied slugfest wouldn't be complete without a little behind-the-scenes intrigue and off-the-field wackiness.

Dr. R.B. Fouch of Minneapolis made a bacon slab out of a chunk of black walnut in 1930, hoping it would serve as the annual traveling trophy and allow the winner to "bring home the bacon." It worked well until it disappeared in the early 1940s during a post-game ruckus among fans. Peg Watrous was president of the Wisconsin female students group. She and her Twin Cities counterpart were to conduct a symbolic exchange, but the slab was lost during the melee. The bacon resurfaced in a storage room at Camp Randall Stadium in 1994, complete with scores from every game from 1930 to 1970 mysteriously printed on the back.

While the unknown scorekeeper was doing his/her handiwork, the schools had introduced the much more popular Paul Bunyan's Axe in 1948. Wisconsin's National W Club built a new, sturdier tool in 2000 and three years later donated the original version to the College Football Hall of Fame in South Bend, Indiana.

Minnesota held a convincing 36-16-5 record before the 6-foot wooden trophy was created, but Wisconsin has shaved that deficit in half since by a 33-23-3 margin.

One of the most fascinating matchups took place at the Metrodome in 2005, a 38-34 Badgers victory that ended in an unbelievable, almost surreal, fashion.

Wisconsin stole this game when freshman Jonathan Casillas blocked Justin Kucek's punt and sophomore Ben Strickland recovered the pigskin in the left corner of the end zone with 30 seconds left. The series of events that led up to that play were nearly as unpredictable.

Gary Russell scored from 1 yard out, one of 18 running calls during a 19-play, 80-yard march that ate up 7:48 of the clock to push Minnesota's lead to 34-24 with 3:27 remaining. Richfield, Minnesota, native John Stocco then directed Wisconsin on a 71-yard drive, hitting Brandon Williams on a 21-yard strike to make it 34-31. More importantly, the possession lasted only 1:17.

Dominic Jones' facemask penalty on the play allowed Badgers punter Ken DeBauche to attempt his onside kick from midfield instead of the 35, and one of the craziest bounces benefited the visitors. Trumaine Banks couldn't handle DeBauche's boot at the Minnesota 38, and an onrushing Badger accidentally kicked it another 30 yards downfield, where Laurence Maroney fell on the ball with 2:10 showing. Maroney, who finished with 258 yards, mustered 9 yards on three carries, with Wisconsin linebacker Mark Zalewski preventing the first down at the 17.

Coach Barry Alvarez decided to go for the block. Strickland and Zach Hampton penetrated up the middle, but Kucek bobbled the snap and scrambled to his right to pick the ball up. That gave Casillas a shot, and he smothered the boot and gave Wisconsin the improbable win in only the fifth meeting in which both teams were ranked in the top 20 since the Associated Press poll started in 1936.

Russell finished with 139 yards and two scores, while Stocco completed 15-of-26 passes for 235 yards, including seven to Williams for 121 yards.

"I stood there numb," said Badgers safety Joe Stellmacher, who registered a game-high 14 tackles. "I just couldn't believe it was happening."

It's not the first time in this series that somebody uttered such words. Minnesota has left with several unexpected, last-minute triumphs.

Future NFL star Rick Upchurch blazed for 167 yards in Minnesota's 1973 win.

One occurred in 1971, when quarterback Craig Curry threw 12 yards to Mel Anderson with nine seconds left to pull out a 23-21 win. Rufus Ferguson gained 211 yards to become Wisconsin's first 1,000-yard rusher since Alan Ameche rumbled for 1,079 in 1952, but the Gophers overshadowed that performance, driving 80 yards in 13 plays for the winning score to send Warmath out with a win in his final game as Minnesota's coach after 18 seasons.

Quarterback Rickey Foggie wreaked havoc with Wisconsin's defense from 1984 to 1987. As a senior, he connected with tight end Craig Otto on a 3-yard score with 36 seconds remaining to lift Minnesota to a 22-19 victory and his fourth straight win over the Badgers. Foggie surpassed 2,000 yards rushing and 4,000 passing for his career in the process.

Richter also remembers the 1961 season finale, a 23-21 Wisconsin upset in Minneapolis in which he caught six passes for 142 yards and two scores from quarterback Ron Miller, who finished with 297 yards.

"I believe that game gave us a boost for the '62 season," Richter said. "It was back and forth. They had already clinched the Rose Bowl berth. Sandy Stephens hit Tom Hall for an 80-yard score, but we came back to win. The Axe wasn't as big of a deal as it is today, but it was always fun. The Axe became highly cherished by both programs during the time when neither was winning as much, so it became a rallying cry and a symbol of success if you had it."

Minnesota didn't have much to rally around in 1993, but it grabbed the Axe with a 28-21 home upset of Pasadena-bound Wisconsin. UW entered 6-0 and ranked 15th (the first time since 1962 that either team was ranked heading into their meeting) but fell behind, 21-0, in the first half and never recovered against the Gophers, 14-point underdogs. The Badgers lost despite generating 625 yards of total offense. Quarterback Darrell Bevell completed 31 of 48 passes for a school record 423 yards (including 156 to Lee DeRamus alone), but he was picked off five times, and tailback Brent Moss rushed for 130 yards.

Scott Eckers passed for 267 yards despite throwing four interceptions for Minnesota, which set a school mark with 36 first downs and tied another with 22 of them through the air.

Wisconsin tied Ohio State two weeks later and finished 10-1-1 after downing UCLA, 21-16, for its first Rose Bowl triumph. The Badgers' setback in the dome prevented them from winning an outright league championship and perhaps a national title, while Minnesota subsequently lost its final three games to finish 3-5 in Big Ten competition and 4-7 overall.

Paul Kratochvil split against the Badgers during his four seasons (1993–96), losing the final two outings, including a 45-28 loss at Madison in his last battle for the Axe.

"I remember my first year on campus, Wisconsin went on to win the Rose Bowl," said Kratochvil, whose brother, Andy, played for the Gophers from 1990 to 1993. "They came into our game undefeated, but we beat them and earned a huge win. It was their only loss of the season. As for the Axe, we won it when they went to the Rose Bowl and the next year we beat them again in Madison, and we ran around the stadium with it and pretended to chop down the goal-posts. People were throwing all kinds of stuff at us."

Scott Nelson helped bring the Badgers back to respectability from 1990 to 1993. The former safety said that the Minnesota series was special on and off the field because of so many interesting connections between the two border schools.

"There were enough guys from Minnesota playing here and vice versa," Nelson said of a rivalry that finished 2-2 during his varsity career. "Winning the game and the Axe means something when you can run across the field and grab it back, and then it's a daily reminder that you'll do whatever it takes to keep it because you don't want to have an empty trophy case."

Nelson recalled many details about the rivalry, especially his final three outings against the Gophers, including the 1991 affair in which Wisconsin snapped a 19-game Big Ten losing streak with a heart-stopping 19-16 victory.

"I rolled my ankle and was sitting out, and Melvin Tucker did a tremendous job," Nelson said. "We were ahead late and he broke up a pass in the end zone. I had never seen a hit like that. Then in '92, we beat them on a cloudy, cold day at Camp Randall. But in '93, we were 6-0 and they beat us up there in a game that both offenses put up crazy numbers. It was disappointing because we could have won the undisputed [league] championship. As it turns out, we finished fifth in the country and could have been the only unbeaten team."

Tom Luckemeyer lettered at Minnesota from 1975 to 1977. He said each of his three outings against the Badgers meant something. "The Wisconsin rivalry wasn't as big because the Badgers and Iowa were down a bit," Luckemeyer said. "But I remember facing Billy Marek [in 1975]. We lost my junior year over in Madison, but then in '77 we beat them to go to a bowl game. We had a big snow the night before that last game and it was like playing on concrete."

Brad Jackomino played in those last two contests and then helped Wisconsin paste the Gophers, 48-10, in 1978. "Minnesota was the big rivalry at the time," said the Rhinelander, Wisconsin, native who owns and operates two fitness centers in the Twin Cities area. "We had a pretty good team during my sophomore year but went in the tank. But we thumped them pretty good in the last game. They beat us my junior year after we had won our first five games and then lost our last six. As seniors, people were calling us out, saying that Minnesota would crush us. But we came together, played a great game, and beat them pretty good."

Butler said that Marek's performance in the 1974 season finale at Camp Randall, a contest in which the tailback from the Chicago area carried 43 times for 304 yards and five touchdowns against Minnesota, was one of the greatest feats he saw as a sports writer.

"It was a drizzly day, so it was tough to hang onto the ball," Butler said of UW's 49-14 win that featured 435 yards rushing. "He [Marek] did all of that despite having a 65-yard touchdown run called back on a penalty. He led the nation in scoring that year and finished with 1,215 yards rushing, 740 of them in the last three games against Iowa, Northwestern, and Minnesota, while scoring 13 TDs."

Neil Graff missed having Marek in the same backfield by a year, having been the Badgers' quarterback from 1969 to 1971. Still, he said those confrontations stood out for many reasons. "I grew up only 15 miles from Minnesota and 10 miles from Iowa, so my dream was to play at Minnesota or a Big Ten school," Graff said of his Sioux Falls, South Dakota, roots. "I visited Nebraska, Iowa State, and Colorado, but I thought the Big Ten was the ultimate conference. I ended up at Wisconsin because there was a great chance that I could play right away as a sophomore, and I fell in love with the place.

"We knew we weren't playing for the Big Ten championship, but we had great games against Minnesota because we were evenly matched," Graff added. "We played for pride and bragging rights. Those games had special meaning because of my history as a youth and having followed Minnesota teams closely, and wanting to play there. So I got extra jacked up to play the Gophers. And playing for the Axe

Paul Bunyon's Axe, the piece of hardware that gets Badgers and Gophers going

was a big motivating factor. The coaches used that as extra incentive. It was a pride thing in getting it back or keeping it. I know that coaches played it up at practices, and people on campus and in the community played it up all week. It showed that there was something else riding on the game besides winning and losing."

Stu Voigt was one of Graff's favorite targets in '69, the former's final season at Wisconsin before his NFL career with the Minnesota Vikings. Voigt has lived in the Twin Cities area since his retirement and knows exactly what Paul Bunyan's Axe means to both sides.

"Minnesota was the rivalry, and it was the last game of the year in those days," Voigt said. "Minnesota had big, strong, physical teams. It was a spirited rivalry. I caught a touchdown pass in that game my sophomore year, which was the time we had a brawl at Memorial Stadium. It was a melee in the second half, and me and several players were involved. The sad thing was that one of our safeties, Melvin Walker, got hit in the air on one play, and came down and severely injured his knee. He had to stay in the hospital and it was so bad that he lost his leg.

"I caught eight or nine passes against them in my last game, but they won [35-10]," Voigt said. "They were among the upper echelon in the league and tied for the title in '67, but Indiana went to the Rose Bowl. My wife is a Gopher, and I'm a Badger. Living over here now, I bump into guys I played against. Badger fans didn't travel as well as they do today, but in those days people would take the train over to Minnesota, probably not more than 1,000. But it was a hard-fought rivalry."

Darrell Thompson was born in St. Louis but was raised in Rochester, Minnesota, so he chose the Gophers over Iowa and Wisconsin among others for his services. Thompson became Minnesota's all-time leading rusher, from 1986 to 1989.

He and the Gophers won three out of four contests, although all four games were decided by a touchdown or less. "Wisconsin wasn't as solid of a program as they are now," Thompson said, "but it was a big deal for Minnesota and Wisconsin kids, and most of us knew about the Axe."

Clarence Stensby mixed it up with the Gophers from 1951 to 1954, winning his first and fourth meetings, and tying the middle two while at Wisconsin. "They had Paul Giel, who was awfully good," Stensby said. "But in 1951, we had the 'Hard Rocks' defense and beat them up there in sub-zero weather. We tied the next two meetings and then beat them decisively my last time."

MORE SERIES HIGHLIGHTS

1897: Wisconsin's Pat O'Dea recorded a 110-yard punt and 55-yard drop-kick field goal in a 39-0 triumph.

1898: Albert "Norsky" Larson's 85-yard touchdown run ignited Wisconsin's 29-0 victory.

1905: A.G. Findlay's 84-yard TD scamper helped the Badgers post a 16-12 win at Minnesota.

1914 and 1919: Minnesota hosted Wisconsin in the Gophers' first homecoming game on November 14, 1914. They downed the Badgers, 14-3, in front of an estimated crowd of 17,000. Wisconsin returned the favor in its initial observance in 1919; however, the Gophers spoiled the celebration with a 19-7 victory. Wally Barr and Paul Meyers collaborated on an 80-yard TD pass, but it was Wisconsin's only bright spot that day.

1926: Wisconsin led, 10-9, despite having no first downs. Malvin Nydahl then returned a punt 60 yards for a score as Minnesota rallied for a 16-10 road decision.

1928: Bronko Nagurski, wearing a back brace, carried Minnesota to a 6-0 victory. He recovered a fumble at the Wisconsin 17 and toted the pigskin six straight times, including the deciding score. He then tackled Frank Cuisinier at the Minnesota 8 late in the game to preserve the victory.

1932: Walter "Mickey" McGuire, a Hawaii native and Badgers senior halfback, scored all three TDs in Wisconsin's 20-13 victory. He returned the opening kickoff 90 yards for a score and hauled in 18- and 14-yard passes from Joe Linfor. McGuire's final score came with less than a minute left. That Gophers team included sophomore guard Milt Bruhn, who later coached at Wisconsin as an assistant and head man (1956–1966).

1934: Visiting Minnesota won its first national title and finished 8-0 after a 34-0 thrashing of the Badgers, who had allowed just 50 points previously.

1935: The Gophers repeated as undefeated champions with an 8-0 mark after posting a 33-7 win over UW in the season finale, leaving the Badgers at 1-7 in Clarence Spears' final year as head coach.

1938: Both teams entered 3-1 with the winner earning the Big Ten title after this season finale. A capacity crowd of 38,511 watched at Camp Randall, but Harry Stuhldreher's No. 12 Badgers fell, 21-0.

1940: Top-ranked Minnesota entered this game 7-0 and cemented a national championship with a 22-13 victory, coming back from a 13-point deficit. A crowd of 33,557, the largest at Camp Randall that season, watched the contest, which marked the 50th anniversary of the teams' first meeting. John Tennant passed to sophomore end Dave Schreiner for a 72-yard Wisconsin TD, but running backs George "Sonny" Franck and Bruce Smith and the blocking of Dick Wildung carried Bernie Bierman's squad to victory.

Gopher Bruce Smith's rushing helped cinch the game in 1940.

1942: The seventh-ranked Badgers raced to a 20-0 lead behind Pat Harder's TD and extra point, Elroy Hirsch's pass to Schreiner, and Ashley Anderson's quarterback sneak. The final was 20-6 as the Badgers finished 8-1-1, including a tie against Notre Dame and a disputed 6-0 loss at Iowa. The Badgers beat Ohio State but finished 4-1 in league play, just behind the 5-1 Buckeyes, who were named the national champions with a 9-1 season mark.

1944: Wisconsin's Earl "Jug" Girard passed and ran for scores, but it wasn't enough as Minnesota claimed 28-26 win in Madison. Wayne "Red" Williams gained 128 yards for the Gophers.

1948: No. 15 Minnesota claimed a 16-0 triumph in the first battle for Paul Bunyan's Axe. It also proved to be Stuhldreher's final game as Wisconsin coach.

1949: Wisconsin finished 5-3-1 and had a chance to share the Big Ten trophy but lost, 14-6, to the Gophers at Memorial Stadium. UM featured such stars as Bud Grant (future coach of the Minnesota Vikings), Clayton Tonnemaker, Leo Nomellini, and Gordy Soltau. Dick Anonsen was a key performer, intercepting three Wisconsin passes.

1950: Wisconsin shut out the visiting Gophers, 14-0, despite Kermit Klefsaas's 121 yards rushing. The Badgers finished 6-3, while Minnesota was 1-7-1.

1951: The "Hard Rocks" defense led eighth-ranked Wisconsin to a 30-6 road victory. Alan Ameche rushed for 200 yards to finish his freshman season, scoring twice. Senior quarterback John Coatta kicked a field goal and scored on a keeper in the final quarter.

1952: Harland Carl ran for 102 yards, including a 55-yard touchdown, and Ameche gained 129 yards and scored twice for No. 13 Wisconsin. But the game ended in a 21-all tie. Burt Hable also intercepted three passes for the host Badgers.

1953: Minnesota tied No. 8 Wisconsin, 21-21 again, to prevent the Badgers from gaining a three-way tie for first place in the Big Ten. Melvin Holme led Minnesota with 121 yards on the ground.

1954: Wisconsin was ranked No. 17 and beat the 10th-ranked Gophers at Camp Randall, 27-0, in Heisman Trophy winner Ameche's last game as a collegian. Playing on a sprained ankle, "the Horse" ran 13 times for just 26 yards but scored two touchdowns, and his teammates carried him off the field on their shoulders. Ameche finished with 439 yards on 84 carries (5.2-yard average) and seven TDs in his career against the Gophers. The Badgers registered a team-record seven interceptions, six against Don Swanson. Clarence Bratt recorded four of them to set a Big Ten standard.

1955: Bob Schultz rushed for 117 yards for host Minnesota, which earned a 21-6 victory in front of almost 63,000.

1958: Dale Hackbart intercepted three Minnesota passes in fifth-ranked Wisconsin's

27-12 win before more than 54,000 at Camp Randall.

1959: UW claimed its first outright league title since 1912. Hackbart scored a TD in No. 9 Wisconsin's 11-7 triumph that clinched the crown. He also registered a two-point conversion, rushed for 74 yards, and passed for 149. Al Schoonover had 103 yards receiving.

1960: Sandy Stephens recorded three interceptions as then No. 4 Minnesota claimed a 26-7 triumph in Madison.

1964: Wisconsin lost a school record-tying six fumbles but managed to pull out a 14-7 win behind Ronald Smith's 160 yards via the ground at Camp Randall.

1966: Host Wisconsin pulled out a 7-6 win in Milt Bruhn's final game after 11 years as coach; he had announced his resignation before the showdown. The game drew 45,373, the lowest total to see a series game since 1950.

1967: Noel Jenke picked off three Wisconsin passes to lift the Gophers to a 21-14 win. John Boyajian passed for 290 yards, and Tom McCauley caught nine passes for 132 yards for Wisconsin.

1968: Jim Carter gained 121 yards rushing, and Barry Mayer added 113 to lift visiting Minnesota to a 23-15 win despite losing five fumbles. John Smith gained 132 yards on the ground for Wisconsin.

1969: Minnesota's Barry Mayer gained 216 yards rushing and 256 all-purpose yards in carrying the hosts to a 35-10 triumph at Memorial Stadium.

1970: Rufus Ferguson rushed for 97 yards, including a 29-yard touchdown, during a 20-point fourth-quarter Wisconsin outburst. This helped the host Badgers give first-year coach John Jardine a 39-14 victory that also included 102 yards receiving from Al Hannah.

1971: John Marquesen finished with 117 yards rushing as Minnesota squeaked by Wisconsin, 23-21, in front of 34,738 fans at home.

1972: Ferguson carried 36 times for a tough 112 yards to finish with 1,004, but visiting Minnesota won, 14-6.

1973: Future Denver Broncos star Rick Upchurch blazed for 167 yards as Minnesota pulled out another close one, 19-17, despite Marek's 131 yards. Attendance reached only 34, 412.

1975: Marek gained 118 yards. He finished his career with 103 carries and 553 yards (5.4-yard average) and six scores against Minnesota. However, the Gophers handled Wisconsin, 24-3, as Greg Barlow rushed for 102 yards.

1976: Wisconsin won, 26-17, behind Larry Canada's 153 yards rushing and Vince Lamia's four field goals (a team record at the time).

1977: The Badgers limited Minnesota to a school record-tying low of 0 yards passing (on three attempts) and set another mark with a .000 completion percentage but still lost, 13-7. It was the second time that Wisconsin accomplished the feat against Minnesota, having shut down the Gophers passing game in 1972. Kent Kitzmann carried 40 times for 154 yards for UM.

1978: Ira Matthews contributed 312 all-purpose yards, registering 134 rushing, 54 receiving, and 124 on returns as Wisconsin rolled, 48-10. Matthews scored three times, including a 64-yard punt return, and ripped off an 82-yard run. Mike Kalasmiki tossed three scoring passes as the Badgers gained 500 total yards, including 113 rushing from Tom Stauss. Marion Barber led Minnesota in rushing with 111 yards.

1979: Wisconsin overcame a 14-0 first-quarter hole, taking a 42-24 lead and holding on for an exciting 42-37 victory. Kalasmiki scored three times, and passed for 252 yards and two touchdowns. Minnesota's Garry White had 230 yards on the ground.

1980: Quarterback Jess Cole led the Badgers to a 25-7 triumph with four touchdowns, including a 52-yard scamper, to finish with 92 yards rushing. Cole's long sprint came with Minnesota ahead, 7-6, with 3:08 remaining in the third quarter. Tim Krumrie registered 17 tackles for Wisconsin.

1981: UW won, 26-21, behind Randy Wright's late heroics. The Badgers trailed, 21-20, when he replaced Cole at quarterback with 1:54 left. Wright hooked up with Michael Jones on a 49-yard play and then hit Jones from 7 yards out for the game-winner, capping an 85-yard march in six plays. Mike Hohensee passed for 254 yards, including 123 to Chester Cooper, and two scores for Minnesota.

The Badgers accepted a bid to their first bowl game since the 1963 Rose Bowl. Meanwhile, the Gophers finished 5-6, in Joe Salem's third season as Gopher's coach.

1982: The Badgers won, 24-0, en route to their first bowl win, a 14-3 decision over Kansas State in the Independence Bowl. Troy King ran for 132 yards against the visiting Gophers. It was Wisconsin's first shutout in the series since 1954.

1983: Wisconsin romped, 56-17, as tailback Gary Ellerson scored three times and Thad McFadden added two touchdowns. It was Wisconsin's biggest scoring output against Minnesota and the most either team had scored against each other since the Gophers' 63-0 decision in the 1890 series opener.

1984: Foggie's two scores and 153 yards rushing lifted visiting Minnesota to a 17-14 victory, the end to Wisconsin's six-game winning streak in the series and a homecoming let-down for the crowd of 78,770.

1985: Minnesota won, 27-18, although Foggie completed only five passes. His aerials, however, went for 242 yards, including an 89-yarder to Melvin Anderson. Gary Couch contributed 124 yards receiving. Larry Emery gained 124 yards rushing for the Badgers.

1987: Chip Lohmiller cranked a 53-yard field goal as the Gophers won, 22-19. Marvin Artley gained 114 yards rushing for visiting Wisconsin.

1988: Lionell Crawford churned for 109 yards rushing during Wisconsin's 14-7 win, snapping the Gophers' four-game winning string in the series.

1989: Host Minnesota claimed a 24-22 triumph behind 143 yards rushing from Darrell Thompson.

1990: Minnesota registered a school-record eight quarterback sacks during its 21-3 victory in Barry Alvarez's first game in the series as Wisconsin's head coach.

1991: Wisconsin pulled out a 19-16 victory in the Metrodome. With 10 seconds left, Wisconsin safety Melvin Tucker jarred the ball loose from Minnesota tight end Patt Evans in the end zone on a fourth-down play from the 11-yard line. Alvarez's first Big Ten victory, this snapped a 23-game road losing streak. It was a costly loss for Minnesota coach John Gutekunst, who was fired at the end of the season. Antonio Carter rushed for 136 yards for the Gophers.

1994: Wisconsin finished 7-4-1 and won the Hall of Fame Bowl, while the Gophers finished 3-8 but claimed a 17-14 victory at Camp Randall Stadium for their only Big Ten triumph despite Terrell Fletcher's 101 yards rushing.

1995: John Hall booted a 60-yard field goal to give Wisconsin a 13-10 halftime cushion. Aaron Stecker bolted 100 yards with a kickoff return to put the Badgers on top for good and rushed for 114 yards as the Badgers claimed a 34-27 triumph. Darrell Bevell hooked up with Tony Simmons on scoring strikes of 62 and 70 yards, and finished with 302 total yards through the air. Jason Maniecki sacked Cory Sauter on Minnesota's final possession to seal the win. Maniecki drove an offensive lineman into Sauter on fourth down at the Wisconsin 20. Sauter passed for 355 yards and finished 20-of-36 with three TD passes, connecting with Tutu Atwell for 148 yards and Tony Levine for 105 more.

1996: Ron Dayne rushed for a Big Ten freshman-record 297 yards in 50 carries to lift Wisconsin to a 45-28 win, offsetting Sauter's 16-of-22 performance for 315 yards, which included 142 to Ryan Thelwell and 105 to Atwell.

1997: Dayne carried 40 times for 183 yards and one touchdown, including eight carries for 36 yards on the final drive, in Wisconsin's 22-21 decision. Badgers quarterback Mike Samuel connected with Simmons on a 53-yard touchdown pass in the first quarter and hit Donald Hayes on a 53-yarder in the second. Simmons and Hayes took the Axe to receivers coach Henry Mason's Madison home after the team returned from Minneapolis. Mason was recovering from surgery but communicated with his position players throughout the game via a cell phone. Atwell eluded the UW defense again, gaining 126 yards receiving and 204 all-purpose.

1998: The eighth-ranked Badgers improved to 9-0, matching the best start in school history, with a 26-7 triumph that featured four Matt Davenport field goals and 133 yards rushing from Dayne.

1999: No. 20 Wisconsin claimed a 20-17 overtime victory on Vitaly Pisetsky's 31-yard field goal, the team's second of eight straight wins to end the season. Pisetsky had tied the game at 17-all with a 36-yarder. Alvarez watched the game on television from his room in the Mayo Clinic, where he was awaiting knee replacement surgery. Thomas Hamner gained 144 yards rushing for No. 25 Minnesota, while Brooks Bollinger and Nick Davis combined for an 81-yard touchdown pass for the Badgers.

2000: Minnesota's Tellis Redmon finished with 211 yards rushing and Ron Johnson had 111 yards receiving. Nevertheless, the Badgers still won in a rout, 41-20, as quarterback Bollinger gained 127 yards on the ground.

2001: Badgers redshirt Anthony Davis carried 29 times for 208 yards and three touchdowns, setting an NCAA freshman record with his 10th game of at least 100 rushing yards, and Lee Evans had nine catches for 151 yards and established the Big Ten single-season receiving record (1,545), but Wisconsin still lost in the dome. With 8:10 left and the Gophers trying to pad a 35-31 lead, Asad Abdul-Khaliq showed off his athletic talents. Minnesota faced a third and 1 at the Wisconsin 3, and Abdul-Khaliq faked a handoff and ran a bootleg to the right. UW end Erasmus James stayed home and was in position to make a tackle at the 13, but the Gophers' signal caller ran away and into the end zone for the 42-31 win. Minnesota had 10 plays of 15 yards or longer for a total of 299 yards, including Abdul-Khaliq's TD tosses of 38, 45, and 59 yards. The Badgers allowed 305 total yards by halftime. Redmon gained 128 yards rushing, and Ben Utecht chipped in 104 receiving for Minnesota.

2002: The host Badgers secured a berth in the Alamo Bowl with a 49-31 victory. Anthony Davis and Bollinger decimated Minnesota's young defense for a combined 413 rushing yards. Davis carried 45 times for 301 yards and five touchdowns, scoring on runs of 4, 1, 25, 1, and 71 yards. In two games against the Gophers, Davis had carried 74 times for 509 yards and eight touchdowns. Bollinger rushed 18 times for a season-high 112 yards and a TD, and completed 6-of-12 passes for 134 yards and another score. Abdul-Khaliq marched the Gophers 80 yards for a touchdown and a 31-28 lead with 12:30 left, but Minnesota failed to score on its final three possessions.

2003: No. 24 Minnesota won, 37-34, on kicker Rhys Lloyd's 35-yard field goal with no time showing at the Metrodome. Benji Kamrath, who hails from Mayville, Wisconsin, guided the Gophers' winning drive. Marion Barber III and Laurence Maroney combined for 274 yards rushing; the latter had 231 total yards for the victors, while Wisconsin's Jim Sorgi threw two of his four touchdowns to tight end Owen Daniels and finished with 305 yards.

2004: The Badgers scored on their first five drives, registering four TDs and a field goal en route to a season-high 525 total yards during a 38-14 win. Fifth-ranked Wisconsin improved to 9-0 for only the third time in school history (1901 and 1998). John Stocco completed 19-of-26 passes for 297 yards. He ran for two touchdowns and threw for one. The Gophers ran seven plays and found themselves behind 21-0 in the first half and finished the game with a season-low 18 rushing attempts for 73 yards. Wisconsin held the ball for an amazing 44:31 for 83,069 at Camp Randall Stadium.

2006: Stocco tied his career high with four touchdown passes as 25th-ranked Wisconsin routed the Gophers, 48-12, in front of a homecoming crowd of more than 82,000 fans at Camp Randall Stadium. The Badgers retained the Axe for a third straight season, and defeated Minnesota for a sixth consecutive time at home. Stocco finished 12-of-19 for 193 yards and extended his streak of TD passes to 16 games. Bruising P.J. Hill rambled for 164 yards rushing, joining Dayne and Anthony Davis as the only freshmen to surpass the 1,000-yard plateau. The Wisconsin defense became only the second team to hold Minnesota under 300 yards of total offense in the last 46 games. Gophers quarterback Bryan Cupito was 13-of-28 for 94 yards and failed to throw a touchdown pass for only the second time in his last 18 games.

ALL-TIME SERIES RESULTS

MINNESOTA LEADS, 59-49-8

November 15, 1890—Minnesota 63, Wisconsin 0
October 24, 1891—Minnesota 26, Wisconsin 12
October 29, 1892—Minnesota 32, Wisconsin 4
November 11, 1893—Minnesota 40, Wisconsin 0
November 17, 1894—Wisconsin 6, Minnesota 0
November 16, 1895—Minnesota 14, Wisconsin 10
November 21, 1896—Wisconsin 6, Minnesota 0
October 30, 1897—Wisconsin 39, Minnesota 0
October 29, 1898—Wisconsin 29, Minnesota 0
November 18, 1899—Wisconsin 19, Minnesota 0
November 3, 1900—Minnesota 6, Wisconsin 5
November 16, 1901—Wisconsin 18, Minnesota 0
November 15, 1902—Minnesota 11, Wisconsin 0
November 26, 1903—Minnesota 17, Wisconsin 0
November 12, 1904—Minnesota 28, Wisconsin 0
November 4, 1905—Wisconsin 16, Minnesota 12
November 23, 1907—Wisconsin 17, Minnesota 17 (T)
November 7, 1908—Wisconsin 5, Minnesota 0
November 13, 1909—Minnesota 34, Wisconsin 6
November 12, 1910—Minnesota 28, Wisconsin 0

November 18, 1911—Wisconsin 6, Minnesota 6 (T)
November 16, 1912—Wisconsin 14, Minnesota 0
November 1, 1913—Minnesota 21, Wisconsin 3
November 14, 1914—Minnesota 14, Wisconsin 3
November 20, 1915—Minnesota 20, Wisconsin 3
November 18, 1916—Minnesota 54, Wisconsin 0
November 3, 1917—Wisconsin 10, Minnesota 7
November 16, 1918—Minnesota 6, Wisconsin 0
November 1, 1919—Minnesota 19, Wisconsin 7
November 6, 1920—Wisconsin 3, Minnesota 0
October 29, 1921—Wisconsin 35, Minnesota 0
November 4, 1922—Wisconsin 14, Minnesota 0
October 27, 1923—Wisconsin 0, Minnesota 0 (T)
October 18, 1924—Wisconsin 7, Minnesota 7 (T)
October 31, 1925—Wisconsin 12, Minnesota 12 (T)
October 30, 1926—Minnesota 16, Wisconsin 10
October 29, 1927—Minnesota 13, Wisconsin 7
November 24, 1928—Minnesota, 6, Wisconsin 0
November 23, 1929—Minnesota 13, Wisconsin 12
November 22, 1930—Wisconsin 14, Minnesota 0
October 31, 1931—Minnesota 14, Wisconsin 0

November 12, 1932—Wisconsin 20, Minnesota 13

November 25, 1933—Minnesota 6, Wisconsin 3

November 24, 1934—Minnesota 34, Wisconsin 0

November 23, 1935—Minnesota 33, Wisconsin 7

November 21, 1936—Minnesota 24, Wisconsin 0

November 20, 1937—Minnesota 13, Wisconsin 6

November 19, 1938—Minnesota 21, Wisconsin 0

November 25, 1939—Minnesota 23, Wisconsin 6

November 23, 1940—Minnesota 22, Wisconsin 13

November 22, 1941—Minnesota 41, Wisconsin 6

November 21, 1942—Wisconsin 20, Minnesota 6

November 20, 1943—Minnesota 25, Wisconsin 13

November 25, 1944—Minnesota 28, Wisconsin 26

November 24, 1945—Wisconsin 26, Minnesota 12

November 23, 1946—Minnesota 6, Wisconsin 0

November 22, 1947—Minnesota 21, Wisconsin 0

November 20, 1948—Minnesota 16, Wisconsin 0

November 19, 1949—Minnesota 14, Wisconsin 6

November 25, 1950—Wisconsin 14, Minnesota 0

November 24, 1951—Wisconsin 30, Minnesota 6

November 22, 1952—Wisconsin 21, Minnesota 21 (T)

November 21, 1953—Wisconsin 21, Minnesota 21 (T)

November 20, 1954—Wisconsin 27, Minnesota 0

November 19, 1955—Minnesota 21, Wisconsin 6

November 24, 1956—Wisconsin 13, Minnesota 13 (T)

November 23, 1957—Wisconsin 14, Minnesota 6

November 22, 1958—Wisconsin 27, Minnesota 12

November 21, 1959—Wisconsin 11, Minnesota 7

November 19, 1960—Minnesota 26, Wisconsin 7

November 25, 1961—Wisconsin 23, Minnesota 21

November 24, 1962—Wisconsin 14, Minnesota 9

November 28, 1963—Minnesota 14, Wisconsin 0

November 21, 1964—Wisconsin 14, Minnesota 7

November 20, 1965—Minnesota 42, Wisconsin 7

November 19, 1966—Wisconsin 7, Minnesota 6

November 25, 1967—Minnesota 21, Wisconsin 14

November 23, 1968—Minnesota 23, Wisconsin 15

November 22, 1969—Minnesota 35, Wisconsin 10

November 21, 1970—Wisconsin 39, Minnesota 14

November 20, 1971—Minnesota 23, Wisconsin 21

November 25, 1972—Minnesota 14, Wisconsin 6

November 24, 1973—Minnesota 19, Wisconsin 17

November 23, 1974—Wisconsin 49, Minnesota 14

November 22, 1975—Minnesota 24, Wisconsin 3

November 20, 1976—Wisconsin 26, Minnesota 17

November 19, 1977—Minnesota 13, Wisconsin 7

November 25, 1978—Wisconsin 48, Minnesota 10

November 17, 1979—Wisconsin 42, Minnesota 37

November 22, 1980—Wisconsin 25, Minnesota 7

November 21, 1981—Wisconsin 26, Minnesota 21

November 20, 1982—Wisconsin 24, Minnesota 0

October 15, 1983—Wisconsin 56, Minnesota 17

October 13, 1984—Minnesota 17, Wisconsin 14

November 9, 1985—Minnesota 27, Wisconsin 18

November 8, 1986—Minnesota 27, Wisconsin 20

November 14, 1987—Minnesota 22, Wisconsin 19

November 12, 1988—Wisconsin 14, Minnesota 7

November 4, 1989—Minnesota 24, Wisconsin 22

November 3, 1990—Minnesota 21, Wisconsin 3

November 16, 1991—Wisconsin 19, Minnesota 16

November 14, 1992—Wisconsin 34, Minnesota 6

October 23, 1993—Minnesota 28, Wisconsin 21

October 22, 1994—Minnesota 17, Wisconsin 14

November 11, 1995—Wisconsin 34, Minnesota 27

November 9, 1996—Wisconsin 45, Minnesota 28

October 25, 1997—Wisconsin 22, Minnesota 21

November 7, 1998—Wisconsin 26, Minnesota 7

October 9, 1999—Wisconsin 20, Minnesota 17 (OT)

November 4, 2000—Wisconsin 41, Minnesota 20

November 24, 2001—Minnesota 42, Wisconsin 31

November 23, 2002—Wisconsin 49, Minnesota 31

November 8, 2003—Minnesota 37, Wisconsin 34

November 6, 2004—Wisconsin 38, Minnesota 14

October 15, 2005—Wisconsin 38, Minnesota 34

October 14, 2006—Wisconsin 48, Minnesota 12

THE GAME:
MICHIGAN vs.
OHIO STATE

"College football is a barbecue joint on the side of the road or a dive bar you find by accident. It is all about time and place." *Detroit Free Press* sports columnist Michael Rosenberg wrote those words several days before the November 18, 2006, showdown between Michigan and Ohio State.

It marked the 38th time that the No. 1 and 2 teams in college football faced off, and the winner would be off to the national championship game.

Both teams entered unbeaten for the third time in their historic series, and it was the fifth occasion that OSU could ruin a perfect season for the Wolverines, who, for the first time since 1969, played the contest without the legendary Bo Schembechler growling along the sidelines or watching from his earthly suite. Schembechler's sad passing the morning before ensured that the sporting world's attention would be focused on Columbus.

An Ohio Stadium record 105,708 fans gathered to watch a game that was sure to be a classic. It was the ninth meeting in which one of the squads was ranked the top team in the land: the honor had been Michigan's in 1947, 1948, and 1997, and Ohio State's in 1954, 1968, 1969, 1973, 1975, and 2006. The game also included the No. 2 team in the country for a fifth time; but never before had the two teams been first and second at the time of their annual grudge match. Tickets were at a premium, with scalpers collecting hundreds and even several thousand dollars apiece.

The Buckeyes entered with the nation's longest winning streak at 18 games; it had been Michigan that ended the school record of 22 in 1969 with a monumental 24-12 upset. Ohio State was attempting to beat the Wolverines for a third straight time, which it hadn't accomplished since 1962, and was chasing its first outright Big Ten crown since 1984.

Jim Tressel's Bucks had already defeated Texas, giving them a chance for two wins against a No. 2 foe in the same season, which no top-ranked team had done since Army in 1945. The respective offenses dominated against two of the country's top defenses, combining for 900 yards and 41 first downs, and the fireworks started early.

Michigan used only 2:28 to take the opening kickoff 80 yards in seven plays for a 7-0 lead, but the Buckeyes converted four third-down plays to tie it on their first drive. They exchanged punts and then freshman Chris Wells bolted 52 yards early in the second quarter to put Ohio State up, 14-7.

With 6:11 left before halftime, Troy Smith hit Ted Ginn Jr. with a 39-yard TD pass on a second-and-inches call to cap a four-play, 91-yard march and push the hosts ahead, 21-7. The Wolverines responded in turn as Chad Henne combined with Adrian Arrington on a 37-yard score to cut the deficit to 21-14. On the Buckeyes' next drive, Smith connected with Anthony Gonzalez four times, including an 8-yard touchdown with 20 seconds left in the half as OSU grabbed a 28-14 advantage.

In the third quarter, Michigan rode running back Mike Hart to close the gap to seven again at 28-21. The Wolverine defense followed up by picking off a tipped pass from Smith, setting up a field goal and a 28-24 game.

The scoring orgy continued. Antonio Pittman added another huge play to Ohio State's ground game, racing 56 yards as the Buckeyes moved ahead, 35-24. Michigan then recovered Smith's fumbled snap from shotgun formation, scoring on Hart's 1-yard plunge, his third TD of the contest, to climb back to 35-30 with 14:41 left. The Wolverines lined up for a two-point try but changed their minds when Ohio State used its second timeout of the half, making it 35-31 with the extra point.

Shawn Crable's late hit on Smith saved Ohio State from disaster after a third-and-15 incompletion; the Buckeyes took advantage of the situation to pad their lead to 42-31 with 5:38 left as Smith set a school record with his 30th TD pass of the season.

Michigan exploited a pass interference call on fourth-and-16 to march in for a score on Henne's 16-yard strike to Tyler Ecker with 2:16 left. Henne then hit Steve Breaston with a two-point conversion to make it 42-39.

Ginn corralled the on-side kick attempt, and Michigan had no timeouts left. Pittman sewed it up with a first down on third-and-2, sending the Buckeyes to the national title game for the second time in five years. Hart finished with 142 yards, while Smith cemented his Heisman Trophy bid, passing for 316 yards to join William "Tippy" Dye (1934–36) as the only Ohio State quarterbacks to beat Michigan three times.

No one appreciates the meaning of the historic victory more than former Buckeyes quarterback Kirk Herbstreit, who finished 0-2-1 against Michigan from 1990 to 1992. In the leadup to the 2006 spectacle, the college football analyst and broadcaster started his column for ESPN.com this way:

"I grew up brainwashed in the Ohio State-Michigan rivalry and it's always been part of my life. My dad was a captain at Ohio State and an assistant coach under Woody Hayes and an assistant under Bo Schembechler at Miami [Ohio]. For the people within this rivalry, every year this game is the Game of the Year and the Game of the Century. As a kid growing up, Ohio State-Michigan was Christmas Day, the biggest day of the year."

The legendary Woody Hayes chats up his boys before the 1956 season.
Quarterback Frank Elwood and All-American guard Jim Parker are to his left.

Some may argue it's been that way since the first meeting in 1897, and particularly since it's been the final game of the regular season for both schools starting in 1935. Michigan holds a 57-40-6 overall advantage, but the series is almost even after the Wolverines' 13-0-2 start through 1918.

The rivalry began to get national attention in the late 1960s; it has enjoyed unprecedented status ever since and deservedly so.

Even though it was the most lopsided outcome in 22 years, Ohio State's 36-point decision to end the 1968 regular season provided the catalyst for the biggest upset of the storied series a year later and catapulted the rivalry to the forefront of the college football landscape.

Hayes' Buckeyes were 8-0 and ranked second heading into the 1968 contest. They dominated the fourth-ranked Wolverines, pounding them, 50-14.

OSU got 34 carries, 143 yards, and four touchdowns from fullback Jim Otis despite 23 tackles by Tom Stincic of Michigan.

However, the ending to that drubbing created controversy and was like throwing gas into an inferno. Otis returned to the game to score the final touchdown, and then Hayes ordered a two-point conversion attempt instead of kicking an extra point, obviously trying to rub salt into the proverbial wound of enemy No. 1. The conversion failed, but Hayes' tart explanation afterward that he couldn't go for three points rightfully enraged Michigan's players and fans, who suffered further when Ohio State moved up to No. 1 and beat Southern Cal, 27-16, in the Rose Bowl.

Despite his 8-2 record against Ohio State, Chalmers "Bump" Elliott was out as Michigan's coach; this development led directly to Schembechler taking over in Ann Arbor. Schembechler had seen the Ohio State program up close—the Barberton, Ohio, native had played under Hayes at Miami (Ohio) and coached under him at OSU before taking the reins at his alma mater for six seasons.

As the 1969 season wound down, it looked like the powerful, top-ranked Buckeyes would steamroll to their ninth win of the year and 23rd straight overall as they visited No. 12 Michigan; with a 7-2 record, the Wolverines were pegged as a 17-point underdog.

Ohio State had outscored its foes by a margin of 371-69, including a 42-14 whipping of 10th-ranked Purdue the week before. The Bucks were prepared to triumph again in front of a college football record crowd of 103,588 at Michigan Stadium.

But a funny thing happened on the way to the massacre. Michigan stunned the crowd by intercepting four Rex Kern passes and two more from reserve Ron Maciejowski. Barry Pierson registered three of the thefts and scooted 60 yards with a punt return to set up a score. UM finished with a 266-22 margin in rushing, while the visitors missed an extra point and failed on a two-point conversion. OSU's Kern was only 6-of-17 passing for 88 yards. Michigan's monumental 24-12 upset victory ushered in the "ten-year war" between the schools, as old friends Schembechler and Hayes engaged in a fierce rivalry.

Despite Michigan's subsequent loss in the 1970 Rose Bowl, the team's landmark victory over OSU resurrected the Wolverines program and established the rivalry as the best in the nation. And Hayes, despite the stunning defeat, went to the grave convinced that no one was better than his 1969 Buckeyes. "That was the best team we ever put together," Hayes maintained with characteristic modesty. "That was probably the best team that ever played college football."

Jim Brandstatter and Michigan won two of three against hated Ohio State, but he and millions of other fans remember that most ballyhooed game in the series, at least north of the border.

"It's considered the watershed game in Michigan history," Brandstatter said of the '69 contest. "Ohio State had won the national championship in '68 and was probably going to be No. 1 again. But we had this confidence that we were going to win that game and knock them off their perch. It's the game that people in Columbus still talk about. It put Michigan back on the map and put Bo [Schembechler] in the spotlight."

The ensuing 10-year struggle is a microcosm of the 100-plus year series, which in turn typified the region's often-antagonistic history. The cities are situated about 200 miles apart on land that the states fought over as far back as the 1780s, and recruiting battles for players have waged ever since, especially for those who have crossed enemy lines.

In 1970, a judge in Columbus dismissed a charge of obscenity against someone who had been arrested for wearing a T-shirt that read, "F--- Michigan" because the message "accurately expressed" local feelings about the university and the state.

It's true that Hayes sometimes had his team stay in Toledo the night before a game in Ann Arbor so the Buckeyes could sleep on Ohio ground. And yes, the most famous story about Hayes' animosity toward the Wolverines, the one about pushing his vehicle across the state line if necessary rather than buying gas in Michigan, may have taken on a life of its own but isn't a tall tale.

The careers of coaches and players have been measured and defined, often harshly, by what they've done or not done in these matchups. In 2003, the highly anticipated 100th meeting, Michigan quarterback John Navarre found himself in the crosshairs of Ohio State's defenders and critical Wolverine supporters.

"Somebody asked about the legacy of John Navarre, whatever that means, would it hinge on this game," said Michigan defensive lineman Grant Bowman, a native of Blacklick, Ohio, prior to the game. "It probably does, and it's probably unfair, but a lot of things are unfair, and that's the way it is and what you have to realize. With a game like this, the opportunities are bigger and the chance for loss is bigger."

The fourth-ranked and defending national champion Buckeyes were 10-1 and hoped to tangle with No. 1 Oklahoma in the Sugar Bowl, but fifth-ranked Michigan (9-2) had other ideas with a conference crown and Rose Bowl shot on the line. Navarre threw for 278 yards, Chris Perry ran for 154 yards, and Braylon Edwards caught seven passes for 130 yards and two touchdowns as the Wolverines earned a 35-21 victory for their first outright Big Ten title since 1997.

Coach Tressel, whose father, Lee, was a big Ohio State fan, said before that encounter, "There is a lot riding on the game, and that's why kids came to Ohio State and why they went to Michigan, to play in games like this. No doubt about it, it's the biggest game ever."

He could have been saying that about almost every game before or since in this series, confrontations that fans have no hesitation identifying as life-changing occurrences. These e-mails from a reader response survey in the *Cleveland Plain Dealer* in November 2005 provide ample proof:

- Steven Miller said, "Fairness has nothing to do with it. It's two storied programs, meeting the last game of the year with both teams fighting for bowl considerations and occasionally a national championship. A rivalry steeped in tradition between two schools bound by proximity playing in a game that can salvage what some might consider a disappointing season (see 2004) or destroy a promising one (see 2003). It's not fair that it defines the season, it's inevitable!"

- Tom Joseph wrote, "Should it define a season? Absolutely! This game is more important to some than any other football game at any level at any time. It's such an intense rivalry that demands the best out of both teams. Year after year—sans the [John] Cooper era—the rivalry not only determines bragging rights, but trips to the national championship games, Big Ten titles, and bowl bids. Without a doubt, it 'defines' the season."

- And Ron Cox added, "This game is the most important day of the year for me. The week leading up to the game is the most important week of the year for me. The month leading up to the game is the most important month of the year for me. To ask such a stupid question as 'should it define a season' is insulting coming from an Ohio newspaper!"

Author Greg Emmanuel expressed it well in *The 100-Yard War*, his 2004 book about the rivalry: "This game has taken root smack dab in the middle of the country, where football is actually more American than apple pie and young fans choose sides as soon as they're old enough to talk."

Longtime Wolverines fan Ken Czasak, who worked at Ulrich's Bookstore on the Michigan campus for 30 years, saw the best and worst of human behavior in the name of school spirit.

"When Bo [Schembechler] arrived, he turned the Michigan program back around," Czasak said. "So with him and Woody, that took the rivalry to a whole new level. It became a deeper level of hate."

He said that it was a challenge to come up with new ways for fans to express their loyalty and/or animosity, depending on the occasion.

"The most unusual item we sold goes back to the days of Woody Hayes," Czasak said. "He was villain No. 1 in the eyes of Michigan fans. He was the lynchpin for a lot of abuse. We had one season where we had toilet paper that had the words 'Wipe Woody' printed on each sheet with a caricature of his face on it. It was wildly popular."

Players from that era knew what was at stake regardless of the outside hoopla surrounding the games. If they didn't remain focused on the task at hand, they faced the wrath of Hayes or Schembechler.

Steve Luke played at Ohio State from 1971 to 1974 and later with the Green Bay Packers. He had been a tight end, linebacker, and center at Massillon High School near Canton. He was 195 pounds and the Buckeyes' starting center for the 1973 Rose Bowl and then switched to defensive back as a junior when the staff saw him perform in agility drills during spring workouts.

OSU almost lost out on Rose Bowl berths during Luke's sophomore and senior seasons because of upset losses at Michigan State. The Buckeyes pulled out narrow victories over Michigan both times to salvage Pasadena trips, even though they ended up losing to Southern Cal both times.

"They were always tough, hard-fought games," Luke said of the dates against the Wolverines. "All three came down to field goals, but Michigan blew theirs. For me, it was a personal thing because Dennis Franklin was Michigan's quarterback, and we had grown up together and talked about going to the same college. But Dennis just wanted to attend Michigan, so that added another dimension to those games for me. I believe he was the winningest quarterback ever at that time, but he lost twice and tied once against us."

Archie Griffin helped the Buckeyes to a 3-0-1 record in the series from 1972 to 1975, a period in which Michigan entered ranked third or fourth every time and Ohio State was No. 1 twice, fourth, and ninth.

"We called this game a separate season," the only two-time Heisman Trophy winner said. "There was the regular season, and then there was the Michigan game. Nothing was as intense as Michigan week, which was a whole different atmosphere."

In his freshman season, Ohio State prevailed, 14-11, at home. Then the top-ranked Buckeyes settled for a 10-all tie in '73. Ohio State held on for a 12-10 decision the next year and finally won a scoring "explosion," 21-14, in '75.

"My first year, we needed two goal-line stands to beat them," Griffin said. "Then they tied us and kept us from winning the national championship. We got four field goals from Tom Klaban to win in '74. My last year, I gained only

46 yards but Pete Johnson had a big game and my brother, Ray, had a key interception after we trailed, 14-7.

"Those were the hardest-hitting games I played in college football, so I was glad they were the last game of the year because I wouldn't have been able to go the next week after two of them," Griffin added. "As a player, you knew you had to be at your best and play even better than you were."

Bill Dufek participated in that hand-to-hand combat at strong-side tackle for Michigan from 1974 to 1978 (he was injured and sat out the 1977 season). Dufek said that he and his teammates knew full well what was in store for them.

"Bo was not a good loser, so we didn't want to disappoint him," Dufek said. "We had a great mutual respect for Ohio State because our programs were so similar and were among the best in the country. There weren't a lot of cheap shots and chippy plays. We knew each other so well and that made them such big games."

The 1970s may have been the heyday for the rivalry, but players from previous eras recall that, even then, the series didn't take a back seat to any others around the country. Former Michigan player Dick Heynen started at offensive and defensive left tackle from 1955 to 1957, lining up next to All-America end Ron Kramer. He blocked for future NFL players Terry Barr and John Morrow.

The Wolverines finished 7-2 his first two seasons and then dipped to 5-3-1, but Heynen, a Grand Rapids native, said that even though every week was tough in the Big Ten, the Ohio State showdown was a notch above the rest.

"We closed practices all week for OSU, and we didn't do that for the other teams," he said of head man Bennie Oosterbaan and his coaching staff. "We always talked about the other teams, but practices for Ohio State were always intense."

Michigan lost two of the three outings in which Heynen saw action, with the road team winning every time. That included a 17-0 Buckeyes triumph in 1955 that knocked the sixth-ranked Wolverines out of the Rose Bowl picture and gave Ohio State an unbeaten league mark.

"I remember we got a bad snow the night before and 'Hopalong' Cassady had a great day [146 yards] in a tough game," Heynen said. "That was the time that Ron Kramer got called for a 15-yard penalty. He kicked the flag and got another penalty, and they drove for a touchdown."

Heynen and Michigan got their revenge at Columbus the next fall, 19-0. "After we scored our last touchdown, I trotted past Woody [Hayes] and asked him what the score was," Heynen said with a devious chuckle. "He came out onto the field and chased me, and I don't know if I ever ran so fast. Then I saw him at a banquet a few weeks later and he said, 'I remember you. You're that

Heynen fellow.' But I'll tell you, those were probably the cleanest, hardest-hitting games we played."

The Buckeyes finished 0-3-1 against Michigan during Robert Momsen's four years at Ohio State; however, he did have the consolation of being a member of the Rose Bowl champions after the 1949 season. Robert and his brother, Tony, played major roles in arguably the most memorable contest in the storied rivalry, as least as far as weather goes—the 1950 Snow Bowl game being on opposite sidelines during a blizzard that dropped 29 inches of snow in the region.

The wintry contest marked Robert Momsen's senior year, one in which he lettered as an offensive tackle and defensive middle guard. The favored Buckeyes jumped ahead, 3-0, after Momsen blocked a punt. Joe Campanella recovered at the Michigan 2-yard line, but the hosts settled for Vic Janowicz's field goal.

Michigan blocked a punt out of the end zone for a safety to close to within 3-2. Then, instead of running out the clock, Ohio State coach Wes Fesler elected another punt attempt just before halftime. Tony Momsen, a center and linebacker, blocked and recovered it in the end zone with 47 seconds left to help put Michigan up, 9-3, a score that held up in the miserable weather that featured swirling 40-mile per hour winds.

Michigan's Chuck Ortmann punted 24 times and Janowicz 21 times for OSU as a reported 50,503 fans braved temperatures that dropped to 5 degrees. The teams combined for 68 yards of total offense: 41 by Ohio State, 27 by Michigan. The Wolverines didn't gain a first down, while Ohio State earned three. Michigan finished 0-for-9 passing, while the Buckeyes had 25 yards through the air on 3-of-18 attempts. Michigan won that dreadful showdown 9-3, which helped the Wolverines give the Momsen family a Rose Bowl title in back-to-back seasons.

"Most people said those were the worst conditions that any college football game was ever played in," Robert Momsen said. "I know they had a heckuva time getting the tarp off the field. The fans helped, but they only got about half of it off because the rest was stuck under snow and ice. Janowicz kicked that 26-yard field goal against a 35-mile per hour wind, and nobody knew if he'd made it until we heard the crowd.

"We felt like we should have won that game, but the funny thing was that Illinois played at Northwestern and was favored by like 26 points, and Northwestern upset them in what we called the Ice Bowl, which was played in sleet and rain. That let Michigan go to the Rose Bowl." His late brother and the Wolverines went on to defeat California, 14-6.

"We had a lot of fun in those days and were both drafted by the NFL," said Robert Momsen, who played with Detroit for one year and San Francisco for two before spending most of his career coaching high school sports in his native

Toledo. "The Rams drafted Tony and he played with Pittsburgh, and then he was in Calgary for three years and won a Grey Cup. But our time in the Big Ten, I can't imagine any conference being any better. Tony always said that we got more publicity from the Snow Bowl game than we deserved."

With such legendary games played for such high stakes over so many years, it's hard to argue with Ohio State and Michigan fans when they say their rivalry is the biggest and best in sports.

"It's two great universities, two historical powers, two great football programs battling it out," Brandstatter said. "For so many years, the winner went to the Rose Bowl and that one game decided the whole ball of wax, which added to the luster. So the stakes got that much higher and the stories got that much better. In the old days, before ESPN, you didn't have Florida-Florida State. The Saturday before Thanksgiving was always Michigan-Ohio State and maybe USC-UCLA, when football was king in the Midwest."

The broadcaster, whose wife, Robbie Timmons, grew up a huge Woody Hayes and Ohio State fan, said that despite the hullabaloo surrounding the games, the players usually worried about what happened on the field and let the fans take care of the rest.

"As players, it was a matter of getting the job done," he said. "There wasn't as much trash talking in my era. We had great respect for Ohio State because they were really good and we couldn't afford to lose. It was emotional, but it was controlled because you had to be on top of your assignments to help the team win.

"As for the fans, there's a real animosity," Brandstatter added. "I mean, people in Columbus don't have any pro teams to root for, so they go crazy. Fans and students call each other bums. At Michigan, they know that OSU doesn't like them, and it's the same down there."

Dave Monnot relished life in the trenches, having served in the Ohio State defensive line for one season before moving to right guard on offense his final three years. No better test existed than when these teams hooked up in a mano-a-mano war for three hours.

"It was a great rivalry," Monnot said. "It was fairly clean because you didn't see a lot of the malarkey you see in other places. Everybody knew what it was about. It was definitely the game that defined every season. This series is why you go to Ohio State. Everybody wants to beat Michigan, so there's no worse feeling than not beating them."

Howard Teifke lettered at Ohio State in 1943 and then served two years in the Army Air Corps, eventually becoming a B-24 gunner over Italy. He returned to OSU from 1946 to 1948, starring at center and linebacker. He and the Buckeyes lost all four times to the Wolverines, including blowouts during his first two tries.

"It was one of those things, but all series go in streaks like that," said Teifke, a native of Fremont, situated between Toledo and Cleveland. "It was a big rivalry when Francis Schmidt was the OSU coach in the 1930s and when Paul Brown was there in the early 40s. I had no intentions of going to college, but the day I graduated my high school coach said that Ohio State was interested. Because of the war, they needed players."

Ohio State–Michigan is always a huge deal, said Teifke. His daughter, Melissa, is a loyal Buckeyes fan who's married to a Wolverine backer. "That happens a lot, especially up around here," said Teifke, who's had season tickets for nearly 60 years. "I want OSU to win, but I don't take it as seriously as some people do. Some folks get so upset over the games. It gets kinda nasty in the stands sometimes. One time up at Michigan, we were treated pretty badly and my wife said she wouldn't go up there anymore.

"Ticket prices for the Michigan game are out of this world," Teifke said. "I once was offered $8,000 for my six tickets. I just couldn't sell them."

It's a feeling the Wolverines share. As current Michigan coach Lloyd Carr said before the 2002 game in Columbus: "You can't buy tradition, and Ohio State–Michigan has it."

MORE SERIES HIGHLIGHTS

1919: Coach John Wilce's team registered the Buckeyes' first win against Michigan, posting a 13-3 decision in Ann Arbor. Ohio State had been 0-13-2 and was outscored 369-21 during the first 15 meetings. Chic Harley contributed a 42-yard touchdown run, an extra point, and four interceptions. He also punted 11 times, including a 60-yarder.

1922: Michigan won, 19-0, as Harry Kipke scored a TD, drop-kicked a field goal, and intercepted two passes as the visitors ruined the Buckeyes' dedication of the new Ohio Stadium.

1926: OSU led, 10-0, after the first quarter but Michigan tied it by halftime. The Wolverines then recovered a fumble at the Ohio State 6 and grabbed the lead on a fourth-and-goal pass from Benny Friedman to Leo Hoffman for a 17-10 margin. The Buckeyes came back for a touchdown, but Myers Clark missed the extra point, handing Michigan a 17-16 victory.

1930–33: Michigan compiled a 31-1-3 record, with its only loss being to Ohio State, 20-7, at home in 1931.

1935: Buckeyes fans tried to bring down the goalposts after their team's 38-0 drubbing of the Wolverines, and a melee lasted for an hour.

1939: Ohio State raced to a 14-0 edge in the first 12 minutes, but that was all the Buckeyes could do as Michigan rallied for a 21-14 decision. Tom Harmon passed to Forest Evashevski for the first score, and holder Fred Trosko scooted 32 yards on a fake field-goal attempt for the winning touchdown in the final 50 seconds.

1940: Harmon moved ahead of Red Grange with an NCAA-record 33 scores, throwing two touchdown passes while completing 11-of-12 tosses for 151 yards to lead Michigan's 40-0 rout. Harmon gained 139 yards rushing, intercepted three passes, averaged 50 yards per punt, and drilled four extra points.

1941: The contest ended in a 20-all tie. It was the first time since the Associated Press poll was established in 1936 that both teams entered ranked, with Michigan at No. 5 and Ohio State at No. 14.

1942: Fifth-ranked Ohio State got two touchdown passes from Paul Sarringhaus, including a 60-yarder, to down fourth-ranked Michigan, 21-7, en route to the national championship. Sarringhaus also caught a scoring toss from wingback Les Horvath, who would win the Heisman two years later.

1944: The lead changed hands five times as Ohio State pulled out an 18-14 victory to finish 9-0 and second in the final AP poll behind Army.

1949: Leo Koceski caught a TD pass from Wally Teninga to help Michigan grab a 7-0 lead; however, Ohio State scored in the fourth quarter. The Buckeyes got a reprieve and a tie when Jim Hague missed the extra point. He got a second chance when officials penalized Michigan for being offsides. That left a tie in the league standings, and because of the no-repeat rule, it allowed Ohio State to go to the Rose Bowl instead of Michigan.

1952: Hayes' second Buckeyes team posted a 27-7 victory, the school's first in the series since 1944. Sophomore quarterback John Borton threw three touchdown passes and ran for a score while the defense forced eight Michigan turnovers to prevent the Wolverines from winning the Big Ten title and going to the Rose Bowl.

1954: The contest was tied at 7-all late in the third quarter when Michigan drove to the Ohio State 1-yard line, where Dave Hill was stopped on a fourth-down play.

The Wolverines disputed the call but to no avail. Ohio State drove 99 yards in 11 plays for the go-ahead score. Howard "Hopalong" Cassady added an insurance touchdown to make it 21-7 as the Buckeyes finished 10-0 and won the national title.

1963: The contest was one of about 35 that were postponed a week after the assassination of President John F. Kennedy. Ohio State won, 14-10, at Ann Arbor.

1964: Michigan won, 10-0, on a touchdown late in the first half after recovering a fumbled punt and a fourth-quarter field goal. Rick Volk recorded two interceptions and knocked down another key pass to stop an Ohio State drive. Michigan finished at No. 4, while the Buckeyes were ranked ninth.

1970: Fourth-ranked Michigan fumbled the opening kickoff, and the No. 5 Buckeyes took advantage en route to a 20-9 victory. Both teams entered unbeaten and untied for the first time in series history. A record 87,331 filled the Horseshoe as the Buckeyes scored 10 points in the fourth quarter, while the Wolverines missed an extra point. Leo Hayden led Ohio State with 118 yards rushing. Wolverines quarterback Don Moorhead was only 12-of-26 for 118 yards, and Michigan gained a measly 37 yards rushing. However, Stanford signal caller Jim Plunkett led his team to an upset of the Buckeyes in the Rose Bowl, ending Rex Kern's record at 27-2 as a starter at OSU.

1971: Michigan was 10-0 and ranked third, while the injury-plagued Buckeyes had suffered three losses before heading to Ann Arbor. Ohio State led, 7-3, after three quarters, but Michigan won, 10-7, as Thom Darden's interception clinched it. However, Stanford pulled another shocker, claiming a 13-12 win for the Roses.

1972: Ninth-ranked Ohio State upset unbeaten and No. 3 Michigan, 14-11, at home, stopping the Wolverines twice on fourth-and-goal from the 1. A field goal in either instance would have sent Michigan to Pasadena. Michigan ran 83 plays and gained 344 yards, compared with the Buckeyes' 44 for 192. Fans tore down the goalposts with 13 seconds remaining as Michigan faced a fourth-and-10 play from the Ohio State 41. But the Buckeyes got trounced, 42-17, by No. 1 Southern Cal in the Rose Bowl.

1973: Top-ranked OSU was 9-0 and had outscored opponents 361-33, while No. 4 Michigan was 10-0. The Wolverines hadn't lost at Michigan Stadium in nearly four years, and a record 105,223 fans witnessed a 10-all deadlock. Archie Griffin gained 163 yards on 30 carries for the Bucks, but quarterback Cornelius Greene's thumb injury prevented them from passing until the final minutes. Neal Colzie intercepted a pass in the end zone in the second half for Ohio State. Michigan's Mike Lantry missed a 38-yard field goal by inches, according to officials, and was wide on a 44-yarder with 28 seconds left. Both teams ended up 7-0-1 in league play, and Big Ten athletic directors (by a 6-4 vote) selected Ohio State to represent the conference in the Rose Bowl. Greene and Griffin then led the Buckeyes to a 42-21 triumph over the Trojans.

1974: Ohio State was ranked fourth and stood 8-1 with its only setback being by three points to Michigan State, and UM was ranked third (10-0). Tom Klaban kicked four field goals, including three from beyond 40 yards, to give the Buckeyes a 12-10 win. Lantry missed a field goal with 18 seconds left. Hayes' bunch went on to lose, 18-17, to USC in the Rose Bowl. The Wolverines compiled a 30-2-1 record from 1972 to 1974 and had no Rose Bowl appearances to show for it.

1975: Ohio State was ranked No. 1 and 10-0, while Michigan was No. 4 and 8-0-2. The Buckeyes hadn't won at Michigan since 1967. OSU earned the hard-fought 21-14 win, but Archie Griffin's career ended after a frustrating 23-10 Rose Bowl loss to UCLA, a team the Buckeyes had beaten in week four.

1976: OSU was 8-2-1 and ranked eighth, while Michigan was 9-1 and fourth. The Wolverines won, 22-0, in Columbus, the first shutout in the series since 1964.

1977: No. 5 Michigan won, 14-6, at Ann Arbor over No. 4 Ohio State. Hayes was put on probation after swinging at an ABC cameraman on the sidelines. Wolverines linebacker Ron Simpkins recorded 20 tackles and recovered a fumble.

1978: Ohio State entered the game 7-2-1 and ranked 16th, while No. 6 Michigan (9-1) won, 14-3, at Columbus. Hayes would erupt again, this time in OSU's upset loss to Clemson in the Gator Bowl, a game in which Hayes hit Tigers linebacker Charlie Bauman after an interception. He also yelled at officials and received two 15-yard penalties. It was a humiliating end to his spectacular career.

1979: Earle Bruce's second-ranked Buckeyes were 10-0 and capped the regular season with an 18-15 victory at Michigan Stadium. Outside linebacker Jim Laughlin blocked a punt with four minutes left, and Todd Bell returned the ball 18 yards for a touchdown to beat the 13th-ranked Wolverines. But Charles White would lead Southern Cal to a 17-16 decision over the Buckeyes in the Rose Bowl.

1980: A 9-1 record and No. 5 ranking didn't help Ohio State as 10th-ranked Michigan posted a 9-3 victory in front of 88,827 at The Horseshoe.

1981: No. 7 Michigan was an eight-point favorite at home and needed a win to clinch a Rose Bowl berth, but Art Schlichter led the unranked Buckeyes to a 14-9 upset, the sixth time in seven years that the visiting team came out on top.

1983: Eighth-ranked Michigan won, 24-21, in Ann Arbor. Jim Lachey, a future NFL standout, was one of the Ohio State messenger guards who took turns bringing in the called play. Lachey was supposed to get the ball on a trick play, the fumblerooski, in which the center appears to snap the ball but leaves it on the ground for a running back to pick up. But center Joe Dooley accidentally kicked the ball after setting it down and Michigan recovered, stopping what could have been the go-ahead touchdown for the Bucks.

1986: Michigan won, 26-24, behind Jim Harbaugh, giving Schembechler his eighth Rose Bowl berth. OSU freshman kicker Matt Frantz just missed a 45-yard field goal in the final minute. Harbaugh had guaranteed a Michigan victory, and

Bo Schembechler is carried from the field by victorious Wolverines
after their squeaker over Ohio State in 1986.

he got help from Jamie Morris, who gained 216 yards rushing. Ohio State's Chris Spielman was valiant in defeat, getting in 29 tackles.

1987: Ohio State had lost wide receiver Cris Carter (for signing with an agent) and entered the game 5-4-1. Bruce was also a lame-duck coach, but the Buckeyes pulled out a 23-20 win at Michigan and the players carried him off the field. He finished 5-4 against the Wolverines and 81-26-1 in nine seasons. Michigan moved ahead, 13-0, but Frantz completed the comeback by hitting a 26-yard field goal with 5:18 left.

1988: John Cooper took over at Ohio State. Buckeye fans liked the fact that Cooper had led Arizona State to a 22-15 win over Michigan in the Rose Bowl after the 1986 campaign, but they had their doubts when his first squad in Columbus finished 4-6-1 after a tough 34-31 loss to the Wolverines. It was Ohio State's first losing season in 22 years.

1991: Michigan won, 31-3, as Desmond Howard's 93-yard punt return touchdown solidified his Heisman Trophy victory party. The Cleveland native also helped hand Cooper his fourth straight setback in the series. Howard caught 134 passes and scored 37 touchdowns during his Michigan career, but the image most fans remember is him striking the Heisman pose after his sparkling runback.

1993: Fifth-ranked Ohio State (9-0-1) needed a win to clinch the Big Ten title over Wisconsin. However, the Wolverines, who had four losses, whipped the Buckeyes, 28-0. Michigan outgained Ohio State, 421-212. Buckeyes quarterbacks Bobby Hoying and Bret Powers combined to throw four interceptions.

1994: Cooper's squad registered its first win against Michigan in his seventh try, posting a 22-6 triumph at home. Marlon Kerner's blocked field goal and Luke Fickell's interception helped the hosts score 10 points early in the fourth quarter to put the game away.

1995: No. 2 Ohio State was 11-0 with wins over six ranked teams, while Michigan was No. 12 under first-year coach Lloyd Carr. He led the Wolverines to a 31-23 victory that got them to the Rose Bowl. Buckeyes star Eddie George won the Heisman after rushing for 1,927 yards and scoring 24 times. *The Lantern*, Ohio State's school paper, described the outcome well with a headline that read, "Deja Blue: Michigan Dashes Ohio State's Rose Bowl Dreams—Again." It was appropriate after Tshimanga "Tim" Biakabutuka riddled the Buckeyes' defense to gain 313 yards rushing, the most ever against OSU and the second-highest single-game mark in Michigan history. Ohio State's final drive was snuffed when Michigan freshman Charles Woodson, an Ohio native, picked off his second pass.

1996: OSU was No. 2 and 10-0 and had clinched a spot in Pasadena, but No. 21 Michigan earned a 13-9 triumph. The Buckeyes piled up a 223-62 edge in total yards but led only 9-0 at halftime. Michigan got a 69-yard touchdown pass and two field goals to win. Ohio State beat Arizona State, 20-17, in the Rose Bowl, but because of the loss to Michigan, the Buckeyes finished second behind Florida.

1997: The fourth-ranked Buckeyes lost, 20-14, to top-ranked Michigan. Woodson led the Wolverines to an 11-0 regular season and a few weeks later helped them claim the school's first national championship since 1948 with a 21-16 win over Washington State in the Rose Bowl. He set up one score against the Buckeyes with a 37-yard pass reception, returned a punt 78 yards for a score and stopped one Ohio State drive with a diving interception in the end zone. Woodson's big plays helped negate David Boston's 56-yard score and a rally from a 20-0 deficit.

1998: This time, Ohio State knocked No. 11 Michigan out of Rose Bowl contention with a 31-16 triumph. The Buckeyes had been ranked No. 1 for 10 weeks but suffered a 28-24 loss to Michigan State two weeks earlier. Boston's 10 catches for 217 yards and two scores helped OSU snap Michigan's 16-game league winning streak despite 375 yards passing from Tom Brady. Ohio State beat Texas A&M in the Sugar Bowl and finished the year No. 2.

2000: Michigan won, 38-26, at Columbus, leaving Cooper with a 2-10-1 mark against the Wolverines. The Buckeyes lost to South Carolina in the Outback Bowl, and Cooper was fired after compiling a 111-43-4 mark in 13 seasons.

2001: Tressel, a former Ohio State assistant and head coach at Youngstown State, was chosen over former Hayes player Glen Mason of Minnesota. At a basketball game in January, the new football coach guaranteed a win over Michigan. He and the Buckeyes followed through on that promise with a 26-20 decision as Jonathan Wells scored the first three touchdowns to help Ohio State to its first win in Ann Arbor since 1987.

2002: Maurice Clarett arrived on the scene, helping No. 2 Ohio State to a 13-0 regular-season mark and a 14-9 win over 12th-ranked Michigan at the Big House. Will Allen intercepted a pass near the goal line as time expired to clinch the win. The Buckeyes then upset Miami in the Fiesta Bowl, 31-24, in double overtime, to snap the Hurricanes' 34-game winning streak. Ohio State had not won a national title since Hayes' last in 1968.

2004: The Buckeyes were only 6-4 but defeated Michigan, 37-21, after the Wolverines had won eight straight games and 13 in a row in league action. Ohio State quarterback Troy Smith accounted for 386 total yards: 241 passing and 145 rushing. The Buckeyes were clinging to a 20-14 lead in the third quarter when freshman Ted Ginn returned a punt 82 yards for a score.

2005: OSU won, 25-21, only its sixth win in Ann Arbor in its last 19 trips dating to the late 1960s. UM gained only 32 yards rushing on 24 carries. Ohio State's Smith passed for a personal-best 300 yards. He completed seven of eight pass attempts, including a 26-yarder to Anthony Gonzalez to the Michigan 4 during a 12-play, 88-yard drive for the winning touchdown with 24 seconds left.

ALL-TIME SERIES RESULTS

MICHIGAN LEADS, 57-40-6

October 16, 1897—Michigan 34, Ohio State 0
November 24, 1900—Michigan 0, Ohio State 0 (T)
November 9, 1901—Michigan 21, Ohio State 0
October 25, 1902—Michigan 86, Ohio State 0
November 7, 1903—Michigan 36, Ohio State 0
October 15, 1904—Michigan 31, Ohio State 6
November 11, 1905—Michigan 40, Ohio State 0
October 20, 1906—Michigan 6, Ohio State 0
October 26, 1907—Michigan 22, Ohio State 0
October 24, 1908—Michigan 10, Ohio State 6
October 16, 1909—Michigan 33, Ohio State 6
October 22, 1910—Michigan 3, Ohio State 3 (T)
October 21, 1911—Michigan 19, Ohio State 0
October 19, 1912—Michigan 14, Ohio State 0
November 30, 1918—Michigan 14, Ohio State 0
October 25, 1919—Ohio State 13, Michigan 3
November 6, 1920—Ohio State 14, Michigan 7
October 22, 1921—Ohio State 14, Michigan 0
October 21, 1922—Michigan 19, Ohio State 0
October 20, 1923—Michigan 23, Ohio State 0
November 15, 1924—Michigan 16, Ohio State 6
November 14, 1925—Michigan 10, Ohio State 0
November 13, 1926—Michigan 17, Ohio State 16
October 22, 1927—Michigan 21, Ohio State 0
October 20, 1928—Ohio State 19, Michigan 7
October 19, 1929—Ohio State 7, Michigan 0

October 18, 1930—Michigan 13, Ohio State 0
October 17, 1931—Ohio State 20, Michigan 7
October 15, 1932—Michigan 14, Ohio State 0
October 21, 1933—Michigan 13, Ohio State 0
November 17, 1934—Ohio State 34, Michigan 0
November 23, 1935—Ohio State 38, Michigan 0
November 21, 1936—Ohio State 21, Michigan 0
November 20, 1937—Ohio State 21, Michigan 0
November 19, 1938—Michigan 18, Ohio State 0
November 25, 1939—Michigan 21, Ohio State 14
November 23, 1940—Michigan 40, Ohio State 0
November 22, 1941—Michigan 20, Ohio State 20 (T)
November 21, 1942—Ohio State 21, Michigan 7
November 20, 1943—Michigan 45, Ohio State 7
November 25, 1944—Ohio State 18, Michigan 14
November 24, 1945—Michigan 7, Ohio State 3
November 23, 1946—Michigan 58, Ohio State 6
November 22, 1947—Michigan 21, Ohio State 0
November 20, 1948—Michigan 13, Ohio State 3
November 19, 1949—Michigan 7, Ohio State 7 (T)
November 25, 1950—Michigan 9, Ohio State 3
November 24, 1951—Michigan 7, Ohio State 0
November 22, 1952—Ohio State 27, Michigan 7
November 21, 1953—Michigan 20, Ohio State 0
November 20, 1954—Ohio State 21, Michigan 7
November 19, 1955—Ohio State 17, Michigan 0
November 24, 1956—Michigan 19, Ohio State 0

Fan fever breaks out at The Game.

November 23, 1957—Ohio State 31, Michigan 14

November 22, 1958—Ohio State 20, Michigan 14

November 21, 1959—Michigan 23, Ohio State 14

November 19, 1960—Ohio State 7, Michigan 0

November 25, 1961—Ohio State 50, Michigan 20

November 24, 1962—Ohio State 28, Michigan 0

November 30, 1963—Ohio State 14, Michigan 10

November 21, 1964—Michigan 10, Ohio State 0

November 20, 1965—Ohio State 9, Michigan 7

November 19, 1966—Michigan 17, Ohio State 3

November 25, 1967—Ohio State 24, Michigan 14

November 23, 1968—Ohio State 50, Michigan 14

November 22, 1969—Michigan 24, Ohio State 12

November 21, 1970—Ohio State 20, Michigan 9

November 20, 1971—Michigan 10, Ohio State 7

November 25, 1972—Ohio State 14, Michigan 11

November 24, 1973—Michigan 10, Ohio State 10 (T)

November 23, 1974—Ohio State 12, Michigan 10

November 22, 1975—Ohio State 21, Michigan 14

November 20, 1976—Michigan 22, Ohio State 0

November 19, 1977—Michigan 14, Ohio State 6

November 25, 1978—Michigan 14, Ohio State 3

November 17, 1979—Ohio State, 18, Michigan 15

November 22, 1980—Michigan 9, Ohio State 3

November 21, 1981—Ohio State 14, Michigan 9

November 20, 1982—Ohio State 24, Michigan 14

November 19, 1983—Michigan 24, Ohio State 21

November 17, 1984—Ohio State 21, Michigan 6

November 23, 1985—Michigan 27, Ohio State 17

November 22, 1986—Michigan 26, Ohio State 24

November 21, 1987—Ohio State 23, Michigan 20

November 19, 1988—Michigan 34, Ohio State 31

November 25, 1989—Michigan 28, Ohio State 18

November 24, 1990—Michigan 16, Ohio State 13

November 23, 1991—Michigan 31, Ohio State 3

November 21, 1992—Michigan 13, Ohio State 13 (T)

November 20, 1993—Michigan 28, Ohio State 0

November 19, 1994—Ohio State 22, Michigan 6

November 25, 1995—Michigan 31, Ohio State 23

November 23, 1996—Michigan 13, Ohio State 9

November 22, 1997—Michigan 20, Ohio State 14

November 21, 1998—Ohio State 31, Michigan 16

November 20, 1999—Michigan 24, Ohio State 17

November 18, 2000—Michigan 38, Ohio State 26

November 24, 2001—Ohio State 26, Michigan 20

November 23, 2002—Ohio State 14, Michigan 9

November 22, 2003—Michigan 35, Ohio State 21

November 20, 2004—Ohio State 37, Michigan 21

November 19, 2005—Ohio State 25, Michigan 21

November 18, 2006—Ohio State 42, Michigan 39

BRINGING HOME THE BUCKET:
INDIANA vs.
PURDUE

It was the Roaring 20s, and the Chicago alumni groups of Purdue and Indiana assigned Russell Gray and Dr. Clarence Jones, respectively, to figure out what kind of trophy would best capture the spirit of both schools and their intrastate football rivalry.

They, in turn, dispatched two men to locate a suitable bucket to go to the winner of the annual showdown. They couldn't have chosen a more appropriate person to lead the search. Indiana alumnus Wiley J. Huddle and his Purdue counterpart, Fritz Ernst, found a moldy, moss-covered water receptacle in a well at a farm between Kent and Hanover in southern Indiana, which had been settled in the 1840s. Legend has it that Confederate General John Hunt Morgan's raiders left it there after moving through the area during the Civil War.

Whatever its origins, the Old Oaken Bucket has symbolized this series since 1925. The refurbished version features a chain with bronze block letters representing each contest: 68 "Ps," 35 "Is," and six "I-Ps."

It's one of the most recognizable trophies in the land, and few rivalries have been fiercer than when the Boilermakers and Hoosiers get together in their traditional regular-season finale.

Only twice has Indiana played with Big Ten Conference title hopes on the line, and the first occurred two days after Thanksgiving, November 24, 1945.

The game had ground to a scoreless tie by halftime, as Indiana freshman halfback George Taliaferro intercepted a Bob DeMoss pass in the end zone, and Bob Ravensberg stole another one. However, future college and pro hall of famer Pete Pihos put Indiana on the scoreboard with a 1-yard plunge in the third quarter and scored again shortly after that to make it 13-0. The second score was set up when Purdue was stopped at its 6 on the kickoff and fumbled, with future major league baseball slugger Ted Kluszewski recovering at the Boilers' 1.

Ben Raimondi passed to Kluszewski to make it 19-0 with five minutes left, and Raimondi connected with Lou Mihajlovich to close out the scoring in front of 27,000 fans at Memorial Stadium in Bloomington. Purdue was limited to 86 total yards, four first downs, and a 1-of-14 pass completion rate that netted minus-2 yards.

Indiana's 26-0 whipping of Cecil Isbell's 18th-ranked Boilermakers allowed the Hoosiers to claim their first crown after 46 seasons in the league. The Hoosiers finished 9-0-1, their first unbeaten campaign. Taliaferro rushed for 100 yards as the Hoosiers claimed their third consecutive shutout to end the season.

An Indiana setback would have handed the Michigan-Ohio State winner the league crown, but the Hoosiers, who finished 5-0-1 to the Wolverines' 5-1 mark, took care of that to close the gap to 24-23 in the all-time series against Purdue.

The Boilermakers finished 7-3, while the Hoosiers ended up ranked fourth in the country.

It took another 22 years for such a scenario to repeat itself, and 1967 marked the first time that the foes played for both the Bucket and the league championship. Harry Gonso passed to Jade Butcher for Indiana's first score, but Perry Williams' run helped tie it. Mike Krivoshia bulled in from 2 yards out, and Terry Cole blazed 63 yards to give the Hoosiers a 19-7 lead, after they missed an extra point and a two-point attempt.

PHOTOS COURTESY PURDUE SPORTS

Cecil Isbell's scoring pass (left) rallied Purdue in 1936; Quarterback Mike Phipps
(right) pulled off a come-from-behind victory for Purdue in 1968.

Third-ranked Purdue closed to within 19-14 on Williams' second TD, but he later fumbled on the Hoosiers' 1-yard line. Cal Snowden sacked Purdue quarterback Mike Phipps to snuff out one drive. Finally, the Boilers drove to the Indiana 22 before time ran out. Williams gained 124 yards and teammate Leroy Keyes added 114, but the Hoosiers held on to share the championship with Purdue and Minnesota, all with 6-1 league marks.

Coach John Pont's Boilermakers could have earned their first outright crown since 1929, but Indiana, which had lost to the Gophers, 33-7, the week before, accepted a berth in the Rose Bowl, where the Hoosiers suffered a 14-3 defeat against top-ranked Southern California. Indiana finished fourth and sixth in the wire service polls, while Purdue captured the ninth position in both.

Ken Kaczmarek was a senior and key member of that Indiana squad's formidable linebacking corps. The South Bend, Indiana, native enjoyed the Hoosiers' magical run to the top.

"I remember that Purdue had to beat us both my junior and senior years to get to the Rose Bowl," Kaczmarek said. "In 1966, we played well and hung in with [No. 2] Michigan State the week before, but we entered the Purdue contest pretty banged up, and they whipped us, 51-6. But in 1967, we were 8-0 and then everything, the dumbest things, went wrong against Minnesota. So we were down most of that week, but we knew if we won that we'd be going to the Rose Bowl. We went to a couple of coaches' houses on Thanksgiving Day, and on Friday we were ready to play.

"Terry Cole had a great game, but they had Mike Phipps and Leroy Keyes, and kept coming back at us," Kaczmarek said. "Our defense was on the field for 105 plays, and they got to our 4-yard line with us ahead, 19-14. They handed off to Perry Williams; I hit him and he fumbled. We ran three plays and punted, so they got the ball back again but didn't get close enough to score."

His father followed Notre Dame when Kaczmarek was growing up. But Kaczmarek chose Indiana because he figured he could start as a sophomore and still major in business. After chosing Indiana, he learned even more about the Bucket.

"Everything came together for us my last year," Kaczmarek said. "Our defense gave up only three touchdown passes all year. We were really quick and did a lot of blitzing. O.J. [Simpson], his longest run against us was 11 yards [in the Rose Bowl]."

Jade Butcher still easily holds the Indiana record for career receiving touchdowns with 30, including three in the Hoosiers' wild 38-35 loss to Purdue in 1968. He led Indiana in receptions all three of his varsity seasons and scored 10 TDs every year, earning All-America honors as a senior. He made a great one-two combination with rushing leader John Isenbarger, who gained 2,453 yards and averaged 5 yards per carry from 1967 to 1969, earning All-America honors as a senior after gaining 1,217 yards.

Butcher also played a vital role in the 1967 showdown against the Boiler-makers, and almost for the wrong reason after his miscue helped botch a two-point attempt because of his absence.

John Isenbarger racked up 2,453 yards for Indiana between 1967 and 1969.

"We had a lot of games where we came from behind, and then the week before the Purdue game we got our butts kicked by Minnesota," Butcher said. "When it came to Purdue week, everybody was talking about the Rose Bowl. We obviously had a lot riding on that game. Then I caught a touchdown pass and we had decided to go for two points, but I always came out for the kicker and nobody told me. Harry Gonso took the snap and rolled left and scrambled for his life before being sacked. I just happened to be watching and standing next to Coach Pont. I'll never forget his look when he saw me. He put his hands on his hips and yelled 'Jade!' But we came back to win.

"The other thing I remember about that game is our fullback, Terry Cole," Butcher added. "He was really nervous beforehand, so I had a feeling and was hoping that Terry would have a good game. He broke two long runs, one about 70 yards and the other about 60, one of them for a TD. That really opened things up and was pretty special."

Butcher lost his final two Bucket games, but he recalled those days fondly. "It's probably one of the greatest rivalries in college football," the Bloomington native said. "Because they're in West Lafayette and we're just down the road, it was always a heated battle. The teams always seemed to get into skirmishes. The Bucket, with the Is and Ps dangling from it, is a pretty neat piece of athletic history."

Students and other fans have stoked the competitive fires from the early days. In the 1930s, Indiana students started a ritual of displaying a dummy they named Jawn Purdue during a torchlight parade through campus. They burned and abused their target before burying him until the next season. The tradition fizzled in the early 1970s.

In 1948, an airplane flew over West Lafayette, dropping leaflets that described Purdue as a "cow college." Boilermakers fans responded by saying that Indiana's campus was home to the "cows," their derisive term for Bloomington coeds. Harry Szulborski was a star halfback for the Boilermakers while many of those mischievous activities took place at both universities. The Detroit native suited up from 1946 to 1949. Purdue fell to Indiana to end his first two seasons, but Szulborski got revenge during his junior and senior campaigns.

Szulborski enjoyed success against the Hoosiers. He carried 34 times for 197 yards in Purdue's 39-0 whitewashing in 1948 and accounted for 110 yards on 20 carries during a 14-6 victory in his last collegiate game. That meant two of his 11 career 100-yard outings came versus Indiana.

"Those were really tough battles," Szulborski said. "They beat us my first two years, but we took them to the cleaners in '48. It's still an intense rivalry for fans."

Alex Agase had the distinction of earning All-America honors at two schools, divided by a stint in World War II. He earned those honors at Illinois in 1942 and '46 and with Purdue in '43. He later coached at Northwestern from 1964 to 1972 and with the Boilermakers from 1973 to 1976.

His only season at Purdue as a player proved to be outstanding, as the Boilermakers finished 6-0 in Big Ten competition and 9-0 overall, culminating with a 7-0 triumph over Indiana. That contest was more than enough to convince Agase that the Bucket Battle was one of the game's best.

"Notre Dame was tough and was always a big game, but it wasn't as big as against the Hoosiers," Agase said. "Purdue–Indiana was vicious. You could really feel the intensity all week long."

Jack Calcaterra could attest to that, having lettered for the Boilermakers from 1964 to 1966, first playing middle guard on defense and switching to right tackle to help protect Bob Griese, earning all-Big Ten laurels on both sides of the ball.

"We clobbered them my senior year, but it was a good rivalry," Calcaterra said, having beaten the Hoosiers all four times. "I had two good friends, John

Heaton and Kevin Duffy, who I played against in high school who were at Indiana. I wrote them a letter that said we were going to kick their asses, all in fun. But they showed it to the coaches and everybody down there was all irate. I didn't find out until later how much commotion it caused. I was all bloody after that game and broke my knuckles. I also wore a helmet that was a little too big, so when the facemask got pushed down, the top of the helmet smashed into the bridge of my nose and never had a chance to heal. But it looked cool, and I still have the scar."

Ken Loushin and Purdue fell during his sophomore and redshirt seasons of 1976–77, but he tasted victory and what it meant to win Bucket games the next two years. The 1979 Boilermakers became the only team in school history to record 10 victories, including a 37-21 decision over Lee Corso's Hoosiers in Bloomington.

"It was really big, and they always made a point to bring up the tradition during a basketball game," Loushin said. "Being from Ohio, I had to learn about the history once I got there. But a lot of guys played against each other in high school, and it meant a lot to them. You definitely wanted to win it or keep it and put a 'P' on the chain."

Jimmy Young's interception for Indiana set off a brawl in 1992.

Joey Eloms played defensive back, wide receiver, and kick returner with the Hoosiers from 1994 to 1997. He then was on the Seattle Seahawks' roster for 18 months and played a season in the XFL before hanging up his cleats.

"All of the time I was growing up, the Indiana-Purdue rivalry was mostly about basketball," said the Fort Wayne, Indiana, native who lives and works in the Detroit area. "But then you see the bucket with the Is and Ps hanging on it and you knew how important football was. The only time we beat them [33-29] while I was there was my freshman year. I never got to actually touch the Bucket after the game, but it was kinda cool to see it. If you won that game, the coach had his job for another year."

Eloms played under Bill Mallory and Cam Cameron, and remembers one contest in particular. "It was my sophomore year, and Mike Alstott was their big star and was just bashing us," Eloms said of the future Tampa Bay Buccaneers standout. "There was one play, a trap off left tackle, and it ended up being just me and him on the outside. I'm 175 pounds and he's a moving freight train, but I hit him as hard as I could. I was the first bee sting he felt. The moral of the story is that it took about seven guys to bring him down."

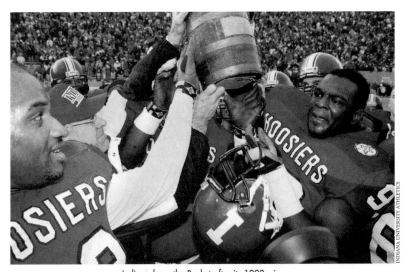

Indiana hugs the Bucket after its 1993 win.

Players aren't the only ones who make a big deal out of such trophy games; coaches often go to great lengths to hype their importance and sometimes celebrate in unusual ways once they have their hands on the coveted symbols.

Lee Corso, better known as one of ESPN's college football analysts in recent years, was Indiana's coach from 1973 to 1982. He posted signs in his office as well as in the locker rooms and bathrooms to get his Hoosiers in the correct frame of mind. So, when he finally won it in his fourth try in 1976, it was easy to see why Corso was so irate when he found out that the Boilermakers hadn't brought the Bucket with them.

"We had lost three in a row, so I went across the field and said, 'Where's the Bucket?'" he said in a 2001 interview. "They said, 'We don't know.' They had won it something like 10 straight times [actually 11 of 13], so they didn't bring it. I just kept saying, 'Where's the Bucket?' The next day I sent an assistant coach to West Lafayette to find the Bucket. They didn't have the Bucket."

Indiana eventually received the Bucket and displayed it in Assembly Hall, the basketball arena, but not before Corso took it home to spend a little personal time with it. "When I finally got it, I slept with it between my legs," he said. "I had the Is and Ps all over my bed. My wife thought I was crazy."

Cameron lettered for Corso in 1982 and 1983, and split against Purdue. He then lost his first four outings against the Boilermakers as the Hoosiers' coach starting in 1996. On the eve of his final Big Ten game and league win as Indiana's coach, a 13-7 decision over Purdue, Cameron said that the series meant everything.

"Having grown up in Indiana, you hear so much about the Indiana-Purdue rivalry," Cameron said in 2001. "There aren't too many families in this state that don't have people on both sides of this game. My father-in-law is a Purdue graduate and has a degree from Indiana. It is something that you hear about 365 days a year."

It was the Boilermakers' turn to celebrate in 2005.

MORE SERIES HIGHLIGHTS

1903: Tragedy struck before the game: At 9:45 a.m. on October 31, a 14-car train carrying the Purdue team, band, and fans into Indianapolis for the game crashed into a section of coal cars that was being backed down the tracks. Thirteen players were among the 16 killed in the mishap, which forced the cancellation of the game.

1925: Both teams were winless in conference action entering the first Bucket meeting, this one at Indiana's new Memorial Stadium in Bloomington. Larry Marks appeared to score on a 90-yard punt return for Indiana, but it was ruled that he stepped out of bounds. The Hoosiers had several other chances, including Louie Briner's three missed field goals, as the game ended in a scoreless tie. So a combined "I-P" was placed on the Bucket.

1926: Chester "Cotton" Wilcox scampered 56 yards for a touchdown and set up a final score on a 30-yard run as Purdue posted a 24-14 victory. Halfback Chuck Bennett registered both Indiana scores.

1929: Purdue came into the game 4-0 in the Big Ten and 7-0 overall, and had locked up its first league championship. The Boilermakers got two scores from Glen Harmeson in finishing off their first perfect season with a 32-0 drubbing of the Hoosiers. Bleachers were erected to accommodate an extra 3,000 to 5,000 fans at Memorial Stadium for the largest turnout of the series to that point. Purdue won the first down count, 12-1, and rushing battle, 243-68. Indiana failed to complete a pass while throwing three interceptions.

1930: Noble Kizer, a Plymouth, Indiana, native, took over from former Notre Dame star and captain Jimmy Phelan as Purdue's new head coach. The Hoosiers were a huge underdog in the contest at West Lafayette after not scoring so far in a conference game. The hosts moved on top, 6-0, in the first half on Lewis Pope's pass to Jim Purvis, but George VanBibber missed an extra point, which would decide the outcome.

Indiana tied it in the fourth quarter on Gene Opask's toss to Vic Dauer, and Ed Hughes' boot won the game, 7-6, for Indiana's first Bucket triumph. However, young men posing as Indiana students had pilfered the coveted traveling prize and taken it back to West Lafayette, but they eventually paid for their sins.

1933: Purdue's 19-3 triumph featured Jim Peelle's 90-yard punt return at Bloomington.

1934: Purdue entered the game at 3-0 in league competition and had a chance to tie Minnesota for the top spot, while Indiana started the day winless and scoreless in Big Ten outings under first-year coach Bo McMillin. It didn't matter as the Hoosiers grabbed a 17-6 decision, highlighted by Don Veller's 82-yard touchdown jaunt.

1935: Indiana clinched its first winning season since 1920 with a 7-0 win on Lewis "Wendell" Walker's pass to Vern Huffman.

1936: Purdue suffered another tragedy, this time before the season started. On September 12, a heater ignited gasoline fumes, shooting flames across the team's locker room. Six players were hospitalized with burns to their feet and legs, and two of them died. The Boilermakers rebounded from the incident as both foes entered with 3-1 league and 5-2 overall marks for this encounter at Ross-Ade Stadium, where 32,000 (7,000 over capacity) fans watched on a rainy, chilly afternoon.

There was no score at halftime as snow started to fall, but Purdue bolted to a 13-0 advantage after a blocked punt set up the second score. Indiana shaved it to 13-7 and Huffman hooked up with Robert Kenderdine for a second time. But the extra point failed, leaving it knotted at 13. The Hoosiers capitalized on a Purdue fumble, taking a 20-13 lead on Huffman's third touchdown pass. Purdue rallied on Cecil Isbell's second scoring pass to Jim Zachary, and Isbell made the point-after with a minute left to secure a 20-all finish, the first tie since the inaugural Bucket game in 1925. George Fowler uncorked an 84-yard punt for Indiana, while Huffman registered a 92-yard kickoff return.

Hall of Famer Pete Pihos helped Indiana whip the Boilermakers in 1945.

1938: The Boilermakers won, 13-6, as Jack Brown raced 100 yards for a touchdown with a kickoff return.

1940: Adolph "Cobb" Lewis set up the game's only score—Gene White's 33-yard field goal—as Indiana won it with just 14 seconds left, in the rain and pending darkness at West Lafayette. It was the Hoosiers' first win on the road in this series since 1930.

1943: No. 3 Purdue took a 7-0 halftime cushion on Sam Vacanti's pass to Frank Bauman and held on, stopping Indiana's last-ditch pass on a fourth-and-inches call on the last play of the game. The Boilermakers shared the Big Ten title, their first since 1932. It also was Purdue's first perfect mark (9-0) since 1929.

1946: Indiana claimed its third straight triumph, 34-20, crawling out of a 13-0 hole to finish 6-3 overall. Ned Maloney raced 90 yards with a fumble return for the Boilermakers. It was the first time since 1925 that Purdue failed to win a conference game.

1948: Purdue routed the Hoosiers, 39-0, the largest victory margin in the series up to that point. Szulborski rushed 34 times for 194 yards, and Norbert Adams toted the pigskin 24 times for another 148 yards as the Boilers outgained Indiana, 524-70, in total yards. The Boilermakers ran 85 times for 454 yards while holding the Hoosiers to four first downs, a dubious school record.

1949: Szulborski and John Kerestes combined for 217 yards on the ground to lift Purdue to a 14-6 win.

1950: Both schools whipped Notre Dame, giving the Hoosiers their first win against the Irish since 1906. However, the Boilermakers had gone winless since their Oct. 7 upset over Notre Dame in week two of the 1950 season, and Indiana had only one victory after their 20-7 upset of Notre Dame heading into the Bucket battle. Purdue stole a 13-0 victory on John Durham's 85-yard kickoff return and Curt Jones' 26-yard interception run in conditions that featured a temperature of 15 degrees and 25-mph winds. Indiana completed 2-of-13 passes for 10 yards.

1951: Purdue pulled out a 21-13 verdict, which didn't sit well with some folks: A melee broke out with 10 seconds remaining that included fans, players, and an official. Phil Klezek topped the Boilermakers with 106 yards rushing.

1952: Purdue jumped to a 14-0 lead, only to see Indiana tie it and grab the upper hand on a safety. The Boilermakers responded as Rex Brock, a brother of baseball Hall of Famer Lou Brock, scooted 24 yards for a 21-16 margin. Purdue then stopped the Hoosiers on the last play from the Boilers' 4-yard line. Purdue tied Wisconsin at 4-1-1 for the crown, but the next day conference ADs gave the Badgers the nod for the Rose Bowl.

1953: The Boilermakers committed 16 penalties and still won easily, 30-0 in front of 33,000 at Bloomington.

1955: Purdue pulled out a 6-4 victory in Bloomington. Boilermakers quarterback Len Dawson was tackled twice for safeties, one intentionally late in the game as Purdue chose not to risk a blocked punt.

1956: Mel Dillard gained 130 yards on 24 tries in Purdue's 39-20 defeat of the Hoosiers.

1957: Purdue claimed its 10th straight win in the series, 35-13, a result that led to several fights involving almost 500 fans; the state police were forced to step in. Thomas Ciukaj returned a blocked punt 13 yards for one Purdue score.

1958: The eighth-ranked Boilermakers were 6-1-1 and the Hoosiers entered the game with a 5-3 record. The foes each missed extra points and made two-point conversions to force a 15-all tie at the intermission. That's how the game ended. Jack Laraway's 27-yard touchdown with a blocked punt aided Purdue's cause.

1959: Bernie Allen's 41-yard field goal lifted Purdue to a 10-7 decision in the final contest played at the original Memorial Stadium.

1960: No. 13 Purdue allowed 32 yards rushing on 26 attempts during its 35-6 triumph, which featured 111 yards rushing from Willie Jones.

1962: Marvin Woodson's 92-yard interception return for a touchdown came off a deflection late in the first half and ignited Indiana's 12-7 victory—its first since 1947. The Hoosiers then stopped Purdue near their 5-yard line as time expired.

1963: Rich Badar's second score closed Indiana's gap to 14-13 with less than three minutes remaining. He then passed to Trent Walters for a two-point conversion. However, Purdue dashed the Hoosiers' hopes when Gordon Teter raced

68 yards with the ensuing kickoff, putting the Boilers 25 yards away and setting up Ron DiGravio's second scoring toss to Randy Minniear for a 21-15 victory. Minniear finished with 106 yards on three receptions.

1964: Teter ran for 126 yards on 31 attempts as host Purdue edged the Hoosiers, 28-22, in front of almost 60,000.

1965: Purdue eked out a 26-21 decision after letting a 20-0 advantage early in the second quarter wilt away. Purdue finished 7-2-1, its best mark since 1943. John Kuzniewski scored two touchdowns and gained 105 yards rushing for the Boilermakers, who won in Bloomington for the ninth straight time. Meanwhile Indiana's attack featured 75- and 25-yard scoring passes from Frank Stavroff to Bill Malinchak.

1966: Purdue, ranked 10th, already had clinched the Rose Bowl berth because the no-repeat rule made Michigan State ineligible. Boilermakers star Bob Griese scored 21 points on two touchdowns, a field goal, and six extra points during a 51-6 romp in which they tallied a record 34 points in the second quarter. Griese completed 11-of-21 passes for 255 yards and two more scores. Purdue then beat Southern Cal, 14-13, in Pasadena.

1968: Indiana, the defending Big Ten champ, lost, 38-35, to No. 12 Purdue after holding an 18-point cushion early in the second half. The Hoosiers cruised to a 21-10 lead on two Gonso touchdown passes and Bobby Pernell's 64-yard run. Gonso then hooked up with Butcher for a second scoring play for a 28-10 margin. Keyes then got busy for Purdue, setting up a score and registering his second touchdown to make it 28-24. The Gonso-to-Butcher combination worked again to give Indiana an 11-point margin, but Phipps and Keyes completed a 58-yard score and then Keyes reached the end zone a fourth time from 1 yard out to complete the rally. Butcher's three scoring receptions set a school record that he tied the next year and has been equaled five other times. Chuck Kyle set a Purdue mark with 27 tackles. Keyes finished with 140 yards on 28 carries, adding 149 yards receiving.

1969: Purdue fell behind, 14-0, but charged back to take a 24-21 halftime lead en route to a 44-21 victory. Phipps finished with four touchdown passes for the No. 17 Boilermakers, who said goodbye to future College Football Hall of Famer Jack Mollenkopf as coach two weeks later. The latter finished with an 84-39-9 mark in 14 years before a record Indiana crowd of 56,223.

1970: Stan Brown returned a kickoff 100 yards for a Purdue touchdown and Otis Armstrong gained 168 yards rushing on 23 carries in this 40-0 whitewashing of Indiana.

1971: Purdue scored on 67-, 70-, and 44-yard plays in the second half, but it wasn't enough to overcome a 31-10 deficit and eventual 38-31 setback. The game ended ugly as a fracas broke out during the final minute after Purdue quarterback Gary Danielson ran out of bounds on the Indiana sideline. The benches emptied and fans joined in. The scrum ended with a Purdue cheerleader being knocked unconscious, a spectator going to the hospital, and Purdue Pete, the Boilermakers mascot, getting his huge head smashed in. Darryl Stingley caught four passes for 108 yards in a losing effort.

1972: Armstrong shredded Indiana's defense for school records of 276 yards rushing and 312 all-purpose yards during a 42-7 blitz at Ross-Ade Stadium. Armstrong scored three times to break the career rushing TDs standard of Wisconsin's Alan Ameche. Tim Racke intercepted three Indiana passes. Purdue coach Bob DeMoss resigned a week later, while Indiana's John Pont stepped down to become the head coach and athletic director at Northwestern.

1973: Corso took the reins at Indiana, while Agase did the same at Purdue. The Boilermakers won their first meeting, 28-23, behind Pete Gross's 29 carries for 147 yards rushing and quarterback Bo Bobrowski's 114 yards on the ground.

1974: Purdue scored the last 15 points to secure a 38-17 triumph in the 50th Bucket game, giving the Boilermakers a 34-13-3 advantage. Scott Dierking rushed for 129 yards, and Larry Burton caught three passes for 100 yards for the gold and black.

1975: Indiana's Courtney Snyder rumbled for 211 yards, but it wasn't enough to prevent a 9-7 Purdue victory in Bloomington.

1976: Steve Sanders accumulated 24 total tackles during the Hoosiers' 20-14 road triumph.

1977: Indiana posted its first back-to-back series wins in 31 years with a 21-10 victory in Jim Young's first Bucket game as Purdue's head man. Tailback Darrick Burnett rushed 43 times for 195 yards for the Hoosiers. Purdue's Freddie Arrington registered 23 tackles.

1978: No. 18 Purdue almost didn't have a trophy with which to celebrate after its 20-7 win in front of the largest crowd (69,918) ever in West Lafayette and the biggest to witness a Bucket game. The prized possession was stolen on October 28, but the kind culprits left $90 to pay for the busted-up display case in the Indiana Union and an apology note for the mess. The perpetrators turned themselves in and were required to write a history of the Bucket and perform public service duties during the upcoming holidays in penance, and the trophy was returned to Bloomington until the Boilermakers won it back shortly thereafter. Mike Augustyniak led the way for Purdue with 135 yards rushing, while Wally Jones added 103.

1979: Bowl bids and the Big Ten co-championship were on the line. Augustyniak scored three times, and Mark Herrmann finished 25-of-40 for 269 yards to help No. 12 Purdue gain a 37-21 victory. Ben McCall led the Boilermakers with 20 carries for 148 yards.

1980: Purdue overcame a 10-0 second-quarter deficit to edge the Hoosiers, 24-23. Steve Corso, the coach's son, brought Indiana to within one with 17 seconds left; however, Tim Clifford's pass to a wide-open Bob Stephenson was tipped by linebacker Mike Marks. The Hoosiers recovered an onside kick, but Marks blocked Don Geisler's 59-yard field-goal try. Lonnie Johnson gained 220 yards rushing in a losing effort. Herrmann completed 19-of-23 attempts for 323 yards for Purdue, including eight to Dave Young for 148 yards.

1982: Indiana claimed a 13-7 decision, its second in a row and fourth in seven years in the series, despite Cliff Benson's eight catches for 159 yards. But it wasn't enough to save Lee Corso's job; he was fired 24 days later.

1983: *Indianapolis Star* columnist Bill Benner said it best as both of the hapless rivals entered the contest in the midst of abysmal losing seasons: "It has been said that this is a game where you can throw out the records. For this, we can be thankful." However, the game defied low expectations, as Purdue went on to win a wild one, 31-30. The Boilers led, 31-17, and held on. Indiana scored, recovered an onside kick, and scored again with 2:18 showing. The Hoosiers failed on a two-point play, and Purdue pounced on a second onside kick before running out the clock. The Boilermakers tied the mark of 32 first downs against Indiana, as Mel Gray carried 36 times for 176 yards and Lloyd Hawthorne chipped in 109 yards.

1984: Purdue rallied from a 14-0 hole in the first 10 minutes to win, 31-24, and end first-year Indiana coach Bill Mallory's season at 0-11. Rodney Carter carried 23 times for 148 yards for Purdue, which also got 16 solo tackles from Jason Houston.

1985: Ray Wallace gained 140 yards on only 19 attempts and Carter caught nine balls for 113 yards in helping Purdue to a 34-21 win.

1986: The Boilermakers won, 17-15, in Leon Burtnett's final game as their coach. Freshman Scott Schult blocked Pete Stoyanovich's 34-yard field-goal attempt in the final seconds to preserve the Boilermakers' fourth straight win in the series. Rod Woodson caused a fumble, registered seven unassisted tackles, gained 93 yards rushing, and caught three passes for 67 yards for the victors. Indiana qualified for the All-American Bowl, where it lost, 27-13, to Florida State.

1987: Indiana, which had downed Ohio State for the first time since 1951 and defeated Michigan for the first time since 1967, finished off its 8-3 regular season with a 35-14 triumph over Purdue. Anthony Thompson led the offense with three touchdowns, while Brian Dewitz picked off two passes and recorded one of Indiana's four fumble recoveries. Indiana also blocked two field goals. The Hoosiers then suffered a 27-22 loss to Tennessee in the Peach Bowl.

1988: The Hoosiers blasted Purdue, 52-7, their biggest winning margin in a Bucket game. Indiana's largest margin had been in its 37-0 win in 1917. Thompson tallied three scores, rushing for 167 yards, in front of 67,861 in West Lafayette. Indiana scored on four of Purdue's six first-half turnovers. Dewitz intercepted two passes, one of which he returned for a touchdown. Indiana then whipped South Carolina, 34-10, in the Liberty Bowl.

1989: Purdue upended 5-5 Indiana, 15-14, and prevented the Hoosiers from earning a spot in the Freedom Bowl. Larry Sullivan kicked a 32-yard field goal with 2:51 left for the deciding points. Thompson returned the ensuing kickoff 64 yards to the Purdue 15, but Scott Bonnell missed a 26-yarder four plays later that sealed the Hoosiers' fate after they had led 14-3 through three quarters. Thompson, the nation's leading scorer and rusher, was held to 97 yards. He finished his career with an NCAA-record 65 touchdowns and 394 points, and was fifth in rushing with 4,965 yards.

1990: Two players from each squad were ejected for fighting during the last two minutes of Indiana's 28-14 triumph. Mike Dumas rumbled a record 99 yards with an interception for Indiana but didn't score. The Hoosiers then lost to Auburn, 27-23, in the Peach Bowl.

1991: Boilermakers kicker Joe O'Leary missed four field goals (two on bad snaps) and failed on one extra point, as Indiana held on for a 24-22 win. The Hoosiers grabbed a 24-6 lead at halftime but survived O'Leary's final miss, a 35-yard attempt, with 28 seconds remaining. Ernest Calloway had 113 receiving yards on just four catches for the Hoosiers, who then blanked Baylor, 24-0, in the Copper Bowl.

1992: Purdue won, 13-10, in another exciting finish. Indiana drove to the Purdue 22, but Bonnell's 39-yard field goal was blocked. The Hoosiers got another chance because Purdue was called for being off-sides on the play. They moved to the Boilermakers' 5, but Jimmy Young intercepted Trent Green's pass and returned it 58 yards. Green tackled Young by the facemask, creating a bench-clearing brawl in which Purdue players rushed across the field. Officials restored order with 16 seconds left after a few harmless punches were thrown. Eric Hunter rushed for a career-high 117 yards, including a 21-yard touchdown, to become the first Purdue quarterback to reach the 100-yard plateau since Bo Bobrowski did it in 1973.

1993: Indiana safety Chris Dyer's vulgarity-laced comments about Purdue and coach Jim Colletto ended up in the *Indiana Daily Student*, enflaming a game and series that didn't need stoking. Fortunately for Dyer, the Hoosiers came back for a 24-17 victory to give the 8-3 team a date in the Independence Bowl, where they were drubbed, 45-20, by Virginia Tech. Meanwhile, Purdue finished 1-10, its first double-digit loss total in school history and first time since 1946 that the Boilermakers didn't win a league contest. It was Purdue's worst overall record since a 0-5 finish in 1907. Corey Rogers gained 123 yards rushing for Purdue.

1994: Alex Smith broke his own freshman record from earlier in the season, gaining 245 yards rushing on 31 carries and scoring twice, including the game-winner in a 33-29 Indiana win. He increased his season total to 1,475 yards, surpassing Minnesota's Darrell Thompson (1,240 in 1986) and setting another league mark for freshmen in a game that included two first-half ties and four lead changes after the break. Lee Brush rambled 85 yards with a fumble return for Purdue.

1995: Mike Alstott gained 264 yards on 25 attempts, scoring three times to carry Purdue to a 51-14 victory.

Indiana's Alex Smith (left) rushed for 245 yards in the 1994 contest.
A great big Bucket of joy (right) for Hoosiers and Boilermakers.

1996: Indiana overcame 10-3 and 16-10 holes to win, 33-16, as it converted 23 points on Purdue turnovers. A Boilermakers highlight occurred when Rick Trefzger connected with Brian Alford on a 90-yard touchdown play, the second-longest scoring pass ever against Indiana, and finished with 301 yards passing. Alford had 162 yards receiving on five catches. It was the final game for both head coaches, Colletto of Purdue and Mallory of Indiana.

1997: A crowd of nearly 47,000 watched as 23rd-ranked Purdue blasted the Hoosiers, 56-7, adding to Indiana's misery with 28 points in the fourth quarter in the 74th Bucket showdown and 100th meeting overall. Indiana's Jay Rodgers completed 28 passes in 49 attempts, while Jason Spear caught a school record 16 for 147 yards. Purdue then defeated Oklahoma State, 33-20, in the Alamo Bowl.

1998: Purdue claimed another one-sided decision, this time 52-7, behind sophomore quarterback Drew Brees and in front of a crowd of 68,512—the hosts' first sellout for a Big Ten game since 1988. Brees passed for 237 yards to give him a league record of 3,753 for the year, which edged the 1988 effort of Iowa's Chuck Hartlieb by 15 yards. It also passed Jim Everett's school mark from 1985. Brees set the Big Ten standards for completions (336) and attempts (516) that were held by former Illinois signal callers Jack Trudeau and Tony Eason, respectively. The Boilermakers used that momentum to upset fourth-ranked Kansas State, 37-34, in a second consecutive trip to the Alamo Bowl.

1999: Both teams entered the game with 3-4 records in conference action, but Vinny Sutherland's 66-yard punt return helped give No. 19 Purdue a 30-24 triumph. The Boilermakers stopped Indiana twice, once on fourth-and-goal and then on a fourth-down play from the Purdue 21. Montrell Lowe rushed 27 times for 135 yards and Randall Lane hauled in six receptions for 113 yards for the Boilermakers. Purdue then lost to Georgia, 28-25, in the Outback Bowl after leading, 25-0.

2000: Purdue, ranked 17th, carried a 5-2 record into the game and was tied with three other teams atop the Big Ten but had beaten all three, so a win over Indiana meant a Rose Bowl berth. The Boilermakers accomplished that feat with a 41-13 trouncing of Indiana at Ross-Ade, the first time since 1967 that the game decided who would go to Pasadena. Lowe carried 38 times for 206 yards and four touchdowns. Purdue then lost to No. 4 Washington, 34-24.

2001: Both teams were assessed 15-yard penalties before the game started because of trash talking. Indiana grabbed a 13-0 lead at the intermission, as it held the Boilermakers to minus-15 yards rushing. Indiana scored on runs by Levron Williams and Antwaan Randle-El and let its defense take care of business in claiming the Bucket for the first time since 1996 in a game played in a horizontal rainstorm. The Hoosiers' defense forced two turnovers and stopped Purdue twice in the red zone in the last 10 minutes. Purdue closed to within 13-7 and appeared ready to finally take the lead after several drives inside the Indiana 30, but Martin Lapostolle stopped Lowe on fourth-and-goal to snuff Purdue's final hope in the six-point setback.

Boilers coach Joe Tiller summed it up after he suffered his first loss in the series: "It's something this team hasn't experienced and this coaching staff hasn't experienced, and it's something that will weigh on our minds for 364 days."

The Hoosiers raced across the field to grab the Bucket, while students tore down a goalpost and carried it toward the Indiana locker room before taking it back to the south end zone.

2002: Purdue regained the Bucket with a 34-10 win behind 131 yards and two touchdowns from Brandon Jones, who averaged 13.1 yards per carry, and 102 from Joey Harris. The Boilers clinched their sixth bowl appearance in six tries under Tiller. They also held Indiana to 29 yards rushing.

2003: John Standeford caught six passes for 151 yards and two touchdowns from Kyle Orton as No. 16 Purdue earned a New Year's Day bowl game with a 24-16 win. Jerod Void added a career-high 141 yards on 31 carries for the Boilermakers. Freshman BenJarvus Green-Ellis carried 35 times for 155 yards and a score for Indiana.

2004: Purdue rolled to a 42-10 halftime lead en route to a 63-24 massacre that featured a Big Ten record 763 yards and 37 first downs. Orton finished 33-of-54 for 522 yards and six touchdown passes, the latter two numbers tying Brees' school marks. Taylor Stubblefield hauled in 14 passes for 138 yards and three scores, making him the NCAA's all-time receptions leader with 309. The 14 grabs are the most ever against Indiana. Kyle Ingraham added 209 yards on 11 catches, and Dorien Bryant chipped in 131, giving the victors three 100-yard receivers for the third time in history. Rob Ninkovich tied a Purdue record with four sacks.

2005: Indiana paid tribute to one of the school's former heroes, Terry Cole, who had helped the Hoosiers earn a trip to their only Rose Bowl after the 1967 season. Indiana players wore a black No. 48 decal on their helmets to honor Cole, who had just died of cancer at age 60. However, Purdue beat Indiana for the eighth time in nine seasons under Tiller, getting three touchdowns from Kory Sheets and two from Bryant in claiming a 41-14 victory.

2006: Sheets blocked a punt to set up Purdue for a 7-0 lead en route to a 28-19 victory. Indiana blew a chance to tie it, fumbling at the Purdue 1-yard line. Indiana's Will Meyers intercepted two Curtis Painter passes in the first half. Redshirt freshman Kellen Lewis ripped off a 62-yard run to set up a field goal for IU. The teams committed five turnovers in a span of seven plays, with two on one play as Tracy Porter returned a fumble 57 yards before Purdue's Jake Standeford batted it out of his hands and through the end zone for a touchback.

Indiana closed to 21-19 with 9:29 left but a two-point try failed. Bryant scored on a 15-yard reverse to make it 28-19 with 4:58 left and that's how it ended to give the hosts their fifth consecutive win in the series. Indiana lost the game but gained 505 total yards, while Purdue had 444 yards. The Boilermakers improved to 8-4 with a bowl bid already in their pocket, while the Hoosiers fell to 5-7 and failed to gain their first bowl appearance since 1993.

ALL-TIME SERIES RESULTS

PURDUE LEADS, 68-35-6	1897—Purdue 20, Indiana 6	1902—Purdue 39, Indiana 0
1891—Purdue 60, Indiana 0	1898—Purdue 14, Indiana 0	1904—Purdue 27, Indiana 0
1892—Purdue 64, Indiana 0	1899—Indiana 17, Purdue 5	1905—Purdue 11, Indiana 11 (T)
1893—Purdue won forfeit	1900—Indiana 24, Purdue 5	1908—Indiana 10, Purdue 4
1894—Purdue won forfeit	1901—Indiana 11, Purdue 6	1909—Indiana 36, Purdue 3

1910—Indiana 15, Purdue 0
1911—Purdue 12, Indiana 5
1912—Purdue 34, Indiana 7
1913—Purdue 42, Indiana 7
1914—Purdue 23, Indiana 13
1915—Purdue 7, Indiana 0
1916—Purdue 0, Indiana 0 (T)
1917—Indiana 37, Purdue 0
1920—Indiana 10, Purdue 7
1921—Indiana 3, Purdue 0
November 25, 1922—Purdue 7, Indiana 7 (T)
November 24, 1923—Indiana 3, Purdue 0
November 22, 1924—Purdue 26, Indiana 7
November 21, 1925—Purdue 0, Indiana 0 (T)
November 20, 1926—Purdue 24, Indiana 14
November 19, 1927—Purdue 21, Indiana 6
November 24, 1928—Purdue 14, Indiana 0
November 23, 1929—Purdue 32, Indiana 0
November 22, 1930—Indiana 7, Purdue 6
November 21, 1931—Purdue 19, Indiana 0
November 19, 1932—Purdue 25, Indiana 7
November 25, 1933—Purdue 19, Indiana 3
November 24, 1934—Indiana 17, Purdue 6
November 23, 1935—Indiana 7, Purdue 0
November 21, 1936—Purdue 20, Indiana 20 (T)
November 20, 1937—Purdue 13, Indiana 7
November 19, 1938—Purdue 13, Indiana 6
November 25, 1939—Purdue 7, Indiana 6
November 23, 1940—Indiana 3, Purdue 0
November 22, 1941—Indiana 7, Purdue 0
November 21, 1942—Indiana 20, Purdue 0
November 20, 1943—Purdue 7, Indiana 0
November 25, 1944—Indiana 14, Purdue 6
November 24, 1945—Indiana 26, Purdue 0
November 23, 1946—Indiana 34, Purdue 20
November 22, 1947—Indiana 16, Purdue 14
November 20, 1948—Purdue 39, Indiana 0
November 19, 1949—Purdue 14, Indiana 6
November 25, 1950—Purdue 13, Indiana 0
November 24, 1951—Purdue 21, Indiana 13
November 22, 1952—Purdue 21, Indiana 16
November 21, 1953—Purdue 30, Indiana 0
November 20, 1954—Purdue 13, Indiana 7
November 19, 1955—Purdue 6, Indiana 4
November 23, 1956—Purdue 39, Indiana 20
November 23, 1957—Purdue 35, Indiana 13
November 22, 1958—Purdue 15, Indiana 15 (T)
November 21, 1959—Purdue 10, Indiana 7

November 19, 1960—Purdue 35, Indiana 6
November 25, 1961—Purdue 34, Indiana 12
November 17, 1962—Indiana 12, Purdue 7
November 30, 1963—Purdue 21, Indiana 15
November 21, 1964—Purdue 28, Indiana 22
November 20, 1965—Purdue 26, Indiana 21
November 19, 1966—Purdue 51, Indiana 6
November 25, 1967—Indiana 19, Purdue 14
November 23, 1968—Purdue 38, Indiana 35
November 22, 1969—Purdue 44, Indiana 21
November 21, 1970—Purdue 40, Indiana 0
November 20, 1971—Indiana 38, Purdue 31
November 25, 1972—Purdue 42, Indiana 7
November 24, 1973—Purdue 28, Indiana 23
November 23, 1974—Purdue 38, Indiana 17
November 22, 1975—Purdue 9, Indiana 7
November 20, 1976—Indiana 20, Purdue 14
November 19, 1977—Indiana 21, Purdue 10
November 25, 1978—Purdue 20, Indiana 7
November 17, 1979—Purdue 37, Indiana 21
November 22, 1980—Purdue 24, Indiana 23
November 21, 1981—Indiana 20, Purdue 17
November 20, 1982—Indiana 13, Purdue 7
November 19, 1983—Purdue 31, Indiana 30
November 17, 1984—Purdue 31, Indiana 24
November 23, 1985—Purdue 34, Indiana 21
November 22, 1986—Purdue 17, Indiana 15
November 21, 1987—Indiana 35, Purdue 14
November 21, 1988—Indiana 52, Purdue 7
November 25, 1989—Purdue 15, Indiana 14
November 24, 1990—Indiana 28, Purdue 14
November 23, 1991—Indiana 24, Purdue 22
November 21, 1992—Purdue 13, Indiana 10
November 20, 1993—Indiana 24, Purdue 17
November 19, 1994—Indiana 33, Purdue 29
November 24, 1995—Purdue 51, Indiana 14
November 23, 1996—Indiana 33, Purdue 16
November 22, 1997—Purdue 56, Indiana 7
November 21, 1998—Purdue 52, Indiana 7
November 20, 1999—Purdue 30, Indiana 24
November 18, 2000—Purdue 41, Indiana 13
November 24, 2001—Indiana 13, Purdue 7
November 23, 2002—Purdue 34, Indiana 10
November 22, 2003—Purdue 24, Indiana 16
November 20, 2004—Purdue 63, Indiana 24
November 19, 2005—Purdue 41, Indiana 14
November 18, 2006—Purdue 28, Indiana 19

The Illini and the Wildcats have been mixing it up since 1892.

HOW SWEET IT IS:
ILLINOIS vs. NORTHWESTERN

Northwestern and Illinois haven't enjoyed prolonged periods of success, and the few they've had have seldom occurred at the same time. But almost every season that the Wildcats or Illini have had opportunities to win Big Ten Conference titles or when bowl trips were on the line, the rival team usually ended those dreams or at least made the journey much more challenging.

Forty-two of their confrontations have been decided by seven points or less, and many of those came down to the final minutes or seconds. That includes their meeting on the final Saturday in October 1995, as eighth-ranked Northwestern traveled to Champaign holding a 5-0 league record and 7-1 over-all mark, while Illinois was struggling to achieve a break-even season.

Anyone expecting an easy Wildcats win was soon disappointed, however, as Lou Tepper's Illini moved out to an early 14-0 advantage in front of 65,425 fans at Memorial Stadium. Gary Barnett's Wildcats bounced back to score first on reserve kicker Brian Gowins' 49-yard field goal and closed to 14-10 after Steve Schnur's 34-yard touchdown pass to D'Wayne Bates. Leading rusher Darnell Autry closed the deal with just six minutes remaining, plunging in from a yard out to provide the deciding points in a 17-14 victory. Autry finished with 151 yards on 41 carries, including 37 yards on the crucial 58-yard march. The Illini kept Northwestern nervous right down to the end; the visitors didn't secure the win until Eric Collier intercepted Illinois quarterback Scott Weaver's desperation pass into the end zone with seven seconds left.

It was Northwestern's closest conference contest and helped catapult the Wildcats to their first Big Ten crown since 1936 and their first Rose Bowl berth since the 1948 season. Paul Janus, a sophomore, was an integral member of that 1995 Northwestern team as a starting offensive tackle and the snapper on kicks. He said that the Wildcats simply did the right things at the right times that season.

"They called us a team of overachievers, and that was right because except for guys like D'Wayne Bates and Darnell Autry on offense and Pat Fitzgerald leading the defense, we weren't a bunch of All-Americans," Janus said. "We didn't suffer any major injuries, but mainly everybody played a part and bought into the system. We didn't blow many teams out, but we did what we had to do to win. We didn't make mistakes at key times, and that's why we came from behind and won a lot of games."

That included the '95 thriller against Illinois, an outcome that Janus helped secure in a big way. "I went up against Simeon Rice much of that game, and he was one of the top defensive players in the country," Janus said of the Illini's all-America linebacker and pass rusher extraordinaire. "I had more butterflies, but I always gave a little more effort going against guys like that. I did whatever I could to block him."

Janus said that's what it usually took to knock off Illinois, too.

"Being from Wisconsin, [playing the Badgers] was my biggest game," he said, "but for most of the guys from in-state, Illinois had more meaning. Playing for the Sweet Sioux Tomahawk meant the records didn't matter, that everyone was going all-out."

That tradition started in 1945 when members of the respective student newspapers came up with a wooden cigar store Indian named "Sweet Sioux." However, the effigy was stolen from Northwestern's showcase a year later, so a tomahawk replaced the statue and has gone to the winner every year since. Ironically, the original trophy was found in '48 but discarded because its bulk made it difficult to transport back and forth.

Illinois leads the series, 51-44-5, overall and 31-27-2 since the trophy took center stage, which always made the school's mascot, Chief Illiniwek, do a special victory dance. While the chief was laid to rest after a basketball game in February 2007, the tomahawk tradition lives on.

Northwestern's only other Rose Bowl appearance occurred on January 1, 1949, and that unit also needed a win against the Illini to secure a trip to Pasadena, this time in the season finale at Evanston. Quarterback Don Burson threw a 23-yard TD pass to Joe Zuravleff, who snared it despite wearing a cast on his broken wrist for one Wildcats score. Chuck Hagmann ran 65 yards after getting a lateral from Loran "Peewee" Day, who had intercepted a juggled Russ Steger pass.

Hagmann had been nursing a bad leg all week, but his effort helped seventh-ranked Northwestern grab a 20-0 halftime lead en route to a 20-7 victory. The Wildcats then downed California and former Northwestern coach Lynn Waldorf, 20-14, for their only Rose Bowl triumph. Frank Aschenbrenner blazed

73 yards for Northwestern's first score, and Art Murakowski bulled in from a yard out. But the upstart Wildcats trailed, 14-13, until the final moments.

"I look back on that team quite a bit," said Frank DePauw, a two-way guard for the Wildcats from 1945 to 1948. "I always felt that Lynn Waldorf sowed the seeds for that team because he had recruited most of the guys, so playing against him added to the excitement and made the victory that much sweeter."

Midwestern teams definitely took their trips to California seriously, winning the first six showdowns under the agreement between the Big Ten and Pacific Athletic Conference (later the Pac-8 and the Pac-10). Illinois claimed two of those victories as the 1946 and 1951 teams dominated UCLA and Stanford by a combined 85-21 score. And the Illini used triumphs over Northwestern as springboards to both dominating performances.

In 1946, Illinois registered a 20-0 victory at NU's Dyche Stadium behind Art Dufelmeier's 123 yards rushing, including a 53-yard touchdown scamper, and 83 more yards from Buddy Young. The Illini went on to whip the 12-point favorite and third-ranked Bruins in the Rose Bowl, 45-14.

"I don't know whether there will ever be another season like 1946," said Tom Stewart, who was a quarterback and cornerback for the Illini from 1946 to 1949. "That's because many top players had come back from the war. How we ever won some of those games, I don't know. We beat Iowa, 7-0, and came from behind to defeat Wisconsin, 27-21. Then Michigan spent almost the entire fourth quarter inside our 20-yard line, but we won, 13-9. Then we played well and dominated the Northwestern game."

Illinois was 4-0-1 and 7-0-1 after a scoreless tie against Ohio State the week before the Sweet Sioux battle in 1951. The Illini clinched a Rose Bowl berth and ended a four-year drought in the series with a 3-0 win against Northwestern. Sophomore place-kicker Sam Rebecca's 16-yard field goal in the second quarter provided the only score, while Al Tate ran for 167 yards to lead Illinois.

Ray Eliot's Illini proceeded to paste Stanford, 40-7, in the 1952 contest in Pasadena behind Bill Tate's two scores and 150 yards rushing, and two Stan Wallace interceptions. Illinois amassed 434 yards of total offense in breaking up a close game with 27 points in the fourth quarter. The Illini finished 9-0-1 for their first unbeaten season since 1927 and the last one in school history.

Al Brosky was one of the nation's top secondary players from his safety spot, where he hauled down an Illinois-record 30 interceptions from 1950 to 1952, an accomplishment that still ranks atop the NCAA record book despite the proliferation of the passing game during the past 55 years.

"I would have rather played Michigan, Ohio State, or Wisconsin because those were the games you had to win if you wanted to be top-notch in that conference,"

Brosky said. "Northwestern wasn't quite as good and they had the smaller stadium and didn't really fit the picture of a big rivalry. But it was tough playing them up on the lakefront. It got down to 30 below with the wind, and I froze my fanny off."

Burt Keddie was a two-way letterman at end for the Wildcats from 1948 to 1950, starting his final two campaigns. He said there were several reasons why playing the Illini was fun, including a 3-0 mark against them during his career.

"Burt Schmidt was a high school buddy of mine who was at Illinois, and I remember the 1949 game," Keddie said of the Wildcats' 9-7 triumph. "We were behind by a point and huddled up, and our quarterback normally didn't kick field goals, especially because he was our second-string kicker, but we decided to try it. We lined up, but instead of staying in tight like I usually did, I moved out more like a flanker. Well, the end, tackle, and linebacker for Illinois shifted my way. Don Burson kicked it, and I swear it never went higher than anybody's helmet, but it hit the crossbar and went over and we won the game.

Illinois back John Karras heads upfield. His 95-yard touchdown run couldn't prevent a Northwestern victory in 1949.

"It was special because I ran over to their locker room before they got out of town, and Burt says, 'Why the hell did you hit me so hard?'" Keddie added. "That's what made it so much fun."

J.C. Caroline played two seasons as a halfback and cornerback at Illinois (1953–54); after school, he spent one season with Montreal of the Canadian Football League before a standout 10-year run with the Chicago Bears. The Columbus, South Carolina, native said that tangling with Northwestern was another tough afternoon in the Big Ten.

"A lot of players on both teams came out of the Chicago

Otto Graham, perhaps the greatest Wildcat ever

area, so they had played against each other before," said Caroline, who coached the Illini secondary from 1967 to 1976 and has remained in the Champaign-Urbana area. "It was like a high school rivalry. The Big Ten was always competitive, and we were proud of playing in the conference because we felt like at least five or six of the teams could play with anybody in the country every year."

Illinois proved that during the 1963 season, upending preseason favorite and fourth-ranked Northwestern by one point in the Illini's league opener. NU grabbed a 6-0 lead on Tom Myers' 29-yard pass to Tom O'Grady in the second quarter, but the extra point was missed. A 32-yard touchdown pass from Ron Fearn to Jim Warren and Jim Plankenhorn's PAT gave Illinois a 7-6 lead. Pete Stamison booted a 24-yard field goal to push the Wildcats back on top, but Plankenhorn answered with a 21-yarder in the third quarter for a 10-9 victory.

Illinois' stingy defense then held on through three Northwestern drives in the final quarter. Middle linebacker and future NFL star Dick Butkus sacked Myers four times, forcing one fumble, and finished with 19 total tackles.

Pete Elliott, the Illini's coach at that time, said the showdowns meant something even though neither program was a title contender most of his seven years at the helm in Champaign (1960–66). "Northwestern was an important game every year even though our teams weren't always that strong," said Elliott, who starred at Michigan from 1945 to 1948 and served as director of the Pro Football Hall of Fame from 1979 to 1996. "We enjoyed mixed results against them, and they had good teams under Ara [Parseghian]."

The schools have seldom cracked the top 10 since then, but those who suited up still liked to brag when they won those skirmishes. Minnesota native Maurie Daigneau played quarterback at Northwestern from 1969 to 1971, directing some of the school's most explosive offensive attacks before the pass-happy 1990s arrived.

"Northwestern wasn't traditionally known for its football program and had trouble beating anybody a lot of the time," Daigneau said. "So every team was a rivalry for us. Things always ebb and flow, but we knew that if we couldn't beat Illinois that we'd be kidding ourselves about beating teams like Michigan or Ohio State. The Illinois game wasn't like, 'If we win any game, it's gotta be that game.' But it was significant because beating them gave us confidence."

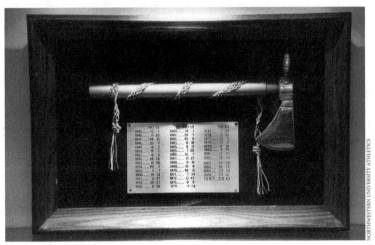

The Sweet Sioux Tomahawk replaced the original cigar store Indian.

Northwestern finished with back-to-back winning seasons in 1970 and 1971 for the first time since 1962–63, and the seven wins in Daigneau's senior year were the most until the 1995 squad won all eight league games and finished 10-2 overall.

"I was extremely fortunate to have played with a bunch of great guys," Daigneau said of those teams under Alex Agase, who starred at Illinois in 1941–42 and '46, and played and coached at Purdue. "We had players such as Mike Adamle, Barry Pearson, Jim Lash, Steve Craig, Joe Zigulich, and Rick

Telander. If I put the ball anywhere near those guys, they'd get it. We had gained confidence and didn't back down to anybody."

The Wildcats have certainly stood up to the Illini often over the years. Northwestern compiled a 2-1 record against Illinois from 1972 to 1974, when Mike Gow showcased his defensive back skills, picking off 19 passes, which stands second only to Brosky's total in team annals. The Michigan native stole four in a victory over Stanford during his senior year.

"We were a losing program back then, so my senior year was our first winning season since 1965," Gow said of the 6-4-1 finish that featured a second win against the Wildcats during his three seasons. "It wasn't a big rivalry to me, but it was an important game and I knew it was a huge game for a lot of the guys I played with."

David Williams agreed with Gow's assessment, even though he and the Illini won all three contests during his illustrious 1983–85 career in Champaign. Besides, he had extra incentive to beat the Wildcats, despite being a California native.

"Northwestern wasn't that good at the time, but the two years before I got there, my brother, Oliver, and guys like Tony Eason beat them pretty good," Williams said. "So I knew I had to make sure we didn't lose to them or I'd hear about it back home."

Illinois didn't lose those games, and Williams was a major reason why, surpassing 100 yards every time they played the Cats, including a school-record 208-yard performance on 11 catches from Jack Trudeau in the 1984 season opener.

"Yeah, I had 11 catches and 200-some yards, but what I remember about that was that I couldn't catch anything that week in practice," Williams said. "Then I dropped five or six passes in the game. I think about what I could have done if I wouldn't have dropped all of those."

Illinois won that contest, 24-16, as Trudeau completed 25-of-39 attempts for 315 yards. Williams then finished a magnificent career. He was inducted into the College Football Hall of Fame in 2006, but he said those contests against Northwestern were tougher than the scores indicated.

"I remember it was later in November and freezing along the lake a couple of times," Williams said. "It seemed like they played harder against us than against other teams, at least from watching them on film. I remember that first game thinking that if we could score a bunch of points we'd be able to sit out, but it was close at halftime and the coaches said, 'You're playing the whole game.' It was always a dogfight because they never played like they were only 2-9."

Brian Galley is an Ottawa, Illinois, native who got his engineering degree from UI in 1980. He has lived in Wisconsin since then, first in Madison and then in Neenah, where he founded the Fox Valley Illini Club in the late 1990s.

"I don't know that I ever considered any team as Illinois' main rival, but they've had the trophy and played interesting games against Northwestern over the years," Galley said. "Unfortunately, neither was that competitive many of the years. I can remember while I was still in college, they tied 0-0 in Champaign on Labor Day weekend. It was an extremely hot day, and it was the most boring football game I've ever seen. Gary Moeller had been brought in to turn the Illini around, but it just never happened. Then they hired Mike White, who had his own problems and issues that led to his downfall, but he brought the program back up again."

The two foes have endured ups and downs, but they've engaged in several exciting finishes since then, including the 1996 game that helped Northwestern claim a piece of a second consecutive Big Ten crown.

The cardiac Wildcats were at it again, scoring with 1:02 left on Adrian Autry's 1-yard plunge to give them a 27-24 win. Autry, subbing for an injured Darnell Autry (they're not relatives), gave the sellout homecoming crowd of 48,187 at Dyche Stadium plenty to cheer about. It was Northwestern's 13th straight league win and assured the No. 11 Wildcats of a bowl bid even though the Illini's Robert Holcombe ripped them for 166 yards rushing.

MORE SERIES HIGHLIGHTS

1893: Northwestern led, 13-10, with about 10 minutes remaining and Illinois knocking at the door from the Wildcats' 12-yard line. The game was called due to darkness, but the referee decided that the 0-all deadlock at halftime would be the official score.

1894: Illinois blasted the Wildcats, 66-0, scoring the most points in any series contest.

1896: Albert Potter recorded an 85-yard run for Northwestern in the Wildcats' 10-4 win.

1923: The great Harold "Red" Grange scored three touchdowns, including a 90-yard interception return, during a 29-0 Illinois win.

1930: Frank Baker caught two TD passes from Ernest "Pug" Rentner and returned an interception for a score during the Wildcats' 32-0 win over Illinois, the Illini's worst defeat under Bob Zuppke to that point. Rentner also returned a kickoff 98 yards, and George Potter scampered 83 yards with another one.

1932: Ollie Olson uncorked an 88-yard punt, the longest ever against Illinois, as the Wildcats won, 26-0 in front of 25,369 in Champaign.

1934: Les Lindberg didn't score, but his 69-yard burst helped the Illini to a 14-3 road triumph with 36,000 in attendance.

1936: Fourth-ranked Northwestern posted a 13-2 triumph en route to winning the Big Ten title at 6-0 and finishing 7-1 overall.

1941: Five days before the Illini's season finale at Northwestern, longtime Illinois coach Bob Zuppke announced his resignation. A crowd of 26,000 watched as the 10th-ranked Wildcats sophomore Bill DeCorrevont scored three TDs in the hosts' 27-0 whipping. Zuppke finished 131-81-13 in 29 seasons, which included seven conference winners and two unbeaten teams.

1943: Eddie Bray returned a kickoff 90 yards for a score, but that was the only highlight for Illinois during the 53-6 drubbing the No. 9 Wildcats gave them.

1947: The last-place Wildcats intercepted three Perry Moss passes, including a 32-yard TD scamper from Loran Day late in the first half. Day added a 71-yard gain during Northwestern's 28-13 upset of No. 12 Illinois.

1949: The Illini's Ron Clark gained 106 yards rushing and John Karras bolted 95 yards for a touchdown on a kickoff return, but Northwestern prevailed, 9-7, as nearly 68,000 fans showed up at Memorial Stadium.

1950: Northwestern again pulled a surprise, hanging on for a 14-7 victory, although Illinois was at the Wildcats' 7-yard line when time expired. Karras ran for 118 yards for the Illini, who led, 7-0, at halftime. Sixth-ranked Illinois could have clinched a Rose Bowl berth with a win but finished 4-2, while the Wildcats ended 3-3.

1952: Clarence DeMoss of Illinois accumulated 151 yards on the ground, but it wasn't enough as Northwestern came out on top, 28-26.

1954: Northwestern won, 20-7, despite giving up 259 yards passing to Hiles Stout and 136 yards receiving to Dean Renn, along with a record six fumbles, a dubious distinction they've tied three times.

1955: Bobby Mitchell's 107 yards rushing for Illinois couldn't prevent a 7-all deadlock.

1957: Linebacker Ray Nitschke (a future Green Bay Packer and member of the Hall of Fame) rushed for 170 yards from his fullback spot, including an 84-yard touchdown scamper, in his final game as a collegian. Illinois routed Northwestern, 27-0.

Ray Nitschke became renown as a middle linebacker in the NFL, but as an Illinois fullback in 1957 his 84-yard touchdown run helped bury the Wildcats.

1959: Ray Eliot's last game as coach resulted in a spirited 28-0 Illinois victory over the eighth-ranked Wildcats that included Bill Brown's 69-yard scoring run. Brown, a future standout with the Minnesota Vikings, finished with 164 yards while John Counts chipped in 109.

1960: Dick Thornton returned a kickoff 83 yards and Curtis Duncan added a 77-yard kick return as Northwestern pulled out a 14-7 victory.

1964: Future Cincinnati Bengals star Bob Trumpy contributed 106 yards receiving as third-ranked Illinois grabbed a 17-6 win. Northwestern's highlight was a 78-yard pass play from Tom Myers to Ron Rector.

1965: Jim Grabowski, another future Packer under Vince Lombardi, bludgeoned the Wildcats for 187 yards rushing during a 20-6 Illinois win in Evanston, which also featured 112 yards receiving from John Wright Sr. Rick Venturi and Ron Rector connected for an 80-yard pass play for Northwestern.

1967: Rich Johnson led the Illini with 157 yards rushing in their 27-21 victory.

1968: Illinois claimed a 14-0 decision behind Johnson's 119 yards.

1972: The Illini won handily, 43-13, as Mike Wells gained 105 yards rushing. It was their largest victory margin over the Wildcats since 1915.

1974: Jim "Chubby" Phillips led the charge with 107 yards rushing in Illinois' 28-14 victory.

1975: The Illini's 28-7 triumph featured Lonnie Perrin's 174 yards rushing.

1976: Phillips got in the act again, gaining 118 yards during a 48-6 Illinois win, a game that also included Marty Friel's 128 yards in receptions and Perrin's record-tying four TDs. It was Illinois' first three-game winning streak in the series since 1963 to 1965.

1978: The dreadful contest, called "The Futility Bowl," fittingly ended scoreless despite Vince Carter's 107 yards rushing for UI.

1979: Illinois claimed a 29-13 triumph to snap a 19-game league winless streak in Gary Moeller's finale as Illini coach after three terrible seasons. Mitchell Brookins blasted for 180 yards via the ground for the victors. Sam Poulos caught 13 passes for the Wildcats.

1980: Illinois won, 35-9. Junior college transfer Dave Wilson was the new Illini quarterback under first-year coach Mike White and, although the results weren't spectacular, Illinois overcame a 9-0 halftime deficit.

1981: Illinois won, 49-12, at icy, dark Dyche Stadium. Despite the conditions, the teams combined for 110 pass attempts, including 70 in the first half. Tony

Eason threw for 409 yards, including 279 before the break. He completed a 68-yard strike to John Lopez, who wound up with 134 yards.

1982: Illinois won, 49-13, as running backs Richard Ryles, Thomas Rooks, and Dwight Beverly combined for more than 200 yards rushing and Eason passed for 245. Sandy Schwab tied an NU record with two scoring tosses in his first game.

1983: No. 4 Illinois won, 56-24, despite having clinched a trip to the Rose Bowl a week earlier. Still, an estimated 30,000 Illini faithful (out of an announced attendance of 52,333) squeezed into Dyche Stadium for this season finale. The visitors accumulated 662 yards of offense, the second-most in team annals and most since 1944, as Illinois became the first school in Big Ten history to beat all nine conference foes in the same year. Illinois gained 223 yards rushing and 408 total yards in the first half. Rooks scooted for a 68-yard TD and finished with 138 yards rushing, while Jack Trudeau passed for four scores and 131 yards to David Williams.

1985: Trudeau finished 22-of-29 for 307 yards and three TDs during a 45-20 shellacking that included Williams' 122 yards.

1986: Northwestern earned a 23-18 triumph at Memorial Stadium as John Duvic booted three field goals. The Illini were slow in sending the tomahawk to Evanston, but a sports information department staff member finally delivered it.

1987: The Wildcats prevailed, 28-10, at Dyche, the first time since 1969–70 that they had won back-to-back games in the series. Northwestern coach Francis Peay and his squad finished 2-6 in the Big Ten and 2-8-1 overall, while Illinois stumbled at 2-5-1 and 3-7-1 under White. Northwestern rushed for 295 yards as Mike Greenfield became the school's single-season rushing leader for quarterbacks to finish his career with 904 yards. Mike Piel registered five tackles for loss for Illinois.

1988: Illinois won, 14-9, when safety Marlon Primous jarred the ball loose from Cats tight end Bob Griswold at the Illini 2-yard line on a fourth-down play in the final minute. The win clinched a bowl berth for Illinois as Keith Jones gained 118 yards rushing to offset Ira Adler's three field goals.

1989: Illinois won, 63-14, scoring 42 points in the first half and gaining a Citrus Bowl bid. Jeff George completed 15-of-18 pass attempts, including three for scores, before the break. It was No. 11 Illinois' biggest scoring output since 1944 and the most points the Illini had registered in a Big Ten outing since putting up 64 against the Wildcats in 1908. Doug Higgins set an Illinois mark with nine extra points, which Neil Rackers equaled against Virginia in 1999.

1990: Howard Griffith ripped the Wildcats for 263 yards rushing on 37 carries to lift No. 22 Illinois to a 28-23 victory. His performance was the school's best until Robert Holcombe's 315 yards against Minnesota in 1996.

1991: Northwestern knocked off 17th-ranked Illinois, 17-11, in the rain at home despite Steve Feagin's 118 rushing yards.

1992: First-year Northwestern coach Gary Barnett led the Wildcats to a 27-26 victory at Champaign, using a 21-0 blitz in the fourth quarter to overcome Kevin Jackson's 102 yards rushing. Lee Gissendaner of the Wildcats registered a 39-yard punt return and caught two touchdown passes, while Chris Gamble caught 10 balls for 146 yards and a score. Barnett and Illinois head man Lou Tepper were on Bill McCartney's staff at Colorado from 1984 to 1987.

1993: Damien Platt hustled for 118 yards running, and Mikki Johnson contributed three sacks in Illinois' 20-13 home triumph.

The Wildcats celebrate beating the Illini at home.

1994: Illinois won, 28-7, and a week later became bowl-eligible, eventually beating East Carolina in the Liberty Bowl. Johnny Johnson finished 19-of-29 with 256 yards and two TDs against the Wildcats. Simeon Rice recorded four tackles for lost yards, including three sacks.

1997: Northwestern won, 34-21, for its first three-game winning streak in the series since Ara Parseghian was leading the Wildcats from 1960 to 1962. First-year Illinois coach Ron Turner had served on Dennis Green's Northwestern staff in 1981–82.

1998: Rocky Harvey finished with 132 yards rushing as Illinois squeaked out a 13-10 decision.

2000: Running back Damien Anderson scored four times in leading the No. 23 Wildcats' 61-23 rout that gave them a 6-2 Big Ten mark and a share of the league title with Michigan and Purdue. Illinois dropped to 5-6 and was eliminated from bowl contention after giving up 35 first downs—an NU record.

2001: Kurt Kittner established an Illini record by completing 76% of his passes (33-of-43) as the 10th-ranked hosts pulled out a 34-28 victory to finish 7-1 and grab first place in the Big Ten. Kittner tossed four TD passes as Illinois ended up with 570 total yards. Brandon Lloyd caught 12 balls for 140 yards, while Walter Young added 123 yards in receptions and John Gockman nailed a 52-yard field goal.

2002: Antoineo Harris rumbled for 178 yards as the Illini earned a 31-24 win in front of only 25,134 fans in Evanston. Jon Beutjer threw for three scores and completed 21-of-34 for 282 yards for Illinois, which survived despite Brett Basanez's 368-yard aerial show for NU.

2003: Northwestern won, 37-20, in Champaign, rushing for 444 yards and a record 26 first downs. The Wildcats overcame a 13-7 halftime deficit despite not throwing a pass in the second half. Jason Wright gained 251 yards on 42 tries and scored four TDs. Leading rusher Noah Herron added 163 yards, making Northwestern bowl-eligible for the first time since 2000.

2004: Northwestern entered this game at Ryan Field (the new name for Dyche Stadium) 4-3 and 5-5, while Illinois was 1-6 and 3-7. The Illini fell, 28-21, in overtime, leaving the tomahawk in Evanston while Turner got the axe after seven seasons. Pierre Thomas gained 131 yards for Illinois, but Jeff Backes returned a punt 73 yards for a score to ignite the Wildcats.

2005: High-scoring Northwestern pounced on the Illini, 38-21, to finish the regular season at 7-4 before losing to UCLA in the Sun Bowl. Basanez threw for two touchdowns and ran for two as the Wildcats pulled away from a 24-21 halftime cushion. Northwestern registered 36 first downs and gained 596 totals yards, including 356 rushing. Tyrell Sutton led the Cats with 212 yards rushing as Illinois finished 2-9 under first-year coach Ron Zook. Basanez became the third QB in league history to reach the 10,000-yard mark in career passing, joining Iowa's Chuck Long and Purdue's Drew Brees.

2006: Northwestern entered the 100th meeting in the series with a 3-8 mark under first-year coach Pat Fitzgerald. The two-time national defensive player of the year for the Wildcats in the mid-1990s replaced the late Randy Walker in July. Illinois was also 1-6 in league play and 2-9 overall.

The UI Spirit Squad fires up the crowd at Memorial Stadium.

Illini quarterback Isiah "Juice" Williams gained 48 yards rushing but completed a paltry 4-of-17 passes. Sutton needed 110 yards rushing to reach 1,000 but fell just three yards short for the victors. The Wildcats jumped out to a 14-0 margin in the second quarter, but Rashard Mendenhall rambled 86 yards for a TD as Illinois ripped off 16 straight points, including a safety. Joel Howells then booted a 36-yard field goal with 10 seconds left for a 17-16 Northwestern lead at the break. NU's defense then shut the Illini out in the second half for a 27-16 victory, its fourth straight in the series. Illinois rushed for 207 yards but got only 70 through the air.

ALL-TIME SERIES RESULTS

ILLINOIS LEADS, 51-44-5

October 12, 1892—Illinois 16, Northwestern 16 (T)
October 21, 1893—Illinois 0, Northwestern 0 (T)
November 3, 1894—Illinois 66, Northwestern 0
November 23, 1895—Illinois 38, Northwestern 4
November 7, 1896—Northwestern 10, Illinois 4
October 20, 1900—Illinois 0, Northwestern 0 (T)
October 26, 1901—Northwestern 17, Illinois 11
November 22, 1902—Illinois 17, Northwestern 0
October 31, 1903—Northwestern 12, Illinois 11
November 12, 1904—Northwestern 12, Illinois 6
November 21, 1908—Illinois 64, Northwestern 8
November 13, 1909—Illinois 35, Northwestern 0
November 12, 1910—Illinois 27, Northwestern 0
November 18, 1911—Illinois 27, Northwestern 13
November 23, 1912—Northwestern 6, Illinois 0
October 18, 1913—Illinois 37, Northwestern 0
October 24, 1914—Illinois 33, Northwestern 0
October 23, 1915—Illinois 36, Northwestern 6
November 4, 1922—Illinois 6, Northwestern 3
October 27, 1923—Illinois 29, Northwestern 0
October 22, 1927—Illinois 7, Northwestern 6
October 27, 1928—Illinois 6, Northwestern 0
November 2, 1929—Northwestern 7, Illinois 0
October 18, 1930—Northwestern 32, Illinois 0
October 31, 1931—Northwestern 32, Illinois 6
October 15, 1932—Northwestern 26, Illinois 0
November 11, 1933—Illinois 3, Northwestern 0
November 10, 1934—Illinois 14, Northwestern 3
November 2, 1935—Northwestern 10, Illinois 3
October 24, 1936—Northwestern 13, Illinois 2
November 6, 1937—Illinois 6, Northwestern 0
October 22, 1938—Northwestern 13, Illinois 0
October 28, 1939—Northwestern 13, Illinois 0

November 9, 1940—Northwestern 32, Illinois 14
November 22, 1941—Northwestern 27, Illinois 0
November 7, 1942—Illinois 14, Northwestern 7
November 20, 1943—Northwestern 53, Illinois 6
November 25, 1944—Illinois 25, Northwestern 6
November 24, 1945—Northwestern 13, Illinois 7
November 23, 1946—Illinois 20, Northwestern 0
November 22, 1947—Northwestern 28, Illinois 13
November 20, 1948—Northwestern 20, Illinois 7
November 19, 1949—Northwestern 9, Illinois 7
November 25, 1950—Northwestern 14, Illinois 7
November 24, 1951—Illinois 3, Northwestern 0
November 22, 1952—Northwestern 28, Illinois 26
November 21, 1953—Illinois 39, Northwestern 14
November 20, 1954—Northwestern 20, Illinois 7
November 19, 1955—Illinois 7, Northwestern 7 (T)
November 24, 1956—Northwestern 14, Illinois 13
November 23, 1957—Illinois 27, Northwestern 0
November 22, 1958—Illinois 27, Northwestern 20
November 21, 1959—Illinois 28, Northwestern 0
November 19, 1960—Northwestern 14, Illinois 7
October 7, 1961—Northwestern 28, Illinois 7
October 6, 1962—Northwestern 45, Illinois 0
October 5, 1963—Illinois 10, Northwestern 9
October 3, 1964—Illinois 17, Northwestern 6
November 20, 1965—Illinois 20, Northwestern 6
November 19, 1966—Northwestern 35, Illinois 7
November 18, 1967—Illinois 27, Northwestern 21
November 16, 1968—Illinois 14, Northwestern 0
October 11, 1969—Northwestern 10, Illinois 6
October 10, 1970—Northwestern 48, Illinois 0
October 30, 1971—Illinois 24, Northwestern 7
November 4, 1972—Illinois 43, Northwestern 13
November 24, 1973—Northwestern 9, Illinois 6

ILLINOIS vs. NORTHWESTERN

November 23, 1974—Illinois 28, Northwestern 14
November 22, 1975—Illinois 28, Northwestern 7
November 20, 1976—Illinois 48, Northwestern 6
November 19, 1977—Northwestern 21, Illinois 7
September 9, 1978—Illinois 0, Northwestern 0 (T)
November 17, 1979—Illinois 29, Northwestern 13
September 6, 1980—Illinois 35, Northwestern 9
November 21, 1981—Illinois 49, Northwestern 12
September 4, 1982—Illinois 49, Northwestern 13
November 19, 1983—Illinois 56, Northwestern 24
September 1, 1984—Illinois 24, Northwestern 16
November 23, 1985—Illinois 45, Northwestern 20
November 22, 1986—Northwestern 23, Illinois 18
November 21, 1987—Northwestern 28, Illinois 10
November 19, 1988—Illinois 14, Northwestern 9
November 25, 1989—Illinois 63, Northwestern 14
November 24, 1990—Illinois 28, Northwestern 23

October 26, 1991—Northwestern 17, Illinois 11
October 24, 1992—Northwestern 27, Illinois 26
October 30, 1993—Illinois 20, Northwestern 13
October 29, 1994—Illinois 28, Northwestern 7
October 28, 1995—Northwestern 17, Illinois 14
October 26, 1996—Northwestern 27, Illinois 24
November 8, 1997—Northwestern 34, Illinois 21
October 3, 1998—Illinois 13, Northwestern 10
November 20, 1999—Illinois 29, Northwestern 7
November 18, 2000—Northwestern 61, Illinois 23
November 22, 2001—Illinois 34, Northwestern 28
November 23, 2002—Illinois 31, Northwestern 24
November 22, 2003—Northwestern 37, Illinois 20
November 20, 2004—Northwestern 28, Illinois 21 (OT)
November 19, 2005—Northwestern 38, Illinois 21
November 18, 2006—Northwestern 27, Illinois 16

Garrett Rivas exults after kicking the overtime field goal that gave Michigan the victory in its 2005 match with State.

BUNYAN AND BROTHERS:
MICHIGAN STATE vs. MICHIGAN

"**Michigan has always been** the big brother, and Michigan State was the little brother," said Ken Czasak, a longtime Wolverines fan: "So State always pointed their finger at Michigan, which was their whole deal. Michigan had always been the powerhouse, except for the 1960s when State was the big dog. Michigan always had the bull's-eye on its back. State fans looked at them as the big bully, so knocking them down meant putting another notch in their belt. It's for state bragging rights, so it's always been important. But Ohio State and Michigan was like two adults going at it. It was the crown jewel and the games were more hotly contested because everything was on the line, and that wasn't usually the case with Michigan State."

Objective observers, regardless of whether they bleed maize and blue or green and white, would agree with most of those sentiments. However, unlike most familial rivalries, these Big Ten siblings, who live only 60 miles apart, don't really care if they ever make nice.

The Wolverines have relished the role as eldest relative, posting a 66-28-5 overall record in a series that has been played every year since 1910 except for the war years of 1943–44. Nobody understands the complicated dynamics of such a relationship more than the Brandstatters.

Art Brandstatter Jr. played offensive and defensive end and was a place-kicker at Michigan State from 1959 to 1961, earning all-Big Ten honorable mention laurels as a senior. His father and namesake starred for the Spartans from 1934–36, winning all-America honors as a fullback after his senior campaign. Meanwhile, Art's younger brother, Jim, played at sworn enemy Michigan and became a starter at offensive tackle under Bo Schembechler after future Pro Football Hall of Famer Dan Dierdorf graduated.

"I think Michigan–Michigan State is still big and was a huge rivalry when

I played," Art Brandstatter Jr. said. "[Clarence] 'Biggie' Munn was an assistant coach at Michigan before he became head coach and athletic director at Michigan State. There were a lot of things that fueled the rivalry."

So it was easy to see why he chose MSU rather than those bad guys in Ann Arbor. "My dad played here. Dr. John Hannah had been president at Michigan State and recruited my father," Brandstatter said. "I visited Notre Dame but never went to Michigan. I grew up here, so it was almost preordained that I played for the Spartans."

One would think the same thing about his younger brother, but Jim Brandstatter chose a different path and never regretted it, especially considering that the Wolverines won two of three times against Michigan State during his varsity career.

"Being from East Lansing, this game was just as huge as Ohio State, but because it happened in the middle of the season and OSU was at the end, the impact and dynamics were different," said Jim Brandstatter, who's covered many of those battles for radio and television since his playing days ended. "It didn't get the national attention, but in the state of Michigan it was more contentious. It was clearly intense—they [MSU] don't like us and they like nothing more in the world than to beat us, and I'm not telling stories. Michigan has had a lot of success, but it was absolutely a knock-down, drag-out battle like Ohio State. It was like battling against your neighbor."

Because of Michigan's dominance, several Spartans triumphs have created better storylines. One such occurrence was the 1999 showdown in front of 76,895 fans at Spartan Stadium. Enthusiasm was sky high on both sidelines, and rightfully so. The foes entered the game with 5-0 records, with the Wolverines ranked third and the Spartans ranked 11th, the first time since 1961 both met as unbeatens.

Left-handed quarterback Bill Burke and 6' 6" wide receiver Plaxico Burress turned in two of the best individual performances in series history, carrying the Spartans to a 34-31 triumph. Burke completed 21-of-36 pass attempts for a school record 400 yards, breaking Ed Smith's mark of 369 set back in 1978. Burress corralled 10 of those tosses for an amazing 255 yards and one of Burke's two touchdowns. It was Burke's 10th consecutive game with at least one TD pass, while Burress edged past Andre Rison's receiving yardage record of 252, which the latter set in the 1989 Gator Bowl.

Michigan, which kept with its quarterback rotation of senior Tom Brady and sophomore Drew Henson, fought back but fell short despite Hayden Epstein's 56-yard field goal and Henson's 81-yard hookup with Marcus Knight.

State's euphoria didn't last; the Spartans dropped their next two outings to share second place in the league standings before rebounding for a 10-2 mark and Citrus Bowl victory. Meanwhile, the Wolverines fell the next week and finished 6-2 and 10-2 with an Orange Bowl trophy.

The 1987 match up actually was bigger for Michigan State. Coach George Perles' Spartans used a 17-11 win over Michigan as a springboard to their first Rose Bowl appearance in 32 years. Strong safety John Miller intercepted four passes and Todd Krumm added two as State picked off a record seven Demetrius Brown tosses. Offensively, Lorenzo White carried 34 times for 185 yards and both touchdowns as the Spartans finished 7-0-1 in league play.

Michigan State then nipped Southern Cal, 20-17, to cap its 9-2-1 season. UM slipped to 5-3 in Big Ten action and to 8-4 overall.

The situation was eerily similar three years later in a scintillating finish at Michigan Stadium. Tico Duckett scored from 9 yards out with 1:59 left for what proved to be the deciding score as State held on for a 28-27 win against the top-ranked Wolverines.

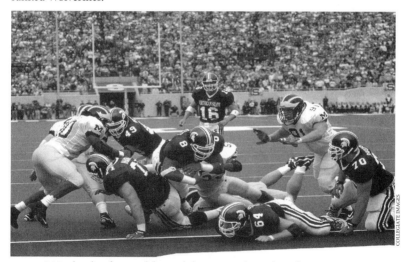

T.J. Duckett dives for a touchdown to help State squeak past the Wolverines in 2001.

Down by seven, Elvis Grbac drove Michigan 71 yards and hooked up with Derrick Alexander for a 7-yard score with six seconds remaining. Michigan coach Gary Moeller decided to go for two and the win. Grbac tried to hit Desmond Howard, but the pass fell incomplete and drew cries for a pass interference call against Michigan State's Eddie Brown. The incompletion stood, and apologies the next day from Big Ten supervisor of officials David Parry didn't soothe the Wolverines' feelings.

The contest had been tied at 14-all when the fireworks started as each team scored two touchdowns in the final 6:03. Hyland Hickson gave the visitors a 21-14 advantage with a 26-yard run, but Howard returned the ensuing kickoff 95 yards. The Spartans and Wolverines finished 6-2 and shared the Big Ten crown with Iowa and Illinois.

Mike Iaquaniello was along for both of those rides under Perles, lettering all four years from 1987 to 1990, the last two and a half seasons as a starter at safety. He said that the hard-nosed Perles, a former MSU player and assistant, instilled an attitude that convinced the players that they could not only compete with the Wolverines, but beat them.

"He wanted our games to be slugfests and wanted us to outhit people," said Iaquaniello, a Dearborn native whose interception set up a score late in the first half of the 1990 tilt. "His mentality was that we could almost tell opponents what play we were going to run and still gain 6 or 7 yards. He ingrained in us the idea that it wasn't a big deal to beat Michigan because we should expect to do it."

Which the Spartans did, finishing 2-2 during Iaquaniello's tenure while losing the 1989 meeting by a 10-7 score.

Iaquaniello grew up in a Wolverine-friendly environment and was courted heavily by both rivals, so when he chose the Spartans it naturally created an interesting dynamic at family gatherings. "I grew up near Ann Arbor, and our Little League uniforms had something similar to the Michigan helmet on them," Iaquaniello said. "But I had a gym teacher, Mr. John Spain, who had run track for the Spartans and was a big influence on me. I was always wearing an MSU jersey. Michigan State was always the underdog when I was growing up, but I believe that this state is more green than blue. It's been a rabid rivalry, even more so in recent years with the increased media coverage and talk radio. The week leading up to that game is unbelievable. And you can see during the years that State gets off to a great start and that Michigan fans get nervous and know that they could actually lose, things get pretty ugly and personal. But to me and my family, it's a fun thing."

Late-game heroics have also benefited Michigan, including back-to-back wins in 2004 and '05. In the former game, Michigan State cruised to a 27-10 advantage with 8:43 left. Garret Rivas started Michigan's comeback by nailing a field goal with 6:27 remaining. Then the Wolverines recovered an onside kick, and quarterback Chad Henne connected with Braylon Edwards to make it 27-20. That combination clicked again to send the contest into overtime, where the Wolverines emerged a 45-37 winner; Henne and Edwards combined for a 24-yard play in the third overtime period on a third-and-9 play. Edwards finished with 11 catches for 189 yards, while Henne tossed four touchdown aerials.

In 2005, it only took one extra period and Rivas' 35-yard field goal for Michigan to claim a 34-31 victory. Mike Hart rushed for 218 yards on 36 attempts in leading the upset of the No. 11 Spartans, who fell to 4-1. Michigan State kicker John Goss missed two of three field goals, including a 23-yarder early in the fourth quarter. His 37-yard attempt to start overtime sailed wide right. Rivas had also shanked a 27-yarder with 48 seconds left in regulation.

If the rivals' on-field contention is fierce, the schools couldn't agree about much of anything when the Paul Bunyan Governor of Michigan Trophy was proposed in 1953, State's first official season as a member of the Big Ten.

United Press reporter Tom Farrell reportedly suggested that the schools play for a trophy. The Spartans apparently liked the idea more than Michigan did; in any event, Governor G. Mennen Williams loved it and pushed the measure through while officials and school newspapers bickered back and forth. Williams commissioned the carving by an artist in Chicago, who crafted it—out of Michigan pine—for $1,400. It was on the field for that first conference match up, a 14-6 victory for the fourth-ranked Spartans.

Michigan didn't want the trophy to take away from the Little Brown Jug, which had been in place for 50 years against Minnesota, and it already had rejected any overtures of playing Ohio State for such a prize. However, the Wolverines haven't had trouble winning or keeping the huge thing in their possession, holding a 33-19-2 advantage after starting 4-11-2.

All of the fuss, or lack thereof, is about a four-foot-high wooden statue of the legendary figure astride an axe with his right foot planted in the Upper Peninsula and his left in the lower half of the state, hands on hips. The axe is suspended between his legs, the blade down around Mount Pleasant and the end of the handle near Marquette. Flags representing each school also were planted in the base, which sits atop a five-foot stand.

The flags have since disappeared, and fraternity members have kidnapped Bunyan. Old Paul has absorbed a beating; the heavy, oversized trophy must be transported in three pieces, and various mishaps have cost him chunks of his right knee, right arm, and abdomen. Despite his size, Bunyan has enjoyed a much lower profile than other trophies. He is displayed in the Schembechler Hall museum while at Michigan, except for during MSU week when he sits in the meeting room. He adorns the Jenison Fieldhouse lobby while in East Lansing.

Regardless of how much (or how little) most fans know about the trophy's history, the rivalry is as intense as any and provides a drama with many midseason subplots every year.

Ralf Mojsiejenko is from Bridgman, a town of about 2,500 in southwestern Michigan. His high school coach was Jerry Planutis, who gained all-America status as a senior fullback for Michigan State in 1955. The coach inspired Mojsiejenko to join the Spartans' program, where he backed up Morten Andersen as a freshman before taking over the placekicking duties his final three years. He also was the No. 1 punter for four seasons before playing in the NFL with San Diego and Washington.

"Michigan had Ohio State, but our biggest rivalry was always Michigan," Mojsiejenko said. "A lot of my teammates were recruited by both teams, so it really didn't matter what our records were or what the point spread was. We were 19 1/2-point underdogs my senior year, but we handled them [19-7] over in Ann Arbor, and that's what made it so special. I believe I kicked three field goals that day.

"The Notre Dame series is pretty big because I'm only 30 minutes from South Bend, but Michigan was always the game we got up for the most," Mojsiejenko added. "The environment was just different. Before this year's game [2006] people were talking trash and everything. Most of it's done in fun, but some people take it more seriously than others."

Walter Kowalczyk was one member of a talented Michigan State backfield from 1955 to 1957, a stretch in which the Spartans won two of three contests against UM. The right halfback earned honorable mention all-league status his first two seasons and then was a first-teamer and gained all-America recognition as a senior, leading the Spartans in rushing and scoring.

"We lost to Michigan my sophomore year, but then we handled them pretty good my last two seasons," said Kowalczyk, who gained 113 yards in MSU's 35-6 triumph that helped the Spartans claim a No. 3 ranking in the final polls behind Auburn and Ohio State, which grabbed the top spot in the AP and UPI polls. "One game that stands out was against Ron Kramer, who was much more of an offensive threat. We ran at him and I remember him saying, 'Why don't you guys run the other way for a change. I'm tired of getting my ass chewed out by the coaches.' We kept running at him."

Kowalczyk said that although every week was a dogfight, coach Duffy Daugherty and the Spartans took a little extra satisfaction from beating their intrastate foes.

"It was a vicious rivalry and we beat the living daylights out of each other, but after the games there wasn't any animosity and we shook hands," Kowalczyk said. "You didn't have all of the dancing and celebrating like you see today because Duffy wouldn't have any of that. But I remember one of our coaches calling Michigan folks 'self-satisfying, egotistical bastards' when they got too much of themselves, and anytime their fans get out of line I'll say that and it usually shuts them up."

Ellis Duckett was born in Texas but has lived in Michigan since moving there at age 5. Michigan State recruited him as a running back, but he became a standout at offensive and defensive end from 1952 to 1954, which spanned the final two years of Clarence "Biggie" Munn's coaching tenure and the first season under Daugherty.

"It was quite intense," Duckett said of the grudge matches. "As a ball player in those days, we didn't get caught up in all of the hype. We were too involved in the games. If I'm not mistaken, we beat them three out of four years I was there."

Duckett was correct. The Spartans defeated Michigan his first three seasons in East Lansing before suffering a 33-7 loss during a 3-6 showing in 1954, the school's first losing record since 1940.

Pete Elliott played for four years at Michigan (1945–48) and never lost to Michigan State, which fell by 40-0, 55-7, and 55-0 counts the first three times. "This series was about equal to Ohio State at one point, so it was big," Elliott said. "It was a matter of bragging rights and pride."

Boris "Bo" Dimitroff's ancestors came from Macedonia and settled in the Detroit area, where he learned all about this series and was recruited by both programs after earning all-state honors as a center-linebacker in high school.

"I believe it's gotten more intense since I played, unfortunately for Michigan State. They've been so mediocre most of the last 40 years," said Dimitroff, who lettered in 1964–65. "Like any of the good college football rivalries, you don't stand on the fence with this one. You're either yellow and blue or green and white. I never knew what the heck maize was for a color anyway."

Those could be construed as fighting words in Michigan, as could some of the reasons Dimitroff selected the Spartans over the Wolverines.

"My high school coach, Jack Hudnut, was a diehard Wolverines fan and I hated to break his heart because I worshipped him, but both schools were recruiting me," Dimitroff said. "After the frenzy died down, there were a couple of weeks left so I took a Saturday and went over to Ann Arbor. Everybody seemed so uptight, aloof, or condescending, like all of the kids were putting on an act. It just wasn't my style and I hated the visit. The next Saturday, I went to East Lansing and there were a lot more people smiling, and the girls were prettier. And then I asked myself which team would I rather not play against, and that was State, so that's where I went."

Dimitroff was a key backup at all three offensive line positions his junior season and then garnered all-Big Ten honors and honorable mention all-America status at center as a senior.

The Spartans lost, 17-10, in 1964 but bounced back to claim a 24-7 victory over Michigan en route to the league crown and national championship laurels in '65, an October contest he can't forget.

Michigan State took advantage of six Michigan fumbles. The Wolverines finished with minus-39 net yards rushing. The Spartans finished the regular season undefeated and shared the No. 1 ranking with Alabama despite losing, 14-12, to UCLA in the Rose Bowl.

"It had rained Wednesday through Friday, and part of the controversy was that they didn't put the tarp down on the field, hoping to slow down all of our all-American skill players," said Dimitroff, who's held Michigan State season tickets since his playing days. "We were kicking the daylights out of them and it was in the second half. Now keep in mind that I hadn't had a bad snap in two years, but we had set up for a field goal in all of this slop. Dick Kenney was our kicker, a bare-footed guy from Hawaii. Our quarterback, Steve Juday, was the holder. As God is my witness, the ball got stuck in the mud, like a divot in golf, and I snapped it over Steve's head. But he got it and lobbed it to Clint Jones, who made a first down, and we went on to score a touchdown. I went off the field and Duffy [Daugherty] and the other coaches were laughing.

"The second memory I have of that game happened in the final 30 seconds or so," Dimitroff recalled. "We had the ball on our own 40 and (MSU fullback) Bob Apisa calls a timeout. We're thinking, 'Are you nuts?' Those guys were angry enough and now they had another shot to hit us. It wasn't until the next day in films that we saw it, but they had all 11 guys up at the line hoping to get their last licks in on us. So, we're all standing up there punching each other and Apisa takes the dive off right guard and goes 60 yards for a score. If that wasn't like putting salt into an open wound."

Dimitroff said it was a raucous ride back to the MSU campus for the Spartan players, who could scarcely suppress their urge to celebrate. "We always stopped for ice cream in Pinckney on the way home," Dimitroff said. "But we hadn't even gotten out of the parking lot when the Rolling Stones' 'Get Off My Cloud' comes on the bus radio full blast, and we don't know the words but we're all screaming and the bus is rocking back and forth."

Don Dufek Sr. remembers a few rocking times, too, while lettering as a full-back and defensive back for the Wolverines from 1948 to 1950. Michigan won his first two encounters by six points each before suffering a 14-7 setback.

"Ohio State was a big rivalry, and a lot of guys from Ohio have played at Michigan, but I've always said that Michigan State was the biggest," said Dufek, whose wife is a State graduate. "An in-state rivalry always takes precedence. And personally I felt it was always bigger than Ohio State. The Wolverines and Buckeyes always had a bearing on conference and national titles, but Michigan–MSU involved state bragging rights because there's such a huge divide. Not just in football and basketball, but in politics and everything else. That line exists

360 days a year, which is different than one week a year like Ohio State."

Dufek's sons, Don (1973–75) and Bill (1974–78) also starred with the Wolverines. Don Jr. finished with 175 total tackles and four interceptions from his secondary spot, while Bill led Michigan's vaunted running game from his position at strong-side offensive tackle.

Bill Dufek and the Wolverines conquered the Spartans every time except for his final meeting, when he was injured. That's when Kirk Gibson and Ed Smith ignited Michigan State's 24-15 victory.

"Most people in Michigan think that State is a sleeping giant," Bill Dufek said. "When you put on the film, you could see that this rivalry was a notch above any other and just like Ohio State. They played you tough until the last whistle, and if you didn't know that then you were in for a rude awakening because they were going to give you their best shots."

MORE SERIES HIGHLIGHTS

1902: Al Hernstein scored seven touchdowns as Michigan whipped the Spartans, 119-0, under their original name of Michigan Agricultural College.

1907: Michigan captain Paul Magoffin scored five times during the Wolverines' 46-0 verdict.

1908: Michigan State and Michigan battled to a scoreless deadlock, the only time in the first seven meetings that the Spartans didn't lose. An estimated 6,000 fans attended.

1913: Michigan State grabbed its first win, 12-7, handing the Wolverines their only setback of the season. The Spartans finished 7-0-0, their first unbeaten and untied campaign—an accomplishment they wouldn't repeat until the 1951 and '52 teams both finished 9-0 and claimed pieces of the national title.

1915: The Spartans dominated during a 24-0 victory, their largest margin over the Wolverines until 1951 (25-0). Jerry DaPrato combined for a 153 yards rushing and receiving, scored all three touchdowns, and drop-kicked a 23-yard field goal.

1924: Michigan won, 7-0, as Herb Steger caught a 47-yard touchdown pass with less than three minutes left in the dedication game of Michigan State's new stadium. It was Michigan's first trip to East Lansing in 10 years, and 22,000 fans showed up.

1930 and 1931: The foes battled to 0-0 ties. Michigan finished 8-0-1 in 1930 and

8-1-1 in '31while the Spartans were 5-1-2 and 5-3-1 those seasons.

1933: Michigan State lost, 20-6, but it was the first time since the 1918 meeting that the Spartans had scored a touchdown.

1934–37: Coach Charlie Bachman led the Spartans to four consecutive wins over the Wolverines after Michigan State had won only twice in 28 previous attempts. Bachman's squads compiled a 28-6-2 overall mark during that span. The 1934 win (16-0) was the school's first against Michigan since 1915.

1935: Al Agett scored on a 46-yard run, and Dick Colina reached paydirt on a 60-yard punt return and caught a touchdown pass from Kurt Warmbein in MSU's 25-6 victory.

1937: Michigan State's 19-14 triumph came in front of an opening-day crowd of 63,311 in Ann Arbor and marked the first time since the turn of the century that Michigan had lost four straight to the same foe. Eugene Ciolek raced 89 yards for a score to highlight the Spartans' performance.

1938–1942: Fritz Crisler led Michigan to five straight wins.

1939: Tom Harmon collaborated with backfield mate Forest Evashevski for two TD tosses and scored a third touchdown during Michigan's 26-13 win.

1940: Michigan pulled out a 21-14 victory as Harmon scored all three touchdowns. His key blocker was quarterback and captain Evashevski, who later coached at Iowa.

1947: The Wolverines blasted the Spartans, 55-0, the most recent of four times that Michigan had scored that many points in a series game and the second in a row after a 55-7 decision the year before.

1950–52: Michigan State swept the Wolverines, 66-20, finishing with 8-1, 9-0 and 9-0 season records under Munn. However, the Spartans weren't officially part of the Big Ten for football at that point, so they weren't eligible to participate in the Rose Bowl despite garnering national championship recognition in 1951 and '52.

MSU's 14-7 verdict in 1950 marked the first of three times that it would knock off a Michigan team that was ranked in the top five. The Wolverines were

No. 3 while Michigan State entered the game at No. 19. Michigan's Bill Billings was forced to punt 11 times in the 25-0 setback in '51.

1954: Tom Hendricks scored on a 67-yard punt return as Michigan bounced the Spartans, 33-7, in front of more than 97,000.

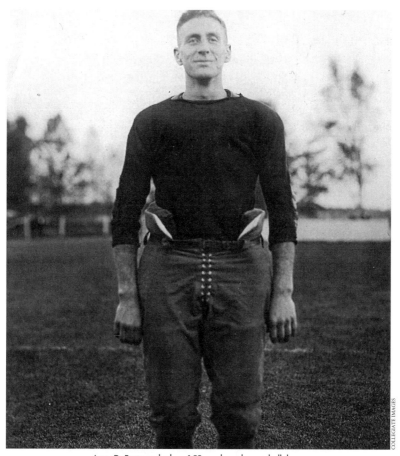

Jerry DaPrato racked up 153 yards and scored all three
touchdowns in the Spartans' 1915 shutout victory over Michigan.

1955: Michigan earned a 14-7 decision, the Spartans' only loss during a 9-1 campaign. Michigan State finished a game behind Ohio State but reached the Rose Bowl because of the no-repeat rule. The Spartans nipped UCLA, 17-14, for their second win over the Bruins in three seasons, beating them, 28-20, after the 1953 season.

1958: Dean Look blazed 92 yards for a score on a punt return for the No. 14 Spartans, while No. 16 Michigan's Gary Prahst scrambled 42 yards with an interception, but the rivals had to settle for a 12-all tie.

1959: Bob Suci helped the Spartans to a 34-8 decision with a 93-yard interception return for a score, the second-longest in team history.

1960: Michigan's Dennis Fitzgerald bolted 99 yards for a kickoff return touchdown, the longest ever against Michigan State. However, the Spartans prevailed, 24-17, as Carl Charon gained 124 yards on 14 carries in front of 76,490, the largest crowd ever in East Lansing to that point.

1962: Sherman Lewis accounted for 20 of Michigan State's points during its 28-0 victory, which also featured Dewey Lincoln's 139 yards rushing on only seven carries.

1964: A brief melee occurred before the game when the No. 9 Spartans ran through the Michigan players' warmup drills. Dick Sygar, who was involved in those pregame festivities, caught a touchdown pass from Bob Timberlake and threw a 31-yard TD pass to John Henderson that helped the seventh-ranked Wolverines rally from a 10-3 fourth-quarter deficit to take a 17-10 victory.

1966: The Wolverines' Stan Kemp punted 11 times as they fell, 20-7. Bob Apisa carried 18 times for 140 yards for top-ranked State.

1969: Don Highsmith rushed for 129 yards and scored two touchdowns, and Bill Triplett carried 18 times for 142 yards as Michigan State handed the Wolverines their only league loss, 23-12. No. 13 Michigan managed only 7 yards passing.

1970: Sixth-ranked Michigan won, 34-20, despite Eric Allen's 156 yards on 23 carries.

1973: No. 5 Michigan scooped up six Spartan fumbles en route to a 31-0 triumph, which also featured David Brown's 53-yard punt return for a score.

1974: Michigan got what it figured was revenge with a 21-7 victory. Michigan State athletic director Burt Smith was one of those who voted (by a 6-4 margin) to send Ohio State to the Rose Bowl instead of the fourth-ranked Wolverines the year before.

1975: Rob Lytle carried 20 times for 111 yards, and Gordon Bell was right behind with 19 tries for 105 yards during eighth-ranked Michigan's 16-6 triumph over No. 15 MSU.

1976: No. 1 Michigan won easily, 42-10, grinding out 442 yards rushing. Lytle busted loose for 180 yards on only 10 carries, while Harlan Huckleby chipped in 23 attempts for 126 yards. Jerry Zuver also scored on a 60-yard interception return.

1978: Eddie Smith and Kirk Gibson (soon to be a major league baseball star) led Michigan State's 24-15 win over the No. 5 Wolverines. Gibson caught five passes for 82 yards and a score for the unranked Spartans at the Big House. The rivals shared first place in the Big Ten at 7-1, but the Spartans were on NCAA probation and weren't eligible for the trip to Pasadena. Smith completed 20-of-36 passes for 248 yards.

1980: Morten Andersen cranked a 57-yard field goal for the Spartans and Ted Jones caught five balls for 109 yards, but Michigan pulled out a 27-23 triumph. It was the first time since 1967 that neither teams was ranked heading into their meeting.

1981: Butch Woolfolk gained 253 yards rushing on 39 carries to lead No. 6 Michigan's 38-20 decision. Bryan Clark of MSU passed for 316 yards but threw three interceptions.

1982: John Leister completed 32-of-46 passes for 272 yards for the Spartans, with Darrin McClelland catching 10 of them and Ted Jones adding nine for 123 yards. However, Michigan earned a 31-17 win.

1984: Bobby Morse's 87-yard punt return for a touchdown helped the unranked Spartans grab a 19-7 win over No. 13 Michigan.

1986: Greg Montgomery uncorked a Michigan State-record 86-yard punt, but it was the lone highlight during No. 4 Michigan's 27-6 win.

1988: No. 17 Michigan upended the Spartans, 17-3, en route to claiming the Big Ten crown at 7-0-1, while Michigan State settled for second place at 6-1-1.

1991: Jim Miller completed 30-of-39 passes for 302 yards, but fifth-ranked

Michigan walked away with a 45-28 triumph.

1992: Mitch Lyons grabbed 12 passes for 119 yards for the Spartans, but MSU came up way short in a 35-10 setback. Derrick Alexander returned a punt 80 yards for a score for Michigan.

1994: Tyrone Wheatley scampered for 153 yards in 23 carries, and Tim Biaka-butuka added 15 attempts for 141 yards as No. 7 Michigan doubled up the Spartans, 40-20. Remy Hamilton booted four field goals for the winners. Nigea Carter caught six passes for 145 yards for Michigan State.

1995: Derrick Mason jump-started the Spartans with three punt returns for 106 yards in their 28-25 victory over the seventh-rated Wolverines, a game that also featured Michigan's Alexander racing 80 yards for a score on a punt return. Tony Banks hit 26-of-34 passes for 318 yards and no interceptions for Michigan State, connecting with Muhsin Muhammad eight times for 116 yards.

1996: No. 9 Michigan won a wild 45-29 decision despite Mason's 10 catches for 151 yards for Michigan State. Scott Dreisbach tossed four touchdown passes for the Wolverines, who picked off four of Todd Schultz's passes.

2000: Michigan, ranked 16th, pulled out a 14-0 victory despite 292 yards and 26-of-37 passing from Ryan Van Dyke.

2001: Epstein knocked a 57-yard field goal through for Michigan, which also received five tackles for loss and three sacks from Shantee Orr. Sixth-ranked UM fell, 26-24, as State's T.J. Duckett ran the ball 27 times for 211 yards.

2006: Michael Hart carried 22 times for 122 yards as the No. 6 Wolverines rushed for 211 yards en route to a 31-13 victory and Michigan's first 6-0 start since its national championship season of 1997. Michigan ran 42 times and attempted only 17 passes, but three of Henne's tosses went for scores, including two to Mario Manningham. Michigan State dropped its third consecutive game after a 3-0 start, helping seal coach John L. Smith's fate.

Sparty rallies the Michigan State faithful.

ALL-TIME SERIES RESULTS

MICHIGAN LEADS, 66-28-5

October 12, 1898—Michigan 39, Michigan State 0
October 8, 1902—Michigan 119, Michigan State 0
October 12, 1907—Michigan 46, Michigan State 0
October 10, 1908—Michigan 0, Michigan State 0 (T)
October 15, 1910—Michigan 6, Michigan State 3
October 14, 1911—Michigan 15, Michigan State 3
October 12, 1912—Michigan 55, Michigan State 7
October 18, 1913—Michigan State 12, Michigan 7
October 17, 1914—Michigan 3, Michigan State 0
October 23, 1915—Michigan State 24, Michigan 0
October 21, 1916—Michigan 9, Michigan State 0
October 20, 1917—Michigan 27, Michigan State 0
November 23, 1918—Michigan 21, Michigan State 6
October 18, 1919—Michigan 26, Michigan State 0
October 16, 1920—Michigan 35, Michigan State 0
October 15, 1921—Michigan 30, Michigan State 0
November 4, 1922—Michigan 63, Michigan State 0
October 27, 1923—Michigan 37, Michigan State 0

October 11, 1924—Michigan 7, Michigan State 0
October 3, 1925—Michigan 39, Michigan State 0
October 9, 1926—Michigan 55, Michigan State 3
October 8, 1927—Michigan 21, Michigan State 0
November 17, 1928—Michigan 3, Michigan State 0
October 5, 1929—Michigan 17, Michigan State 0
October 4, 1930—Michigan 0, Michigan State 0 (T)
November 14, 1931—Michigan 0, Michigan State 0 (T)
October 1, 1932—Michigan 26, Michigan State 0
October 7, 1933—Michigan 20, Michigan State 6
October 6, 1934—Michigan State 16, Michigan 0
October 5, 1935—Michigan State 25, Michigan 6
October 3, 1936—Michigan State 21, Michigan 7
October 2, 1937—Michigan State 19, Michigan 14
October 1, 1938—Michigan 14, Michigan State 0
October 7, 1939—Michigan 26, Michigan State 13
October 5, 1940—Michigan 21, Michigan State 14
September 27, 1941—Michigan 19, Michigan State 7
October 3, 1942—Michigan 20, Michigan State 0

September 29, 1945—Michigan 40, Michigan State 0

November 9, 1946—Michigan 55, Michigan State 7

September 27, 1947—Michigan 55, Michigan State 0

September 25, 1948—Michigan 13, Michigan State 7

September 24, 1949—Michigan 7, Michigan State 3

September 30, 1950—Michigan State 14, Michigan 7

September 29, 1951—Michigan State 25, Michigan 0

September 27, 1952—Michigan State 27, Michigan 13

November 14, 1953—Michigan State 14, Michigan 6

November 13, 1954—Michigan 33, Michigan State 7

October 1, 1955—Michigan 14, Michigan State 7

October 6, 1956—Michigan State 9, Michigan 0

October 12, 1957—Michigan State 35, Michigan 6

October 4, 1958—Michigan 12, Michigan State 12 (T)

October 3, 1959—Michigan State 34, Michigan 8

October 1, 1960—Michigan State 24, Michigan 17

October 14, 1961—Michigan State 28, Michigan 0

October 13, 1962—Michigan State 28, Michigan 0

October 12, 1963—Michigan 7, Michigan State 7 (T)

October 10, 1964—Michigan 17, Michigan State 10

October 9, 1965—Michigan State 24, Michigan 7

October 8, 1966—Michigan State 20, Michigan 7

October 14, 1967—Michigan State 34, Michigan 0

October 12, 1968—Michigan State 28, Michigan State 14

October 18, 1969—Michigan State 23, Michigan 12

October 17, 1970—Michigan 34, Michigan State 20

October 9, 1971—Michigan 24, Michigan 13

October 14, 1972—Michigan 10, Michigan State 0

October 13, 1973—Michigan 31, Michigan State 0

October 12, 1974—Michigan 21, Michigan State 7

October 11, 1975—Michigan 16, Michigan State 6

October 9, 1976—Michigan 42, Michigan State 10

October 8, 1977—Michigan 24, Michigan State 14

October 14, 1978—Michigan State 24, Michigan 15

October 6, 1979—Michigan 21, Michigan State 7

October 11, 1980—Michigan 27, Michigan State 23

October 10, 1981—Michigan 38, Michigan State 20

October 9, 1982—Michigan 31, Michigan State 17

October 8, 1983—Michigan 42, Michigan State 0

October 6, 1984—Michigan State 19, Michigan 7

October 12, 1985—Michigan 31, Michigan State 0

October 11, 1986—Michigan 27, Michigan State 6

October 10, 1987—Michigan State 17, Michigan 11

October 8, 1988—Michigan 17, Michigan State 3

October 14, 1989—Michigan 10, Michigan State 7

October 13, 1990—Michigan State 28, Michigan 27

October 12, 1991—Michigan 45, Michigan State 28

October 10, 1992—Michigan 35, Michigan State 10

October 9, 1993—Michigan State 17, Michigan 7

October 8, 1994—Michigan 40, Michigan State 20

November 4, 1995—Michigan State 28, Michigan 25

November 2, 1996—Michigan 45, Michigan State 29

October 25, 1997—Michigan 23, Michigan State 7

September 26, 1998—Michigan 29, Michigan State 17

October 9, 1999—Michigan State 34, Michigan 31

October 21, 2000—Michigan 14, Michigan State 0

November 3, 2001—Michigan State 26, Michigan 24

November 2, 2002—Michigan 49, Michigan State 3

November 1, 2003—Michigan 27, Michigan State 20

October 30, 2004—Michigan 45, Michigan State 37 (3 OTs)

October 1, 2005—Michigan 34, Michigan State 31 (OT)

October 7, 2006—Michigan 31, Michigan State 13

HOG HEAVEN:

IOWA vs. MINNESOTA

As Bryan Skradis recalls it, the attempt to create a new football tradition at the University of Iowa didn't quite replace the real thing.

"They started playing Iowa State again my first year and tried to build that up, but unequivocally Minnesota was our chief rival," Skradis said. "It was a big week. I remember assistant coach Bernie Wyatt wearing his letterman's jacket to practice that one Thursday, so the coaches made sure we knew about it. I made a tackle along the sidelines on a kickoff during my freshman season and got a 15-yard penalty, but it was worth it because I hated those guys. The goofy Gophers had a bunch of cheap-shot artists who'd punish you standing around the pile, so those games were bloodbaths."

Skradis is an Omaha native who suited up for Iowa from 1977 to 1979 and '81, receiving a medical hardship after sitting out the 1980 campaign because of an injury. He easily could have been referring to games played decades earlier, such as those in the mid-1930s.

Minnesota bludgeoned the Hawkeyes, 48-12, en route to winning the Big Ten title and the 1934 national championship. The Gophers amassed an astounding 595 yards, all rushing. Julius Alphonse, Stan Kostka, and Francis "Pug" Lund surpassed the 100-yard mark in front of 52,000 fans at Iowa's homecoming.

Bernie Bierman's squad battered the hosts, especially Iowa standout running back Ozzie Simmons, which elevated the already emotionally charged Hawkeyes crowd. Some of them vowed revenge the next season. Iowa Governor Clyde L. Herring and folks south of the border also remained rankled because a Minnesota representative had ardently supported Iowa's recent suspension for slush-fund violations.

So as the teams prepared to tangle for a second straight season in Iowa City in 1935, Minnesota Governor Floyd B. Olson proposed a friendly wager to his counterpart in an attempt to defuse tensions between the teams and their followers: The winner would take home a prize hog.

The Gophers entered the game 5-0, and the Hawkeyes were 4-0-1. Minnesota won the contest, 13-6, on its way to the second of three consecutive national crowns. As a present, Allen Loomis, owner of the Rosedale Farm near Fort Dodge, Iowa, donated a boar named Floyd. Supposedly, some Hawkeye backers wanted to rename the hog Hawkeye Honor, but Herring liked the fact that the pig and the Minnesota governor shared the same name. Thus, the annual prize was called Floyd of Rosedale.

Mission accomplished, at least as far as the game itself was concerned. However, the mischief began shortly thereafter, and the legend of Floyd grew exponentially.

A grumpy Iowa fan complained that using the pig as a trophy constituted gambling, but that didn't stop Herring from eventually having his aides load the 220-pound porker into a truck for his long ride northward. When Herring herded the animal into Olson's office in St. Paul, Minnesota, someone decided that a city ordinance had been broken. Both charges were dismissed, but the governor had had enough of actual livestock and commissioned a 15 $\frac{1}{2}$-inch bronze statue to become the traveling trophy.

As for the real hog, he became well-traveled, too. First, 14-year-old Richard Jones won him in an essay-writing contest and sold him to the University of Minnesota. J.B. Gjerdrum, a breeder who lived near Mabel, Minnesota, not far from the Iowa border, paid $50 for the popular pig. Sadly, Floyd lived only about

Some pig: The famous Floyd of Rosedale

a year longer; legend has it that he died of cholera after his vaccination for the disease was accidentally skipped. He was buried in a nearby field, with no headstone erected to mark his resting place and chronicle his spot in Big Ten football lore.

Still, history remains a huge part of the annual confrontations that continue to be among the most heated in the country. The outcomes seldom attracted as much attention as Floyd had, but the 1960 clash was one that did. Iowa was ranked No. 1 and Minnesota sat in the No. 3 position as both teams came into the game with 6-0 marks for a match up on the first Saturday in November. It was a cold, windy day in Iowa City. Minnesota trailed, 10-7, after Joe Williams' 26-yard run but got the upper hand at 13-10 when Sandy Stephens capped an 11-play, 81-yard march. Roger Hagberg's 42-yard run helped give the Gophers a 10-point cushion. They went on to a 27-10 victory as Hagberg finished with 103 yards on 15 carries.

The Gophers then lost to Purdue, 23-14, to eventually share first place with Iowa. They were ranked fourth heading into their regular-season finale against Wisconsin. UM beat the Badgers, regained the top spot in both wire service polls, and won the national title (which was also decided by ballot in those days). Good thing, because Minnesota suffered a 17-7 setback to Washington in the Rose Bowl. Iowa followed with wins over Ohio State and Notre Dame to finish 8-1 in Forest Evashevski's final season, giving him a 52-27-4 record through his nine years.

David Lothner said that the 1960 showdown was the pinnacle of his sophomore season and one of the most special in Minnesota annals.

"We had a lot of injuries going into that game, but everybody was fired up and we got it done," Lothner said. "Of all the games that year, that one was the clincher and let us take over the No. 1 spot. Iowa was always tough to play, especially because you had so little room behind your bench. Those fans were very supportive of their team, and we didn't want to get hit by any tomatoes or cabbage. Luckily, I didn't suffer any direct hits."

Although the Hawkeyes have enjoyed more feast than famine during the past quarter-century, wild and unusual circumstances have been numerous in this series, which reached 100 games in 2006. Take the 1986 edition. Minnesota sported a 5-2 conference record and was coming off a 20-17 upset of Michigan. Iowa, the defending Big Ten champion, was 4-3 and trying to recover from several key injuries.

Iowa trailed, 17-0, at halftime as Minnesota's Chip Lohmiller kicked a Big Ten-record 62-yard field goal. Peter Marciano ignited the Hawkeyes' comeback with an 89-yard punt return for a touchdown, but Iowa still trailed, 24-13, after three quarters. However, Hawkeyes quarterback Mark Vlasic finished 15-of-21, including 11 straight completions, for 99 yards and a score in the second half to help the visitors claim a 30-27 triumph in front of a record crowd of 65,018.

The outcome turned dramatically after Iowa's Rob Houghtlin missed a potential game-winning boot from 52 yards away. He got a second chance when Minnesota was whistled for having 12 men on the field, an unsportsmanlike conduct penalty that moved the Hawkeyes 15 yards closer. Houghtlin didn't miss his second opportunity.

Dave Croston was a three-year starter at left offensive tackle at Iowa in the mid-1980s, winning his final two chances against Minnesota, including that barn burner in '86 that sent Iowa to the Holiday Bowl.

"I remember that my roommate, Jeff Drost, gave a historic pep talk, basically going nuts for 10 minutes, at halftime," said Croston, who later played for the Green Bay Packers. "We put Mark [Vlasic] in and everything turned around. Then I was walking off the field after Rob [Houghtlin] missed that first field goal, but they had 12 guys on the field and he made the second kick."

Croston also attended the wild 2002 tilt at the Metrodome, which sent No.

Gopher Bob McNamara gained 227 yards in Minnesota's 1954 win.

6 Iowa to the Orange Bowl with a 45-21 win. The Hawkeyes rushed for 365 yards and recovered four Gophers fumbles. Fred Russell gained 194 yards and Jermelle Lewis added 101. Quarterback Brad Banks threw two touchdown passes and ran for two as Iowa clinched at least a share of its first conference title in 12 years.

"I was sitting way up in the top of the stands somewhere, and it was amazing to watch," Croston said. "Fans carried part of the one goalpost up the walkway and out of the stadium. They were playing that high-pitched noise on the loudspeakers, but it didn't help get people to cooperate."

Croston said that was only one example of how crazy things can get when it comes to this series.

Croston had an unpleasant day on the field his first time around, too. "I had been hurt most of the 1984 season but was back for that game," he said of the eventual 23-17 setback to the Gophers. "I had a guy get blocked into the outside of my injured knee. My knee brace absorbed the hit and broke, which saved me from worse damage, but it kept me out of the Freedom Bowl."

Louis Matykiewicz also witnessed highs and lows against the Gophers, sandwiching a 27-0 victory in between two defeats from 1952 to 1954.

"In those days you didn't exchange game films, so one of our assistant coaches had scouted them," Matykiewicz said of preparations for Iowa's win late in his junior year. "Minnesota ran a form of the single-wing offense with all-America halfback Paul Giel. Our coach picked up on the fact that Giel always wet his fingers before a running play, and when he didn't it was a pass."

Matykiewicz and the Hawkeyes then suffered a disheartening 22-20 loss in his final showdown in the Twin Cities.

"We ran up and down the field and finished with something like 500 yards, but they got a safety and beat us," Matykiewicz said. "I remember lining up on the left side and running down on punt coverage. I was going to lay the guy out and somebody else hit him and I got knocked in the face and broke my nose. We were wearing white and I had blood all over my jersey. My picture was inside the next issue of *Sports Illustrated*."

Tom Luckemeyer didn't gain such notoriety, losing two of his three contests against Iowa as a three-year starter at defensive back for the Gophers from 1975 to 1977. As a senior, he and the Gophers entered their annual scrum having beaten UCLA and Washington at home; two weeks later, they would stun top-ranked Michigan. However, they didn't enjoy their trip to Iowa City at all, falling, 18-6. Luckemeyer, whose father, Dick, played for Minnesota in 1941–42, suffered an even worse fate.

"Earlier in the game I had dinged up my shoulder," Luckemeyer said. "Then I was making a tackle and one of our safeties came in and hit me with his helmet and broke four of my ribs. I went to the sidelines thinking I had just gotten the wind knocked out of me. I told the trainer that my shoulder was bothering me and about the pain in my diaphragm and he knew right away. I had hurt my pancreas, and my spleen had ruptured. I was in surgery before the game got over and spent a couple of weeks in the hospital. Luckily, I had been born with two spleens—they told me that about 12 percent of people have an extra one."

Despite the beating he took, he remembers those years fondly.

"My dad had replaced Bruce Smith at running back [in 1942], so I always dreamed of playing for the Gophers," Luckemeyer said. "It was always a tough game against Iowa, but I enjoyed the bus rides and the pomp and circumstance going to all of the Big Ten venues. I remember as a freshman when they brought the pig trophy into the locker room, so the Floyd of Rosedale was a big deal. Iowa and Wisconsin are our neighbors, so we always wanted to beat them."

Minnesota was winless against Iowa during Paul Kratochvil's tenure with the Gophers from 1993 to 1996, but that doesn't mean the games weren't special.

"They always filled up Kinnick Stadium, and it seemed like it was always half and half when they came up to the dome," Kratochvil said. "There are probably 30,000 Iowans that make the trip. It's a huge game and the fanfare is incredible."

Darrell Thompson, who starred at Minnesota after nearly becoming a Hawkeye, couldn't agree more. "Iowa was my favorite place to play," Thompson said. "I loved Hayden Fry and came an inch away from going there. They had been to the Rose Bowl the year before and had guys like Chuck Long, Ronnie Harmon, and Larry Station. Kinnick Stadium was a fun environment, but we had to band together because it could get a little hostile down there. The fans are literally 10 to 12 feet away from the field, and they're laughing and calling you names. It was almost like being at a basketball game."

Bud Sueppel has been one of the most ardent supporters of players who've worn the black and gold. After all, he has lived in Iowa City his entire life and has attended every game, home and away, during the past 35 years or so.

"I remember the 1990 game up there. Minnesota won, 31-24, but we already knew we were going to the Rose Bowl," said Sueppel. "One time they called Iowa twice for penalties because of crowd noise. And the way I was yelling, they could have called us for another one. I know that we've had twice as many fans as them up there, so the last couple of years their new athletic director has notified us that they'll only sell us 5,000 tickets. The last couple of times that we've beaten them we've knocked them out of a better bowl game, so they're probably a little bitter. Minnesota is Iowa's biggest rival because it's been a home game many times. A lot of fans from northern Iowa flock to Minnesota once a year because they can't get tickets to home games."

Steve Smith is a Burnsville, Minnesota, resident who has been a longtime Hawkeyes fan. Smith has owned season tickets since 1980, Hayden Fry's second year as coach. Smith also owns a place in Keokuk, Iowa, so he attends most Hawkeyes home games, too. But one recent tussle between the Hawkeyes and Gophers stands out.

"I was at the 2002 game in the Metrodome, the one that Iowa won to finish 8-0 in the Big Ten and went to the Orange Bowl," Smith said. "The cheerleaders were carrying banners and the fans rushed the field and tore down the goalpost and tried to haul it out of the stadium. They actually got parts of it out into the corridor. The security guards were all like 75 years old and couldn't do much. To get the fans to leave, they turned on a high-frequency thing. That pissed the fans off even more. It was a crazy scene."

Not so out of the ordinary when it comes to these teams and their faithful followers. Smith, like most folks, caught clips on television or read about Fry's humorous display leading up to the 1982 contest, the first match up in the Dome.

"Joe Salem, the Minnesota coach at the time, had said something in passing about Iowa being a bunch of hicks or something. So Hayden showed up at a press conference the day before the game with a cowboy hat and overalls on, and a straw between his teeth," Smith related. "I have a picture of that."

Another fond memory is the story about Forest Evashevski apparently pulling one over on his team before its 7-0 road defeat of the Gophers in 1956; the Hawkeyes had been battered in a 17-14 loss to Michigan the week before and needed a little something extra to get them ready to face unbeaten Minnesota.

"The story goes that he got off the bus and didn't have his ID, so the security guard wouldn't let him in," Smith said. "He told the players and that got them all fired up and ready to go. It turns out that Evy did have his badge in his pocket; it was a psychological ploy."

Iowa then held off Ohio State to clinch its first outright league crown in 35 years and whipped Notre Dame to reach the Rose Bowl. The Hawkeyes blasted Oregon State, 35-19, for their first title in Pasadena.

Sherwyn Thorson lettered in football as an offensive guard and linebacker from 1959 to 1960 under Evashevski and in '61 under Jerry Burns. Thorson also won an NCAA heavyweight title in wrestling as a senior at Iowa, so he knows how rugged the Big Ten was.

"We beat the Gophers handily during my sophomore season," the Fort Dodge resident said of the 33-0 victory. "My junior year, they beat us but then lost to Purdue to tie for the league title. But Minnesota was one of the two games I missed that year with an injury. Then they knocked us off my senior year. It always seemed like Minnesota looked down at us, so it was a big rivalry."

Jack Mulvena played the same positions and lettered the same three seasons as Thorson, but he suited up for the Gophers and understandably carried a little different perspective.

"Iowa wasn't as gentlemanly as Wisconsin," said Mulvena, a Delaware native who resides in Florida. "In '59, we were mostly sophomores and outmanned, and Iowa's guys were unfriendly. There were a couple of unsportsmanlike things that happened and we had a couple guys all bloodied up. They were pretty good every year and beat us, 33-0.

"We also used an open huddle at the time, where everybody lines up in a couple of rows facing the other team and our quarterback, Sandy Stephens, called the plays with his back to the opponent," Mulvena added. "One time, one of their guys just walked up to us in between plays and said we didn't even know how to huddle up right. They just didn't show any respect."

However, Mulvena and his mates got the better of Iowa his final two seasons and won the national championship in 1960. "We remembered what happened the year before, when they were No. 1 and we were ranked third," Mulvena said. "It wasn't necessarily revenge, but we used those things to our advantage. It was a rough rivalry, and some dirty things went on."

Lonnie Rogers played defensive back and halfback, and punted for the Hawkeyes from 1961 to 1963. He said that those games weren't always pretty, but that was life in the Big Ten back then.

"Iowa and Minnesota played a lot of good games that went back and forth, most of them defensive struggles," said Rogers, who coached at South Dakota and Northern Arizona with Salem, who later led the Gophers from 1979 to 1983. "I remember in 1962 that several teams hadn't scored against Minnesota and we went up there to face guys like Carl Eller and Bobby Bell. It was a heckuva game, but unfortunately for us, yours truly fumbled the ball going in for a score that I believe would have tied it in the third quarter. We ended up losing, 10-0, and I made the front page of the *Minneapolis Star-Tribune.*"

MORE SERIES HIGHLIGHTS

1901: Minnesota won, 16-0, after saying it would lodge a complaint if Iowa used Clyde Williams, the Hawkeyes' best player, who was deemed ineligible because he had played baseball in North Dakota under an assumed name.

1909: Minnesota whipped the Hawkeyes, 41-0, as Lisle Johnston scored five touchdowns, including 55- and 65-yard punt returns. It was the second of four straight shutouts as the Gophers started 6-0.

1911: Iowa lost, 24-6, but Willis "Fat" O'Brien kicked 45- and 52-yard field goals, the first points that Iowa scored against the Gophers since 1892. O'Brien's 52-yarder was the longest in the nation that season.

1916: Halfback Joe Sprafka scored four touchdowns during Minnesota's 67-0 rout, one of the Gophers' four shutouts that season, as Iowa failed to gain a first down until the fourth quarter.

1918: Iowa had lost its first 12 games against the Gophers in a series that started in 1891. The Hawkeyes finally won, 6-0. Fullback Fred Lohman scored the game's only points in the third quarter, while the Hawkeyes didn't allow Minnesota inside their 30.

1919: Iowa won at Minnesota for the first time as Aubrey Devine booted a game-winning 33-yard field goal for a 9-6 win with 12,000 in attendance.

1920: The Hawkeyes became the first squad to beat the Gophers for a third straight time, posting a 28-7 home victory.

1921: Devine accounted for all of Iowa's points during its 41-7 thrashing of the Gophers. He scored four touchdowns and drop-kicked four extra points to go with two TD passes to end Lester Belding. It was the largest scoring output that Minnesota had given up to that point in its history. Devine accumulated 464 all-purpose yards at Northrop Field.

1922: Gordon Locke scored three touchdowns to ignite Iowa's 28-14 homecoming win en route to a 7-0 record, its second unbeaten season.

1924: Leland Parkin rushed 38 times for 163 yards and Iowa's only touchdown in its 13-0 decision, another homecoming triumph, as the Hawkeyes finished 6-1-1 in Burt Ingwersen's first year as head coach.

1928: Iowa earned a 7-6 homecoming victory after both teams entered the game unbeaten. Fred Hovde raced 91 yards with a punt return in the fourth quarter to give Minnesota a 6-0 advantage. Soon thereafter, Oran "Nanny" Pape burst 61 yards for a touchdown to tie it. Starting kicker Willis Glassgow had been injured earlier in the game, which left it up to drop-kicker Irving Nelson. He ran onto the field without his helmet but eventually converted the deciding extra point.

1929: Iowa downed the Gophers, 9-7. Glassgow's second-quarter

Ozzie Simmons was a standout running back for Iowa in the 1930s.

field goal gave Iowa a 3-0 lead that held until Bronko Nagurski bolted 41 yards to push Minnesota ahead 6-3 in the fourth period. Pape scooted 6 yards with 30 seconds left for the Hawkeyes, their last victory in the series for 10 years.

1939: Iowa rallied from a 9-0 deficit after three quarters to post a 13-9 triumph over No. 20 Minnesota. Heisman Trophy winner Nile Kinnick tossed a 45-yard touchdown pass to Erwin Prasse. Kinnick added the extra point and then connected with Bill Green on a 28-yarder for the deciding score. Kinnick and six of his teammates played all 60 minutes. Minnesota had gained its cushion on Joe Mernik's second-quarter field goal and Davenport, Iowa, native George "Sonny" Franck's 7-yard run in the third period. Kinnick completed 15- and 18-yard passes to Floyd "Buzz" Dean, ran for 2 yards, and then hit Prasse to make it 9-6 and drop-kicked the extra point. He then led a 79-yard, game-winning drive.

Nile Kinnick tossed a 45-yard touchdown pass for Iowa in the 1939 meeting.

1940: Franck registered four touchdowns in sixth-ranked Minnesota's 34-6 decision as the Gophers eventually claimed the No. 1 spot and their fourth national championship.

1941: Bruce Smith was only in for seven plays for No. 1 Minnesota, but five of them went for scores during the Gophers' 34-13 triumph. It was the first and only time that the stingy Gophers allowed an opponent to score in double figures in eight games, all victories.

1942: Wayne "Red" Williams gained 149 yards to carry No. 16 Minnesota to a 27-7 triumph.

1943: Minnesota romped, 33-14, as Williams scored four times and passed for another touchdown while rushing for 143 yards. The Gophers weren't ranked heading into this confrontation for the first time since the AP poll started in 1936.

1945: Jerry Niles' screen pass to Nelson Smith was the deciding score in Iowa's 20-19 victory, ending the Hawkeyes' 18-game league losing streak. Iowa had been outscored by a 278-48 margin in its first six games of the season.

1946: Billy Bye gained 112 yards as host Minnesota earned a 16-6 verdict in front of more than 59,000 fans.

1947: Iowa claimed a 13-7 win after head man Eddie Anderson, in his second stint as Hawkeyes' coach, had resigned the day before the game. However, the athletic board didn't accept it and Anderson stayed on for another two seasons. No. 20 Minnesota got 137 yards from Everette Faunce.

1951: Iowa trailed, 20-0, after three quarters but rallied to tie it at 20-all as Bill Reichardt scored on 8- and 37-yard plays. Paul Giel led the Gophers with 166 yards rushing.

1953: Iowa's defense dominated, holding Giel to 14 yards rushing on 13 carries and allowing No. 15 Minnesota to complete only three passes for 22 yards. George "Dusty" Rice scored three times in Iowa's 27-0 win, its largest victory margin in a conference outing since 1922. The Gophers finished with 81 total yards.

1954: Minnesota, ranked 13th, pulled out a 22-20 victory. The Gophers raced ahead, 14-0, on 36- and 89-yard scoring plays from Bob McNamara, who rushed for 115 yards and gained 227 all-purpose yards. Iowa knotted things on scores by Jerry Reichow and Earl Smith. Don Swanson's 27-yard pass pushed Minnesota ahead again before Iowa tied it at 20. Iowa's Smith then had an 81-yard punt return called back on a clipping penalty, and three plays later the Hawkeyes fumbled and fell on the ball in their end zone, giving the Gophers the deciding safety.

1955: Iowa whipped the Gophers, 26-0, as Eddie Vincent threw for one TD and ran for two.

1956: Iowa won, 7-0, and earned its first Rose Bowl berth, forcing six Minnesota turnovers. The sixth-ranked Gophers were unbeaten and would have earned a trip to Pasadena had they won. Minnesota fumbled on the game's fourth play, and the Hawkeyes traveled 38 yards, capping the drive on a 1-yard burst from Fred Harris. William Happel intercepted a Gophers toss at his 1-yard line and UI pilfered another in the final two minutes to preserve the win.

1957: Host Iowa riddled the Gophers, 44-20, ripping off 23 points in the second quarter. Randy Duncan passed for two touchdowns and ran for two more. Jim Gibbons caught nine passes for 164 yards and hauled in both of Duncan's scoring tosses.

1958: Duncan and Willie Fleming led the way in Iowa's 28-6 road decision. Duncan passed for two touchdowns, while Fleming scooted 46 and 63 yards as the Hawkeyes rushed for 305 yards. On New Year's Day, Iowa blasted California, 38-12, in the Rose Bowl.

1964: Minnesota held on for a 14-13 triumph after Iowa's two-point attempt failed. Gary Snook hit Craig Nourse for what was then a school-record 87-yard touchdown pass to shave the Hawkeyes' deficit to one. However, Snook's pass for Karl Noonan was off the mark. Snook finished with 309 yards passing and two scores.

1965: More than 59,000 showed up in a downpour in Iowa City, only to see the foes battle to a scoreless deadlock at the half. Minnesota grabbed a 7-3 lead on a 54-yard pass play and 22 seconds later sewed up a 14-3 verdict, getting a 30-yard run the first play after intercepting a Snook pass.

1966: Minnesota won, 17-0, but it wasn't because of Dave Moreland. The

Hawkeyes' defensive star registered 23 tackles, including 15 solo stops. Robert Stein led the Gophers with five tackles for loss, and Ed Duren contributed a 95-yard interception return.

1967: Mo Forte accumulated 149 yards for the Gophers, who earned a 10-0 win.

1968: The Hawkeyes recorded their first road victory since 1965 and snapped a four-game skid in this rivalry, posting a 35-28 decision after not scoring a TD in the three previous showdowns. Larry Lawrence scored four times, and Iowa gained 319 of its 450 yards on the ground. The Hawkeyes set team marks with 101 offensive plays, including 82 runs. Meanwhile, Wayne King registered 24 tackles for the Gophers. Barry Mayer led Minnesota with 179 rushing and 207 all-purpose yards.

1969: Minnesota entered this contest 0-5-1 overall but whipped the Hawkeyes, 35-8, behind two fumble recoveries and four interceptions. Three of the latter were picked off by Walter Bowser. Iowa's quarterbacks completed only 10 of 42 passes. Meanwhile, Jim Carter ran for four scores and Mayer rushed for 135 yards for the Gophers.

1970: Iowa gained 369 yards rushing, including 161 from Levi Mitchell and 137 from Tim Sullivan. But the Hawkeyes settled for a 14-all tie and couldn't bring the Pig back home. Bill Light finished with a school record 32 tackles, including 17 solos, for the Gophers.

1971: Ernest Cook topped Minnesota with 175 yards as the Gophers handed Iowa a 19-14 defeat.

1972: Coach Cal Stoll's Gophers were 0-5. But quarterback Bob Morgan used a no-huddle offensive attack that gained more than 400 yards rushing as Minnesota routed the Hawkeyes, 43-14. Andre Jackson had 20 tackles for Iowa, which shut down the Gophers' passing game. However, Minnesota got four scores and 173 yards from John King and 135 yards from Doug Beaudoin.

1973: John King rambled for 179 yards, and Larry Powell complemented him with 128 in Minnesota's 31-23 decision.

1974: Minnesota grabbed a 23-17 victory as Rick Upchurch gained 210 yards, including an 86-yard touchdown, and John Jones chipped in 125 yards.

1976: The Gophers, 3-0 in league play and 5-1 overall, took a 12-0 halftime lead. But visiting Iowa registered 15 points in the fourth quarter to win, 22-12. This was the Hawkeyes' first win in the series in eight years.

1977: Iowa downed the Gophers at home for the first time since 1963, hanging an 18-6 decision on Minnesota behind Dave Holsclaw's then-record four field goals. It also gave Iowa its first back-to-back wins in the series since 1958–59.

1978: Minnesota moved ahead, 22-0, in the third quarter and held on for a 22-20 victory as Marion Barber gained 130 yards rushing.

Marion Barber's rushing helped Minnesota shut the Hawkeyes down in 1978.

1979: Minnesota's Elmer Bailey gained 158 yards receiving to lift the Gophers to a 24-7 win, the first time since 1966 that attendance surpassed 60,000 for this game.

1981: Sixth-ranked Iowa overcame a 9-0 halftime deficit to grab a 10-9 margin after three quarters. But Jim Gallery booted his fourth field goal with 2:22 left to give UM a two-point upset win. The Hawkeyes mustered only two first downs and 45 total yards in the first half. Iowa had knocked off Nebraska, UCLA, and Michigan that season, all of which were ranked sixth at the time. Eddie Phillips carried 36 times for 198 yards and a touchdown for the Hawkeyes.

1982: The Hawkeyes gave their 15,000 victory-hungry fans a treat in their first trip to the Metrodome, claiming a 21-16 decision that ended a four-year drought and eased the pain of 11 defeats in their last 13 outings against Minnesota. Gallery booted three field goals and quarterback Mike Hohensee completed 27-of-47 passes for 311 yards, including 104 to Dwayne McMullen. He did, however, throw four interceptions for the Gophers.

1983: No. 11 Iowa tore the Gophers apart with a record 517 yards rushing and seven scores, averaging 11 yards per carry in its 61-10 romp. The Hawkeyes accumulated 656 total yards, only the third-highest total that season. Phillips raced 80 yards for a touchdown on one of his carries.

1984: Billy Happel bolted a school-record 95 yards for a punt-return touchdown, George Davis set an Iowa mark with 18 solo tackles, and Larry Station had 21 total tackles, but the Hawkeyes still lost, 23-17.

1985: Third-ranked Iowa won, 31-9, to reach the Rose Bowl, where the Hawkeyes fell to UCLA.

1987: Chuck Hartlieb completed 26-of-41 passes for 328 yards and two scores as Iowa won by a 34-20 count.

1989: Darrell Thompson gained 122 yards rushing in Minnesota's 43-7 laugher.

1992: Maurea Crain tied a school record with two blocked kicks for Iowa, but the Gophers prevailed, 28-13, as Rob St. Sauver completed 21-of-32 passes for two scores and 261 yards. Aaron Osterman gained 158 of those yards.

1993: Cliff Young scored twice and the Hawkeyes grabbed five interceptions as

Minnesota attempted a Kinnick Stadium record 60 passes in Iowa's 21-3 victory. It was Fry's 200th career coaching triumph and 111th in 15 seasons at UI.

1994: Minnesota's Tim Schade threw for 365 yards and two touchdowns, Osterman had 143 yards receiving, and Chris Darkins rushed for 188 yards; however, the Gophers lost the wildest scoring game in the series, 49-42. Redshirt freshman Matt Sherman threw two touchdown passes and caught a third for Iowa. Sherman finished 13-of-18 for 256 yards as the Hawkeyes capitalized on three Gophers turnovers for 21 points.

1996: Brion Hurley drilled a 50-yard field goal in Iowa's 43-24 verdict despite Ryan Thelwell's 127 yards receiving for the Gophers.

The Hawkeyes go hog-wild.

1998: Thomas Hamner (148 yards) and Byron Evans (108) led the Gophers' potent ground attack, while Luke Leverson had 107 yards receiving in their 49-7 win. Curtese Poole finished with three sacks among his four tackles for loss to lead Minnesota's defense.

1999: Scott Mullen threw for 340 yards and three touchdowns for Iowa, but No. 17 Minnesota came away with a 25-21 triumph behind Billy Cockerham's 122 yards rushing.

2000: Karon Riley set a team record with four quarterback sacks as the Gophers pulled out a 27-24 victory. Travis Cole tossed three touchdown passes and finished with 299 yards for Minnesota.

2001: Ron Johnson tallied 181 yards receiving and Asad Abdul-Khaliq passed for 319 for the Gophers, but Iowa whipped the visitors, 42-24.

2003: At Kinnick Stadium, Abdul-Khaliq completed 28-of-46 passes and one touchdown, including 10 tosses to Jared Ellerson for 159 yards and Aaron Hosack's 124 yards receiving. It wasn't nearly enough; the hosts piled up a 40-22 triumph, which included Nate Kaeding's 55-yard field goal and David Bradley's 75-yard punt.

2004: Sophomore Kyle Schlicher converted a school-record five field goals, including a 49-yarder, and set another Iowa kicking standard with 17 points. The No. 19 Hawkeyes squeaked out a 29-27 win in the Metrodome after holding a 23-10 lead at halftime. Drew Tate threw for 333 yards and TDs of 41 yards to Clinton Solomon and 60 to James Townsend. Solomon finished with nine catches for 157 yards. Laurence Maroney scored three touchdowns and gained 156 yards rushing for the Gophers, who also got 167 yards on the ground from Marion Barber III.

2005: Senior wide receiver Ed Hinkel set a Kinnick Stadium record with four touchdown catches from Tate, who threw for 351 yards. The Hawkeyes exploded past Minnesota, 52-28, which entered the game with the nation's best running attack.

2006: Both teams registered more than 200 yards passing in the first half, which featured four lead changes and Iowa heading for a fifth when Mike Sherels picked off Tate's pass near the goal line to keep Minnesota in front, 20-17. Tate and backup quarterback Jake Christensen were picked off as Minnesota turned those miscues into a 34-17 lead and held on for a 34-24 victory.

ALL-TIME SERIES RESULTS

MINNESOTA LEADS, 59-39-2

November 2, 1891—Minnesota 42, Iowa 4	October 2, 1909—Minnesota 41, Iowa 0
October 26, 1901—Minnesota 16, Iowa 0	October 28, 1911—Minnesota 24, Iowa 6
October 25, 1902—Minnesota 34, Iowa 0	October 26, 1912—Minnesota 56, Iowa 7
October 17, 1903—Minnesota 75, Iowa 0	October 24, 1914—Minnesota 7, Iowa 0
November 24, 1904—Minnesota 11, Iowa 0	October 23, 1915—Minnesota 51, Iowa 13
October 21, 1905—Minnesota 39, Iowa 0	October 28, 1916—Minnesota 67, Iowa 0
	November 9, 1918—Iowa 6, Minnesota 0

October 25, 1919—Iowa 9, Minnesota 6
November 13, 1920—Iowa 28, Minnesota 7
November 5, 1921—Iowa 41, Minnesota 7
November 11, 1922—Iowa 28, Minnesota 14
November 17, 1923—Minnesota 20, Iowa 7
October 25, 1924—Iowa 13, Minnesota 0
November 14, 1925—Minnesota 33, Iowa 0
November 6, 1926—Minnesota 41, Iowa 0
October 22, 1927—Minnesota 38, Iowa 0
October 27, 1928—Iowa 7, Minnesota 6
November 9, 1929—Iowa 9, Minnesota 7
October 24, 1931—Minnesota 34, Iowa 0
October 22, 1932—Minnesota 21, Iowa 6
October 28, 1933—Minnesota 19, Iowa 7
October 27, 1934—Minnesota 48, Iowa 12
November 9, 1935—Minnesota 13, Iowa 6
November 7, 1936—Minnesota 52, Iowa 0
November 6, 1937—Minnesota 35, Iowa 10
November 5, 1938—Minnesota 28, Iowa 0
November 18, 1939—Iowa 13, Minnesota 9
October 26, 1940—Minnesota 34, Iowa 6
November 15, 1941—Minnesota 34, Iowa 13
November 14, 1942—Minnesota 27, Iowa 7
November 13, 1943—Minnesota 33, Iowa 14
November 18, 1944—Minnesota 46, Iowa 0
November 17, 1945—Iowa 20, Minnesota 19
November 16, 1946—Minnesota 16, Iowa 6
November 15, 1947—Iowa 13, Minnesota 7
November 13, 1948—Minnesota 28, Iowa 21
November 5, 1949—Minnesota 55, Iowa 7
November 4, 1950—Iowa 13, Minnesota 0
November 3, 1951—Minnesota 20, Iowa 20 (T)
November 1, 1952—Minnesota 17, Iowa 7
November 14, 1953—Iowa 27, Minnesota 0
November 13, 1954—Minnesota 22, Iowa 20
November 5, 1955—Iowa 26, Minnesota 0
November 10, 1956—Iowa 7, Minnesota 0
November 9, 1957—Iowa 44, Minnesota 20
November 8, 1958—Iowa 28, Minnesota 6
November 7, 1959—Iowa 33, Minnesota 0
November 5, 1960—Minnesota 27, Iowa 10
November 11, 1961—Minnesota 16, Iowa 9
November 10, 1962—Minnesota 10, Iowa 0
November 9, 1963—Iowa 27, Minnesota 13

November 7, 1964—Minnesota 14, Iowa 13
October 16, 1965—Minnesota 14, Iowa 3
October 15, 1966—Minnesota 17, Iowa 0
November 4, 1967—Minnesota 10, Iowa 0
November 2, 1968—Iowa 35, Minnesota 28
November 1, 1969—Minnesota 35, Iowa 8
October 31, 1970—Minnesota 14, Iowa 14 (T)
October 16, 1971—Minnesota 19, Iowa 14
October 21, 1972—Minnesota 43, Iowa 14
October 20, 1973—Minnesota 31, Iowa 23
October 19, 1974—Minnesota 23, Iowa 17
October 25, 1975—Minnesota 31, Iowa 7
October 23, 1976—Iowa 22, Minnesota 12
October 8, 1977—Iowa 18, Minnesota 6
October 14, 1978—Minnesota 22, Iowa 20
October 20, 1979—Minnesota 24, Iowa 7
October 25, 1980—Minnesota 24, Iowa 6
October 24, 1981—Minnesota 12, Iowa 10
October 23, 1982—Iowa 21, Minnesota 16
November 19, 1983—Iowa 61, Minnesota 10
November 17, 1984—Minnesota 23, Iowa 17
November 23, 1985—Iowa 31, Minnesota 9
November 22, 1986—Iowa 30, Minnesota 27
November 21, 1987—Iowa 34, Minnesota 20
November 19, 1988—Iowa 31, Minnesota 22
November 25, 1989—Minnesota 43, Iowa 7
November 24, 1990—Minnesota 31, Iowa 24
November 23, 1991—Iowa 23, Minnesota 8
November 21, 1992—Minnesota 28, Iowa 13
November 20, 1993—Iowa 21, Minnesota 3
November 19, 1994—Iowa 49, Minnesota 42
November 25, 1995—Iowa 45, Minnesota 3
November 23, 1996—Iowa 43, Minnesota 24
November 22, 1997—Iowa 31, Minnesota 0
November 21, 1998—Minnesota 49, Iowa 7
November 20, 1999—Minnesota 25, Iowa 21
November 18, 2000—Minnesota 27, Iowa 24
November 17, 2001—Iowa 42, Minnesota 24
November 16, 2002—Iowa 45, Minnesota 21
November 15, 2003—Iowa 40, Minnesota 22
November 13, 2004—Iowa 29, Minnesota 27
November 19, 2005—Iowa 52, Minnesota 28
November 18, 2006—Minnesota 34, Iowa 24

HEAT RISES IN THE HEARTLAND:
WISCONSIN vs. IOWA

Perhaps no two college football programs have followed such par-
allel paths as Iowa and Wisconsin. Both schools enjoyed stretches of success and
endured hardships during the first half of the 20th century. They often chal-
lenged for the Big Ten title throughout the 1950s, and then fell on mostly tough
times in the 1960s and '70s. Fortunes turned around again in the 1980s for the
Badgers under Dave McClain, and even more so for the Hawkeyes with Hayden
Fry. Wisconsin plummeted again for several years but resurfaced as a postsea-
son presence under Barry Alvarez starting in 1993.

The big difference was that Iowa lost three Rose Bowls (1981, '85, and '90),
while Wisconsin won three (1993, '98, and '99). Still, much of the Badgers'
upswing is because of coaches who formerly worked in Iowa City, starting with
Alvarez, who in turn brought such former players and assistants as Bernie
Wyatt, Dan McCarney, Jay Norvell, and Bret Bielema to Madison to dig the
Badgers out of the doldrums of the Don Morton era.

Such ties have helped make this rivalry, the closest record-wise of any in the
Big Ten at 40-40-2, even more intense—despite the fact that they've only played
for the Heartland Trophy since 2004.

No better examples of this significant and hotly contested series have occurred
than during the 2005 and 2006 seasons. The Hawkeyes and coach Kirk Ferentz, who
also worked on Fry's staff for most of the 1980s, posted a 20-10 victory at Camp
Randall Stadium in 2005. The loss ruined Alvarez's final home game as head coach
after 16 seasons in charge of the Badgers. Iowa became bowl-eligible with its win
against 19th-ranked Wisconsin. UI limited the Badgers to a paltry 19 yards rushing
in front of a record crowd of 83,184.

Wisconsin roared to a 10-0 lead after its first three possessions, gaining 121
yards. However, Iowa's defense took over, finishing with six sacks of John Stocco.

The Badgers gained only 155 yards on their final nine drives.

In 2006, Bielema and the Badgers, who were 6-1 in league play and 9-1 overall with a No. 16 ranking, earned a 24-21 victory at Kinnick Stadium, where Wisconsin had won only twice since 1975.

Redshirt junior Tyler Donovan, filling in for the injured Stocco, completed his first seven passes and finished 17-of-24 for 228 yards and two touchdowns, including a 42-yarder to Luke Swan. Donovan also contributed 61 yards rushing on 13 carries.

Meanwhile, Wisconsin's defense frustrated the Hawkeyes and senior Drew Tate, who completed only 10-of-31 attempts for 170 yards as the Badgers clinched no worse than a second-place tie in the Big Ten. Tate's three TD passes doubled the output that Wisconsin's defense had allowed through its first 10 games.

It was sweet redemption for the Badgers, especially for their seniors, who had never beaten Iowa in their 2003 and '04 meetings. In 2003, the Hawkeyes prevented Wisconsin from earning a New Year's Day berth in the Outback Bowl, rallying for a 27-21 victory at Madison. The Hawkeyes knocked starting signal-caller Jim Sorgi from the game, picked off backup Matt Schabert three times, and deflected Stocco's fourth-down pass from the Iowa 4-yard line on the game's final play.

The next season, Iowa whipped Wisconsin soundly, 30-7, forcing five turnovers and limiting the visiting Badgers to 41 yards on the ground. That brought Wisconsin's 9-game winning streak to an end and cost it a share of the league crown and a Rose Bowl berth.

Another important late-season contest in recent years took place in 1997. Iowa was 6-2 and ranked 12th, while the Badgers were unranked despite a 7-2 mark.

Wisconsin came out on top of a hard-fought contest, 13-10, to end an 18-game winless streak (0-17-1) in the series. The Badgers lost star sophomore running back Ron Dayne to an injury after only seven carries and 24 yards, but redshirt freshman Eddie Faulkner carried 26 times for 119 yards and the Badgers' lone touchdown, a 4-yard run in the second quarter. Iowa also clamped down on UW receivers Tony Simmons and Donald Hayes, who combined for only three catches and 41 yards.

However, the Badgers' defense was stout, shutting the Hawkeyes out in the first half. Then they allowed only 3 net yards in eight plays from the Wisconsin 15 after Matt Bowen returned a Mike Samuel interception 56 yards early in the third quarter. Leonard Taylor blocked Zach Bromert's 29-yard field-goal attempt. Iowa had been ranked second nationally in scoring and ninth in total offense, but the visitors were stuffed on three fourth-down plays. Taylor added an interception and Donnel Thompson recovered a fumble on a kickoff.

Twenty-seven of these showdowns have been decided by a touchdown or less, including the deadlocks in 1967 and 1984. One such meeting happened October 11, 1969, when neither team was going anywhere in the standings—especially the Badgers, who hadn't won more than three games in a season in six years and were sitting at 0-3.

Wisconsin appeared to be heading for another disaster, trailing by 17 points after three quarters. Mike Cilek, subbing for the injured Larry Lawrence, had tossed two touchdown passes to Kerry Reardon that appeared to put the Hawkeyes in control. However, in the final 15 minutes Wisconsin ripped off three touchdowns and a safety of future NFL coach Dennis Green to steal a 23-17 triumph. Alan Thompson rushed for 104 yards; quarterback Neil Graff connected with Randy Marks on a 17-yard, go-ahead touchdown with 2:08 remaining; and Neovia Greyer intercepted a pass in the final minute.

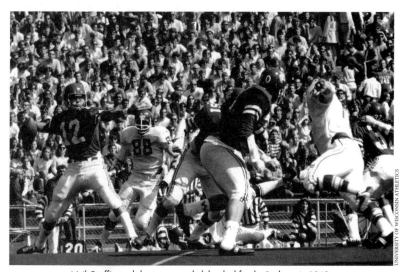

Neil Graff's touchdown pass sealed the deal for the Badgers in 1969.

The decision allowed Wisconsin to snap an 18-game losing streak and 23-game winless string under John Coatta, who was fired after the season. Although on a much smaller stage, the finish was reminiscent of the Badgers' surprising comeback in the 1963 Rose Bowl, in which they fell to Southern Cal, 42-37.

Graff quarterbacked the Badgers from 1969 to 1971 and said that the rally was huge for the moribund program.

"What was unique about that team was that we had a great sophomore class and we hadn't been exposed to all of the losing and that stigma," said the

Sioux Falls, South Dakota, native. "At that time it was Michigan and Ohio State, with the rest of us in the middle of the pack fighting for .500 records. But we had great games with Iowa. After that game in '69, it seemed like everybody in the stadium was down on the field and acting like we'd just won the Rose Bowl, taking down the goalposts and carrying players on their shoulders. As I said, one of the keys was that many of us weren't around for many of those losses, when some guys might have said, 'Here we go again,' and given up. We were down, 17-0, and got a couple of breaks and kept fighting. It's one of my two or three biggest highlights because of the euphoria it created in the stadium and all up and down State Street. It was a neat feeling."

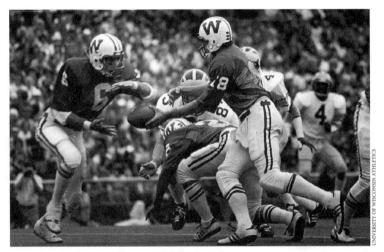

A Badger handoff

Stu Voigt logged 11 productive seasons with the Minnesota Vikings and still lives in the Gopher State. A Madison native and prep athletic star, he was with the Badgers for that rare winning ride, too.

"Wisconsin and Iowa were down and not very good in those days," he said of his letter-winning seasons (1967–1969). "I do remember our game against Iowa in my senior year because I scored a TD and we broke that long losing streak, so that was a big, big victory."

Dave Croston (1984–86) said none of his three meetings against Wisconsin, two double-digit Iowa wins and a tie, elicited rave reviews, but that doesn't mean the games weren't important.

"I know that the Badgers always had excellent athletes and sent a bunch of guys to the NFL, but it was one of those things where Hayden [Fry] always seemed to have their number," Croston said. "The interesting thing about playing up there was that cage or fence they had up where you come out of the locker room. Fans were always throwing stuff at us. In 1983, one of our backup offensive linemen, John Carroll, caught an egg that somebody had thrown at Coach Fry."

The Badgers ended up with major egg on their faces that day as Iowa won, 34-14, finishing with a 9-3 record while Wisconsin ended up 7-4. Bryan Skradis remembered that the contests against Wisconsin were memorable for what happened both on and off the field.

"It was always a tough game," said Skradis, who lettered four times and started three seasons at outside linebacker for the Hawkeyes. "In 1981, if they had beaten us they could have gone to the Rose Bowl, but we won, 17-7, up there. I recall as a freshman walking into the stadium and getting a dress rehearsal of what it would be like. We come out of the tunnel and I'm thinking, 'What the hell is this?' The fans were throwing all kinds of crap at us. They were rabid, all right. I remember them passing bodies through the crowd and then tossing a fake one out of the stadium. And I don't know how it got in there, but they had a beer keg one time. But it was good, clean fun."

The fun of the Wisconsin-Iowa rivalry spans generations. Louis Matykiewicz played quarterback and linebacker for the Hawkeyes during Forest Evashevski's first three seasons, from 1952 to 1954. Iowa, Ohio State, and Michigan State won or shared national titles during the decade. Two words come to mind when Matykiewicz reminisces about the Wisconsin series and Big Ten play in general.

"Alan Ameche," said Matykiewicz, who still attends all Iowa home games and almost every road contest. "We beat them, 13-7, my senior year, but they got us on a tipped pass and beat us, 10-6, when I was a junior. They were exciting games. In those days, the Big Ten was almost strictly a rugged, running league where everybody beat each other up."

Clarence Stensby was an offensive guard and linebacker on those Wisconsin teams, lettering all four years from 1951 to 1954.

"Iowa wasn't as big a rivalry at that time," said Stensby, a Chicago area native. "But they had some great players, like the big lineman [Cal Jones] who died in a plane crash. I also remember running downfield trying to catch up to George O'Brien's 96-yard punt in '52, which is still a Wisconsin record. They played us tough, and I almost got knocked out in one of them."

Another similar skirmish occurred at Iowa City in 1957, one of three occasions during a four-year span that both teams were ranked heading into their meeting. Wisconsin's sophomore-laden squad entered the confrontation at 3-0, having whipped Marquette and West Virginia by a combined 105-19 margin before knocking off Purdue, 23-14, in its league opener.

Meanwhile, the defending Big Ten and Rose Bowl champion Hawkeyes returned 30 of the 44 players who made that most recent trip to California, including future Detroit Lions great Alex Karras at tackle and quarterback Randy Duncan, a future top pick for Green Bay. Iowa had whipped Utah State, Washington State, and Indiana by a 137-34 total.

UI downed the Badgers, 21-7, in front of a record-breaking homecoming crowd of 58,147, stopping the Badgers several times deep in scoring territory. The Hawkeyes moved ahead, 7-0, after their first possession. Wisconsin tied it in the third quarter before Iowa grabbed the lead for good later in that period and sewed it up in the fourth.

The Hawkeyes used 15 plays to go 75 yards for their first score and needed only six plays to travel 76 yards for the eventual game-winner. Bill Gravel sealed the Badgers' fate with a 45-yard interception return. Jon Hobbs scored Wisconsin's lone touchdown on a blocked punt that he fell on in the end zone. Wisconsin's bugaboo was turnovers: It lost two of eight fumbles, while Sid Williams threw three interceptions and Dale Hackbart one. Five of those turnovers occurred in Iowa scoring territory.

Wisconsin finished 6-3, while the Hawkeyes wound up 7-1-1, tying Michigan and losing, 17-13, to Ohio State, the eventual national co-champion.

Pat Richter participated in the series during the early 1960s and later witnessed the rivalry as Wisconsin's athletic director from 1989 to 2003. He said the games have grown exponentially in stature.

"It wasn't as big as the Minnesota series when I played, but Iowa had good teams under Forest Evashevski and his staffs," Richter said. "I broke my collarbone in that game during my sophomore year, and they beat us pretty badly my junior year. Then we won the last one. It was more of a rivalry with the fans, but they had great players such as Randy Duncan, Bernie Wyatt, Paul Krause, and Larry Ferguson.

"Since then, Iowa dominated for quite a while, but it became more intense because of all of the coaching connections with Hayden Fry—Barry [Alvarez], Bernie [Wyatt], Dan McCarney, and now Bret [Bielema], who played there, all came to Wisconsin," Richter added.

The retired Badgers AD said the development of the Heartland Trophy recognizes the importance of the Wisconsin and Iowa match up. "Every team in the Big Ten has a historical rival who they play every year despite the unbalanced schedule, and Iowa, Wisconsin, and Minnesota have two each because they all play each other every year. That's helped the games take on more significance," Richter said.

Scott Nelson was a prep standout at Sun Prairie High School in Wisconsin.

He redshirted during Morton's final season as Wisconsin's coach in 1989 and started most of the next four seasons under Alvarez. His first starting assignment was memorable, even though it resulted in a 30-10 loss at Kinnick Stadium. Nelson recorded his first interception and registered a whopping 23 tackles.

"It was awesome and something I'll always remember, especially because Barry and assistants Dan McCarney and Bernie Wyatt had coached at Iowa before coming to Madison, and everybody was all jacked up," Nelson said. "They had Nick Bell, who was something like 6' 3" and 255, and it felt like 20 of my tackles came against him. And they had Mike Saunders as another running back."

The 1992 showdown was another heartbreaker for the Badgers, who finished 5-6 for their most wins in a season since McClain's final squad posted the same record in 1985. Iowa rallied, and then Carlos James blocked Rich Thompson's 53-yard field-goal attempt after a low snap from center with six seconds remaining to preserve the hosts' 23-22 victory in Iowa City.

Jim Hartlieb drove the Hawkeyes 80 yards in 13 plays, hitting Anthony Dean on a 4-yard pass to cut Wisconsin's lead to 22-21. Hartlieb and Dean then hooked up on a two-point conversion for the deciding points. Hartlieb converted three third-and-10 situations, two on passes and another on a 16-yard scramble, during the crucial drive to finish 31-of-51 for 297 yards passing and 40 yards rushing. Brent Moss ran 25 times for 159 yards and two scores for Wisconsin, which took leads of 12-7 and 22-15 but couldn't hang on.

Longtime Madison sportswriter Tom Butler said that Wisconsin rooters disliked Fry with unusual passion. Losing to the Hawkeyes so many times in a row may have had something to do with it: Iowa was 15-0-1 before falling to Wisconsin in Fry's final two seasons.

"They hated him around here," Butler said. "Fans got pretty ugly. I believe that he or his family had their tires slashed."

However, two Iowa supporters say that things remained predominantly civil despite the usual flare-ups. "Iowa's biggest rivalry is with Minnesota, but as far as fans and traveling, the biggest one is against Wisconsin," Bud Sueppel said. "Wisconsin brings all they can down here, and we do the same at Madison."

"Wisconsin wasn't as heated," said Steve Smith, an Iowa fan who lives in Minnesota. "After all, Iowa won almost 20 straight during one stretch. Madison was always fun and the best place to go, and at that time Wisconsin fans were more worried about dancing and going to the Fifth Quarter celebrations."

Smith has endured the roller coaster ride of emotions since Iowa's long run of success. One of those ups was the 1992 thriller. Wisconsin was leading by seven points with only seconds left, but Iowa scored a touchdown and then went for two points and won it, 23-22.

Then came 1999 and one of the most disheartening down periods, a big game that Smith is glad he didn't attend. "I had tickets to that game at Camp Randall," Smith said of Wisconsin's eventual 41-3 rout. "It was Kirk Ferentz's first year, and Iowa was on its way to a 1-10 record. It was going to be Ron Dayne's coronation, so I sold the tickets to Badger fans and Dayne ran wild."

That, of course, was the day the bruising 260-pound halfback surpassed Ricky Williams of Texas as the all-time NCAA Division I-A career ground-gainer.

Lonnie Rogers has had season tickets since the mid-1980s, but his ties go back to his playing days in Iowa City, where he lettered from 1961 to 1963 under Jerry Burns. "Wisconsin was one of the powers during those years and you had to win those games if you wanted to go anywhere," said Rogers, who lost two of three to the Badgers. "I remember the game my last year down in Iowa City. Wisconsin was ranked No. 2 and they won it, 10-7. We weren't ranked, but it was a good game and we had the ball at their 16-yard line when the game ended. Those were knock-down, drag-out battles."

That's no bull: The Heartland Trophy

Brad Jackomino chose Wisconsin so he could join former Rhinelander High School teammates Dave Crossen and Jim Moore with the Badgers. Jackomino was small at 5' 10" and 220 pounds, but he lettered and survived in the Big Ten from 1976 to 1978 as an offensive guard in a system that took advantage of his athletic ability. It allowed him to pull and get out in space to block on running plays.

"I recall that in the '78 game down there, they scored a late touchdown with something like 1:24 remaining. Iowa fans stormed the field, tore the goalpost down, and carried it off the field, and they called the game," he said of the Hawkeyes' 38-24 triumph.

Such is life in a series in which the winner gains possession of a bull statue that measures 30" tall, 36" long, and 18" deep and weighs 85 pounds. Appropriately, a former Iowa football player, Frank Strub, designed and crafted the trophy. It is mounted on a walnut base, a wood that is native to both states. As Iowa athletic director Bob Bowlsby observed when the trophy was unveiled at the 2004 game in Iowa City, "The Iowa-Wisconsin series has always been one of the most competitive and hard-fought series in college football. The bull symbolizes the kind of games that have been typical when the schools meet."

And don't forget the cock-and-bull stories that go along with it.

MORE SERIES HIGHLIGHTS

1907: Iowa dropped a 6-5 decision in Iowa City in what became known as the "rabbit game." Hawkeyes coach Mark Catlin thought a rabbit jinxed them just before the start of the second half with Iowa on top, 5-0. The critter raced from Wisconsin's goal line the length of the field and between the hosts' goalpost, an omen to Iowa supporters because Harlan "Biddy" Rogers of UW ran back a windblown punt for a long touchdown to tie the game (TDs were worth only five points in those days), and the extra point gave Wisconsin the victory.

1912: Wisconsin ruined the Hawkeyes' first homecoming celebration with a 28-10 decision that ended the Badgers' season at 7-0, the last of the school's three unbeaten seasons; the others were 1901 and 1906.

1924: Leland Parkin gained 170 yards for Iowa. His day featured 17- and 25-yard scores, and a 63-yarder that set up another Hawkeyes touchdown in their 21-7 victory.

1925: Wisconsin escaped with a 6-0 triumph on Robert Kreuz's 1-yard plunge in the fourth quarter after an Iowa punt went out of bounds on the Hawkeyes' 11-yard line in what became known as the "Snow Bowl." Rain turned to sleet and then to snow and blizzard-like conditions during the game in Iowa City on November 7. Thanks to the sloppy weather, the teams combined for 40 fumbles, 26 of them by Iowa. This was the first of three consecutive shutout losses for Iowa to end the season after starting 5-0.

1927: Lloyd Grimm rumbled 95 yards with an interception for Iowa's second score during its 16-0 win.

1928: The foes combined for only seven first downs, but the Hawkeyes fumbled 10 times in dropping a 13-0 verdict, which ended their 6-0 streak to start the season.

1939: Nile Kinnick fired touchdown passes to Dick "Whitey" Evans, Al Couppee, and Bill Green during Iowa's 19-13 victory.

1940: Bill Walker waltzed 66 yards with a blocked punt, and Green scored three times as Iowa won, 30-12.

1942: Wisconsin's only loss of the season (8-1-1) proved to be Iowa's last Big Ten win for more than three years. The Hawkeyes downed second-ranked Wisconsin, 6-0, and dashed the Badgers' national title hopes. A controversial goal-line series ended the first half. Iowa QB Tom Farmer's pass to Bill Burkett resulted in the lone score.

1945: Iowa held the Badgers to 0 yards passing, but it didn't matter as Wisconsin won, 27-7.

1947: No. 19 Wisconsin established a school and Big Ten record with 277 yards on seven punt returns, tying an NCAA mark with three for touchdowns during its 46-14 win. Earl "Jug" Girard had two of them, including an 85-yarder, and finished with three runbacks for 158 yards. Clarence Self led Wisconsin's offense with 138 yards on the ground.

1948: Iowa overcame a 13-0 halftime deficit to down the Badgers, 19-13, in front of 38,000 at Iowa City, a second straight heartbreaking loss for Wisconsin after its 34-32 setback at Ohio State.

1950: Ed Withers intercepted three passes for a Wisconsin record 103 yards in the Badgers' 14-0 triumph. No. 15 Wisconsin claimed its third consecutive triumph to start the season, ruining it for more than 46,000 Iowa fans at Kinnick Stadium.

1951: Wisconsin set a school record for rushing defense, allowing minus-18 yards in 34 attempts in holding Iowa to 82 total yards. The Badgers won, 34-7. Meanwhile, Alan Ameche gained 126 yards rushing as eighth-ranked Wisconsin improved to 6-1-1 for a Camp Randall crowd of nearly 40,000.

1952: George O'Brien uncorked a 96-yard punt and averaged 51 yards per boot during Wisconsin's 42-13 thrashing of the Hawkeyes, which also included Ameche's 125 yards running and 117 from Bill Hutchinson.

1953: A deflected 38-yard scoring pass lifted Wisconsin to a 10-6 decision over UI. A capacity homecoming crowd of almost 53,000 filled Camp Randall.

1954: Iowa posted a 13-7 victory despite Ameche's 117 grueling yards on 26 carries; however, he lost one of two Wisconsin fumbles near the Iowa goal line, this one with about 5:30 left. Iowa took a 13-0 halftime lead over the No. 8 Badgers in front of 52,185 at Kinnick Stadium.

1955: Wisconsin trailed, 14-13, but recorded the game's final 24 points for a 37-14 win. The Badgers received three touchdown connections between Jim Haluska and Dave Howard, covering 42, 16, and 33 yards. Howard finished with 147 yards receiving.

1958: Jeff Langston returned a fumble recovery 21 yards, and Bob Jeter raced 68 yards with a screen pass to help Iowa overcome a 9-point deficit to win, 20-9, in front of more than 65,000 in Madison.

1959: Quarterback Olen Treadway finished 26-of-41 for 304 yards and a score for Iowa, but it wasn't enough to prevent Wisconsin's 25-16 upset of the ninth-ranked and visiting Hawkeyes.

1960: Iowa grabbed a 21-7 advantage, but the Badgers tied it with two fourth-quarter scores. Iowa's Larry Ferguson raced 51 yards with a punt return and gained 29 yards on a pass play, but it was called back. Nevertheless, the Hawkeyes still won when Wilburn Hollis' deflected pass found Sammie Harris for a 28-21 victory.

1962: Matthew Szykowny connected with Ferguson for an 80-yard scoring play, but 10th-ranked Wisconsin routed the visiting Hawkeyes, 42-14, behind Ron Vander Kelen's 202 yards passing.

1964: Wisconsin won, 31-21, but Iowa's Karl Noonan finished with 10 receptions for 155 yards and a touchdown. Ralph Kurek led the Badgers with 103 yards rushing.

1965: Jerry Burns' Iowa squad was a 10-point favorite but found a way to lose a

16-13 decision. The Hawkeyes led, 13-7, with less than five minutes remaining when Burns instructed punter Larry McDowell to take a safety, which made it 13-9. But with 3:42 showing, Wisconsin's Chuck Burt threw a 42-yard TD pass to Lou Jung for the deciding score.

1966: Wisconsin won a defensive slugfest, 7-0, at Iowa City as Tom Schinke picked off three Iowa passes as almost 53,000 showed up for this battle of unranked rivals.

1967: The foes battled to a 21-all tie as Wisconsin's John Smith finished with 157 yards rushing at Camp Randall. It was the only one of 10 games that season the Badgers didn't lose, while Iowa finished 1-8-1.

Ralph Kurek's 103 yards rushing helped Wisconsin beat Iowa in 1964.

1968: Iowa skunked the Badgers, 41-0, as Don Schaffner tied a Wisconsin record with 12 punts. More than 45,000 looked on at Kinnick Stadium as the Badgers' woeful offense was shut out for a third straight week en route to a 0-10 record.

1971: Dave Triplett caught seven balls for 157 yards and an 80-yard touchdown toss from Frank Sunderman as Iowa pulled out a 20-16 victory. Wisconsin received 126 rushing yards from Rufus Ferguson and 124 more from Alan Thompson.

1972: Tony Davis led the Badgers to a 16-14 victory with 115 yards rushing. More than 78,000 attended Wisconsin's homecoming game.

1973: Billy Marek rumbled for 203 yards and scored four times to lift Wisconsin to a convincing 35-7 decision at Camp Randall.

1975: Iowa gained 502 yards of total offense during a 45-28 home triumph. The Hawkeyes hammered Wisconsin with five scores and 439 yards rushing.

1977: The Hawkeyes' 24-8 win was their first in Madison in 19 years. Wisconsin coach John Jardine had announced his resignation that week, which didn't help matters as Iowa's Rod Sears recovered two fumbles, intercepted a pass, and blocked a punt to offset David Charles' 122 yards in pass receptions. Dave Crossen was in on 24 tackles for the Badgers.

1978: Brad Reid scored on an 80-yard jaunt during Iowa's 38-24 triumph that saw UW's David Charles get 134 yards receiving.

1979: Phil Suess' 75-yard hookup with Dennis Mosley ignited Iowa's 24-13 victory, which overshadowed Dave Mohapp's 139 yards on the ground for host Wisconsin.

1981: The Hawkeyes held the Badgers to two first downs and 29 yards of offense in grabbing a 17-0 cushion at the break and held on for a 17-7 victory. Iowa then whipped Michigan State and earned a Rose Bowl berth when Ohio State upended Michigan. But Washington thumped the Hawkeyes, 28-0, in Pasadena.

1982: Iowa pilfered a team-record seven interceptions in claiming a 28-14 home victory to offset Troy King's 127 yards rushing and Randy Wright's 278 yards passing.

1983: Wisconsin's Wright attempted a school-record 54 passes, completing 25 for 325 yards. However, No. 15 Iowa blasted the Badgers, 34-14, in Madison.

1985: Top-ranked Iowa claimed a 23-13 verdict despite Larry Emery's 104 yards rushing for host Wisconsin.

1986: Bud Keyes passed for 218 yards, including 110 to Reggie Tompkins, but visiting Wisconsin still fell to No. 10 Iowa, 17-6.

1987: The Hawkeyes overcame 24 tackles from David Wings to register a 31-10 triumph as nearly 75,000 watched at Camp Randall.

1989: Nick Bell bulled for 217 yards on 31 carries, including three touchdowns, to lead Iowa to a 31-24 road win. Wisconsin drew a season-high 62,402 fans— some 17,000 more than any crowd at Camp Randall during Don Morton's final year as coach.

1991: Iowa stifled Wisconsin's offense, holding the Badgers to 82 total yards in a 10-6 Hawkeyes victory. The host Badgers gained just 36 yards rushing and 46 passing.

1995: Darrell Bevell established a Badgers team record with 35 pass completions and finished with 352 yards. Tight end Matt Nyquist latched onto 13 of them for 140 yards, but Sedrick Shaw rambled for 214 yards on 41 carries to lift Iowa to a 33-20 victory. Iowa also stuffed Wisconsin's running game, limiting the Badgers to minus-18 yards, and Brion Hurley booted a 50-yard field goal.

1998: Iowa's Eric Thigpen finished with 20 tackles, but the ninth-ranked Badgers won in a cakewalk, 31-0. Dayne plowed for 164 yards on 39 carries and Tom Burke recorded five sacks at Iowa City.

1999: Dayne became the NCAA's all-time leading rusher in Division I-A, carrying 27 times for 216 yards and a score to surpass Ricky Williams of Texas. No. 9 Wisconsin's dominating 41-3 triumph gave it the outright Big Ten crown and a Rose Bowl berth against Stanford.

2000: Chris Chambers hauled in a record-tying 13 catches for 191 yards and Brooks Bollinger passed for 292 yards, but Wisconsin had to hang on for a 13-7 victory in front of 62,560 in Iowa City.

2001: Anthony Davis gained 132 yards and the Badgers needed every one of them in a 34-28 win. Brooks Bollinger added 262 yards through the air, including 175 to Lee Evans as a capacity crowd of more than 79,000 looked on at Camp Randall.

2003: Iowa won, 27-21, in Madison, including a 50-yard field goal from Nate Kaeding. Dwayne Smith tallied 119 yards running for the losing Badgers.

2004: Iowa's Drew Tate connected with Clinton Solomon for a second touchdown pass, this one a 51-yarder, to break a 7-all tie in the second quarter. The Hawkeyes dominated after that, running away for a 30-7 victory despite Wisconsin's three interceptions. It was Iowa's 18th straight win at home. UI came in at No. 17 and knocked the ninth-ranked Badgers out of a potential tie for the crown and a Rose Bowl berth. Instead, the Hawkeyes shared the title with the Pasadena-bound Michigan Wolverines.

ALL-TIME SERIES RESULTS

THE SERIES IS TIED, 40-40-2

October 29, 1894—Wisconsin 44, Iowa 0
November 3, 1906—Wisconsin 18, Iowa 4
November 2, 1907—Wisconsin 6, Iowa 5
November 4, 1911—Wisconsin 12, Iowa 0
November 23, 1912—Wisconsin 28, Iowa 10
October 27, 1917—Wisconsin 20, Iowa 0
November 15, 1924—Iowa 21, Wisconsin 7
November 7, 1925—Wisconsin 6, Iowa 0
November 13, 1926—Wisconsin 20, Iowa 10
November 12, 1927—Iowa 16, Wisconsin 0
November 17, 1928—Wisconsin 13, Iowa 0
October 26, 1929—Iowa 14, Wisconsin 0
October 8, 1932—Wisconsin 34, Iowa 0
October 21, 1933—Iowa 26, Wisconsin 7
October 16, 1937—Wisconsin 13, Iowa 6
October 8, 1938—Wisconsin 31, Iowa 13
October 28, 1939—Iowa 19, Wisconsin 13
October 12, 1940—Iowa 30, Wisconsin 12
October 18, 1941—Wisconsin 23, Iowa 0
November 7, 1942—Iowa 6, Wisconsin 0
October 2, 1943—Wisconsin 7, Iowa 5
November 11, 1944—Wisconsin 26, Iowa 7
November 3, 1945—Wisconsin 27, Iowa 7
November 9, 1946—Iowa 21, Wisconsin 7
November 8, 1947—Wisconsin 46, Iowa 14
October 30, 1948—Iowa 19, Wisconsin 13
November 12, 1949—Wisconsin 35, Iowa 13
October 14, 1950—Wisconsin 14, Iowa 0
November 17, 1951—Wisconsin 34, Iowa 7
October 18, 1952—Wisconsin 42, Iowa 13
October 31, 1953—Wisconsin 10, Iowa 6
October 30, 1954—Iowa 13, Wisconsin 7
October 1, 1955—Wisconsin 37, Iowa 14
October 13, 1956—Iowa 13, Wisconsin 7
October 19, 1957—Iowa 21, Wisconsin 7
October 18, 1958—Iowa 20, Wisconsin 9
October 17, 1959—Wisconsin 25, Iowa 16

October 15, 1960—Iowa 28, Wisconsin 21
October 21, 1961—Iowa 47, Wisconsin 15
October 20, 1962—Wisconsin 42, Iowa 14
October 19, 1963—Wisconsin 10, Iowa 7
October 17, 1964—Wisconsin 31, Iowa 21
October 2, 1965—Wisconsin 16, Iowa 13
October 1, 1966—Wisconsin 7, Iowa 0
October 21, 1967—Wisconsin 21, Iowa 21 (T)
October 19, 1968—Iowa 41, Wisconsin 0
October 11, 1969—Wisconsin 23, Iowa 17
October 10, 1970—Iowa 24, Wisconsin 14
October 30, 1971—Iowa 20, Wisconsin 16
November 4, 1972—Wisconsin 16, Iowa 14
November 10, 1973—Wisconsin 35, Iowa 7
November 9, 1974—Wisconsin 28, Iowa 15
November 8, 1975—Iowa 45, Wisconsin 28
November 6, 1976—Wisconsin 38, Iowa 21
November 12, 1977—Iowa 24, Wisconsin 8
November 18, 1978—Iowa 38, Wisconsin 24
October 27, 1979—Iowa 24, Wisconsin 13
November 1, 1980—Iowa 22, Wisconsin 13
November 14, 1981—Iowa 17, Wisconsin 7
November 13, 1982—Iowa 28, Wisconsin 14
November 5, 1983—Iowa 34, Wisconsin 14
November 3, 1984—Wisconsin 10, Iowa 10 (T)
October 12, 1985—Iowa 23, Wisconsin 13
October 11, 1986—Iowa 17, Wisconsin 6
October 10, 1987—Iowa 31, Wisconsin 10
October 8, 1988—Iowa 31, Wisconsin 6
October 14, 1989—Iowa 31, Wisconsin 24
October 13, 1990—Iowa 30, Wisconsin 10
October 12, 1991—Iowa 10, Wisconsin 6
October 10, 1992—Iowa 23, Wisconsin 22
November 18, 1995—Iowa 33, Wisconsin 20
November 16, 1996—Iowa 31, Wisconsin 0
November 8, 1997—Wisconsin 13, Iowa 10
October 24, 1998—Wisconsin 31, Iowa 0
November 13, 1999—Wisconsin 41, Iowa 3

October 28, 2000—Wisconsin 13, Iowa 7

November 3, 2001—Wisconsin 34, Iowa 28

November 2, 2002—Iowa 20, Wisconsin 3

November 22, 2003—Iowa 27, Wisconsin 21

November 20, 2004—Iowa 30, Wisconsin 7

November 12, 2005—Iowa 20, Wisconsin 10

November 11, 2006—Wisconsin 24, Iowa 21

BATTLING FOR THE ILLIBUCK:
OHIO STATE vs. ILLINOIS

Michigan will become Ohio State's longest ongoing rivalry in 2007 as the two juggernauts meet for the 90th consecutive season, a streak that began in 1918. But before the Big Ten Conference's rotating schedule got in the way during 2002–03, that distinction belonged to the Buckeyes' series against Illinois, which had run uninterrupted since 1914.

While nobody would argue that Illinois–Ohio State comes close to "The Game" in magnitude or scope, that gap in the schedule did a disservice to a series that exudes history, especially from the 1920s through the early 1950s, when the Illini and Buckeyes hooked up right before and even after the Ohio State-Michigan game on the schedule.

Ohio State holds a commanding 60-29-4 lead in the series, but the Buckeyes have won only nine of the past 17 contests. And 36 of their encounters have been decided by a touchdown or less.

At stake in the conflict is a trophy called the Illibuck, a 25-pound wooden turtle that's been traded back and forth since the mid-1920s after the original, real-life version died. "If you're a big Buckeye fan, you probably know about the trophy because there were years Illinois–Ohio State was a pretty big thing," OSU historian Jack Park said in a 2005 newspaper interview.

As the story goes, members of the junior honorary societies Atius Sachem of Illinois, and the Bucket and Dipper of Ohio State got together before the 1924 contest and suggested that a snapping turtle, chosen for its toughness and longevity, would make a suitable trophy. But the reptile didn't live up to that reputation, dying in a fraternity bathtub at Illinois during the next school year.

A trophy ceremony, which used to include the puffing of a peace pipe, lives on as students line up at halftime or between quarters and pass the replica backward over their heads to their counterparts whose team won the previous season.

A history of the Illibuck is displayed at Kuhn Honors House on 12th Avenue in Columbus.

Two of the more interesting and significant showdowns that lived up to the trophy's élan occurred in 1943 and '46. The former gave Ohio State its only Big Ten win that season as legendary coach Paul Brown, who led the Buckeyes to the national title a year earlier, finished his third and final season in Columbus with a 3-6 record.

Harold "Red" Grange, aka "The Galloping Ghost"

Illinois' Eddie McGovern ripped off a 63-yard scoring run, but Dean Sensanbaugher and Ernest Parks did more damage for the Buckeyes with more than 150 yards rushing apiece. Fans and players at The Horseshoe believed the game had ended with a 26-all tie when officials called the teams back onto the field because of an Illinois penalty on the final play. Eighteen-year-old freshman Ohio State quarterback John Stungis then booted a 35-yard field goal, handing the hosts a 29-26 decision in what became known as the "Fifth Quarter" victory. Several Illini players had already hopped in the showers when the teams were notified of the offsides penalty.

Ninth-ranked Illinois returned the favor against No. 13 OSU at Champaign three years later, using late-game theatrics to secure a victory. This virtually sewed up a trip to the 1947 Rose Bowl, the first one played under the Big Ten's agreement with the Pacific Coast Conference.

Ohio State fullback Joe Whisler ran for 123 yards, but the Buckeyes' upset bid ended inside the Illini 10-yard line. Julius Rykovich pilfered a George Spencer pass intended for Jameson Crane and returned it 98 yards to snuff out Ohio State's bid, giving the hosts a 16-7 victory on a foggy, rainy afternoon. It was the Illini's first win in the series since 1934.

Tom Stewart was a freshman quarterback and defensive back on that 1946 Illinois squad. "It was the night before the game, and our stadium superintendent called the Air Force base to see about the weather," said Stewart, who coached high school football from 1952 to 1983. "Keep in mind, weather forecasting wasn't as sophisticated as it is today. Well, it rained cats and dogs all night, so we played in a quagmire."

Howard Teifke spent that afternoon on the other sideline. He lettered for the Buckeyes four times (1943 and 1946–48).

"They had good teams and great players such as Buddy Young," said Teifke, who split four games against Illinois, winning the first and last meetings. "Rykovich returned that interception for a touchdown when we were down on their goal line. That really ruined our season because then Michigan blew us out the next week."

O. Landis Hurley was a reserve offensive and defensive lineman for two years at Illinois before starting both ways his senior season of 1940. That was coach Bob Zuppke's second-to-last of 29 campaigns with the Illini. Hurley idol-

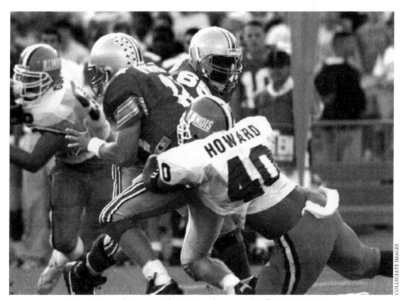

Dana Howard stops an Ohio State advance as the Illini win in 1994.

155

ized the great Red Grange as a youngster in his small hometown of Farmer City, 25 miles northwest of Champaign, where the "Galloping Ghost" ran roughshod over Big Ten defenses in the 1920s.

"Ohio State had a heckuva good team, so they were our real rival in those days," Hurley said from his home in Savannah, Georgia. "We always played them late in the year. We weren't that talented, so they beat us every time. It was a tough league of mostly old-fashioned, single-wing football."

The situation didn't change much as Woody Hayes grabbed the reins at Ohio State in 1951. Illinois had handed the Buckeyes their first league loss, 14-7, the previous season. Then Hayes' first bunch battled the third-ranked Illini to a scoreless tie, holding star runner Johnny Karras to minus-11 yards on 14 carries. That proved to be the only blemish in Illinois' eventual 9-0-1 season record.

Al Brosky snagged three interceptions to help eighth-ranked Illinois upset then-No. 1 Ohio State during his sophomore season of 1950 and remembers how rugged those contests were.

"They always used to ring that huge bell over in Columbus when they won," Brosky said. "Well, nobody scored and we tied them [in 1951] and they must have felt like it was a moral victory or something because we had been unbeaten, so they rang that damn thing anyway. Those were always good games."

J.C. Caroline burst into the limelight in a big way as a sophomore at Illinois in 1953, and the third-ranked Buckeyes were the target on that October 10 afternoon in Columbus. The Illini's starting left halfback and cornerback, Caroline gained 192 yards, scoring twice including a 64-yard jaunt, to lead a 41-20 triumph. He also had a 60-yard run called back because of a penalty. Mickey Bates chipped in 152 yards and four scores as Illinois rushed for 432 yards.

"As the visiting team, we were supposed to come out and warm up at the nearest end zone, but then they came out and made us move down to the other end," Caroline recalled. The snarky maneuver only motivated the Illini more. "They had the big reputation and everything, so we wanted to beat them anyway. But because of their attitude, by the time that game started we were really hot and came out fired up. They were one of the big honchos in the Big Ten, so it was a big rivalry."

Illinois later lost to Wisconsin in Madison to finish 5-1 in league play. The Illini had to settle for a tie for first place with Michigan State, which was picked to represent the Big Ten in the Rose Bowl despite being on probation most of its first season as an official member of the conference. Illinois wound up 7-0-1 overall and ranked seventh, while Ohio State ended with a 4-3 league record and 6-3 overall.

The 1960s weren't much to talk about around Champaign, except for '63, which featured a key early-season match up with OSU in Columbus. The Bucks had a 10-point lead in the fourth quarter only to see Illinois bounce back to take a 20-17 advantage. However, Ohio State's Dick Van Raaphorst drilled what was then a Big Ten record 49-yard field goal in the final two minutes to salvage a tie.

Illinois finished 5-1-1 in conference action and earned the Big Ten crown and Rose Bowl berth over the Buckeyes, who were 4-1-1.

Pete Elliott coached at Illinois for seven seasons, leading the Illini to four winning records, including three straight from 1963 to 1965 highlighted by a Big Ten title and a defeat of Washington in the Rose Bowl. Elliott said that Ohio State was always important for Illinois.

"We tied them once and beat them only once, in my last year," Elliott said. "There's a great picture after that game of Woody [Hayes] walking off the field with the big scoreboard in the background reading, 'Illinois 10-9.'"

George Catlett witnessed those games and many more before and since at Memorial Stadium. He heard of Grange's exploits from his father and watched the college game during the Depression, serving as student manager at Illinois from 1936 to 1938. He had season tickets for many years and was a member of the university's Athletic Board from 1961 to 1965, including one year as its president. So he followed UI athletics closely, and football in particular.

"Rivalries have changed over the years, but Michigan was the biggest competition when I was in school," Catlett said. "Michigan and Ohio State were the big games, especially at Champaign, and there's still no comparison. Illinois fans got madder at Woody Hayes than anybody. One time, Ohio State was ahead, 40-6 or 50-6 or something like that, and he put his first-stringers back in to parade down the field again. Many haven't forgotten that yet. People around here always hated Hayes and the Michigan coaches."

Illinois defensive back Mike Gow remembers well his first experience against the Hayes-led Buckeyes. "It was my first trip to Columbus," he said of the eventual 26-7 loss in 1972. "I remember it like it was yesterday. The first play, they sent Archie Griffin around my end on a sweep. Here comes guard Kurt Schumacher, who became an all-American, and 280-pound fullback Pete Johnson. My baptism was me hitting the turf and reaching for air."

Griffin gained 192 yards rushing in that game, and the Buckeyes mauled Illinois all four times during his illustrious career, also winning by margins of 30, 42, and 37. However, Griffin said it wasn't in Ohio State's nature to take any games lightly.

"We had decent games against Illinois," Griffin said. "My senior year, they played us really tough in the first half before we won pretty easily. Then you had the Illibuck, which gave you something else to play for and was a big game at one time. If you talked to the coaches, it was always a big game."

The intensity of the contest has continued, including several offensive barn burners like Ohio State's 49-42 victory in 1980. OSU bolted to a 35-7 advantage and held on for dear life as Illinois quarterback Dave Wilson went wild, completing 43 of 69 passes, six for touchdowns, and gaining 621 yards, all school records. Wilson also established an Illini mark with 344 yards in the second half. He equaled records with three TD passes in a quarter and five in a half.

Wilson completed 10 passes in a row at one point for the visitors, who registered 36 first downs, 26 through the air. Joe Curtis caught 10 passes, while Mike Martin, Lee Boeke, and Greg Dentino each surpassed the century mark in receiving yardage.

Doug Donley and Gary Williams accomplished the same feat on the ground, with 137 and 120 yards, respectively, as Art Schlichter passed for 284 yards and tossed four touchdown passes for the Buckeyes.

In 1983, No. 19 Illinois knocked off sixth-ranked Ohio State, 17-13, only its fifth home victory against the Buckeyes since 1934.

All-America wide receiver David Williams and Illinois won two of three games from 1983 to 1985, but all of them were decided by seven points or less.

"They were always near the top of the conference, but we took it to them twice," Williams said. "And in the '84 game, we were up by three touchdowns in the first half, but Keith Byars gained 274 yards and scored five touchdowns, and they won something like 45-38. We were on their 15-yard line with no timeouts left when the game ended. All three of those games came down to the final drive."

Byars broke Griffin's single-game mark of 246 yards in the 1984 showdown. He also tied Pete Johnson's record of five TDs, including a 67-yard burst that he finished with one shoe. Mike Tomczak of Ohio State added 236 yards passing, including 134 to future NFL star wide receiver Cris Carter.

Thomas Rooks chewed up 168 yards rushing for Illinois, which also got four touchdown aerials and 313 yards passing from Jack Trudeau. Cap Boso caught 10 passes for Illinois.

In 1985, Illinois grabbed a 14-0 lead only to see the Buckeyes proceed to score 28 unanswered points. However, the Illini rallied to tie it and then got a game-winning, 37-yard field goal from Chris White as time expired to surprise the fifth-ranked visitors, 31-28. Trudeau completed 28-of-40 passes for 294 yards, 131 to Stephen Pierce. Carter finished with 147 yards receiving for the Buckeyes.

Ohio State piled up winning streaks against Illinois of 15 games from 1968 to 1982 and 10 from 1935 to 1945, while Illinois had runs of three in a row from 1923 to 1925 and 1927 to 1929. The Illini enjoyed their biggest streak of five straight from 1988 to 1992. Three of those wins came at Columbus, where, surprisingly, the Illini have won 17 times compared to 12 times at home in the series.

In 1991 at Memorial Stadium, Chris Richardson connected on a 41-yard field goal with 36 seconds left for a 10-7 Illinois victory. The Buckeyes' Roger Harper intercepted two passes, but Jason Verduzco still completed 28-of-41 tries for 272 yards, 19 of his tosses going to his running backs. The 20th-ranked Illini upset No. 11 Ohio State despite only 84 yards rushing.

Illinois stunned the 21st-ranked Buckeyes a year later, 18-16, on Richardson's 21-yard field goal with 4:56 left. Before the clock ran out, however, the Illini had to watch as OSU's Tim Williams, who had made three field goals earlier, missed a 44-yarder with 53 seconds remaining. Jeff Arneson had rumbled 96 yards for a touchdown with one of Ohio State's fumbles deep in Illinois territory, this one on the first drive at the Horseshoe. Dan "Big Daddy" Wilkinson recorded three sacks for the Buckeyes.

Steve Havard led the ground game as Illinois stomped Ohio State in 1999.

Dave Monnot played one season as a defensive tackle, but he made his mark at Ohio State as a three-year starter and letter winner at offensive right guard; the Buckeyes finally upended Illinois in his last shot in 1993 after three straight setbacks.

"We always seemed to move the ball against Illinois, but we'd turn it over or miss field goals or something," Monnot said. "They had Jeff George and [Jason] Verduzco at quarterback, and they had really nasty defenses with guys like Mel Agee, Dana Howard, Kevin Hardy, and John Holecek.

"Howard's motor never stopped," Monnot added. "In 1991, it was one of his first Big Ten games and my fourth or fifth game as a guard. We had enjoyed pretty good success scripting our first 15 plays, and we ran a lot of traps. On one, my job was to slide through the A gap and seal off the linebacker, then get out of the way because Butler By'not'e would be coming through the hole. Well, Howard obliterated me and made the tackle. He finished with more than 20 tackles that day."

Howard registered 20 solo stops and 24 overall, and running back Kameno Bell latched onto 12 of Verduzco's passes.

Brian Galley, who earned his engineering degree at Illinois, said it was a wonderful stretch for Illini fans. "Illinois had Ohio State's number from the mid-1980s to the mid-1990s," Galley said. "Unfortunately, Illinois has pretty much hit rock bottom since then."

Buckeyes starting quarterback Steve Bellisari was suspended after his arrest for drunk driving before a 34-22 loss to No. 12 Illinois in '01. Illinois quarterback Kurt Kittner registered four scoring passes against Ohio State for the second time in three seasons, finishing with 274 yards. Walter Young accounted for 133 yards receiving.

Jonathan Wells ripped the Illini for 192 yards rushing, and Michael Jenkins had 155 yards receiving, but it wasn't enough to keep Ohio State from slipping to 4-4 in Jim Tressel's first Big Ten season as coach, although the Buckeyes bounced back to upset Michigan a week later at Ann Arbor.

Ohio State has claimed its share of hard-fought wins, including the 2002 showdown at Illinois. OSU claimed its fifth victory of six regular-season outings that it won by a touchdown or less; the Buckeyes were en route to the national championship game against Miami.

The second-ranked Buckeyes survived in overtime, 23-16, as Maurice Hall scored on an 8-yard run and Illinois quarterback Jon Beutjer's last pass was batted

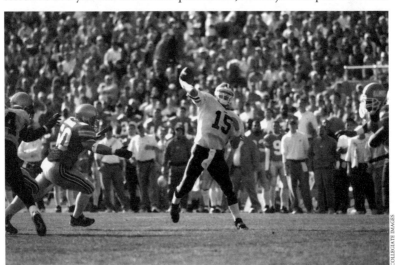

Kurt Kittner threw four touchdown passes in 2001 to help Illinois pull off a 34-22 win over the Buckeyes.

down. John Gockman's 48-yard field goal on the final play of regulation had tied it at 16-all. Beutjer was 27-of-45 for 305 yards and connected with Walter Young on 10 passes for 144 yards. He was, however, sacked six times.

Jenkins anchored the Ohio State air game with 147 yards receiving, while David Thompson led the Buckeyes' defense with 3.5 sacks.

Kittner missed that excitement by one year, but he created enough of his own in helping Illinois fashion a 2-2 record against Ohio State. In a rare turn of events, the home team lost all four Illinois-OSU showdowns from 1998 to 2001.

"Ohio State was always ranked in the top 25 and had pretty good teams," Kittner said. "It was a big step for our program if we could beat them. It was crazy because there aren't a lot of teams that go in and win in The Horseshoe, and we did it twice."

So what if Ohio State has won more than twice as many meetings as the Illini? So what if this series will never reach the heights of the Bucks' big showdown against Michigan? None of that means that players and fans alike haven't taken this rivalry seriously. The original Illibuck mascot didn't last long, but the battle for the turtle, even a wooden one, will remain a big piece of the Big Ten landscape for years to come.

MORE SERIES HIGHLIGHTS

1919: Illinois upset Ohio State to share the national championship with Harvard and Notre Dame. The Illini claimed a 9-7 victory in this season finale against Chic Harley and the Buckeyes, who had gone unbeaten in 1916 and 1917 (a combined 15-0-1) and were looking to do the same in this contest at Columbus. The Buckeyes led, 7-6, with less than two minutes showing. Bob Fletcher, who hadn't kicked a field goal before but had to step up because Illinois' top two kickers were injured, knocked through a 25-yarder with 12 seconds left. Local newspapers reported a Buckeyes' victory in early editions, including a headline that read, "Ohio State Smears Illinois."

1921: Illinois entered the season-ending contest winless in league play, while Ohio State was unbeaten. However, Don Peden and Lawrence Walquist combined for a wild 40-yard pass for the game's only score and a stunning 7-0 Illini victory. What made the outcome even more startling was the fact that Walquist wasn't supposed to catch the ball. It was intended for Dave Wilson, who fell down. Walquist latched onto the pigskin after it went through the hands of a Buckeyes defender.

1924: Red Grange's 34-yard touchdown run was the only score in Illinois' 7-0 win as more than 27,000 watched in Champaign.

1925: Grange gained 103 yards rushing to lead Illinois to a 14-9 win at Ohio Stadium, his last collegiate game.

1930: Illinois had recorded three consecutive shutouts from 1927 to 1929, but Wes Fesler ignited the Buckeyes with 12 points in the first quarter. They held on for a 12-9 win.

1934: Illinois pulled out its "Flying Trapeze," a play that featured three laterals and a forward pass. Jack Beynon, who had originally gone into the secondary as a potential receiver, made the 36-yard touchdown pass to a wide-open Gene Dykstra to complete the play and give the Illini a 14-13 victory.

1942: No. 10 Ohio State's 44-20 road win featured 122 yards rushing from Thomas James against the 13th-ranked Illini.

1945: Oliver Cline gained 124 yards to aid ninth-ranked Ohio State's 27-2 home win in front of more than 70,000 fans.

1948: Dike Eddleman, who uncorked an Illinois-record 88-yard punt a week earlier against Iowa, boomed an 86-yarder and averaged 53 yards on his kicks. Alas, it didn't matter much; Ohio State won, 34-7.

1949: John Karras bolted 95 yards to score on a kickoff, but Illinois fell to the No. 11 Bucks, 30-17.

1951: Third-ranked Illinois entered this game 4-0 in league play and 7-0 overall but settled for a scoreless tie in Columbus, where Ohio State's Fred Bruney registered three interceptions. The Illini still won the Big Ten crown at 5-0-1 and finished 9-0-1 after whipping Stanford, 40-7, in the Rose Bowl.

1952: Robert Watkins gained 100 yards to help Ohio State to a 27-7 victory. He would be a key ingredient when the teams met two years later, gaining 112 yards in OSU's 40-7 romp.

1956: Illinois fielded one of the country's top offensive backfields with Bobby Mitchell and Abe Woodson at halfback, Ray Nitschke at fullback, and Hiles Stout at quarterback. But it was reserve Harry Jefferson who opened the scoring with a 44-yard touchdown jaunt to make it 6-0 after only three minutes. Ohio State soon took control, however. Jimmy Roseboro plunged over to complete a 79-yard scoring drive and tie it up. The Buckeyes then scored after forcing two turnovers to increase their lead to 19-6. OSU quarterback Frank Elwood scored the final TD after an 85-yard drive to make it 26-6. Roseboro ran for a game-high 101 yards, and fullback Galen Cisco added 98. All-America guard-linebacker (and future all-pro) Jim Parker spearheaded Ohio State's defensive charge.

1957: Donald Clark finished with 133 yards rushing to lead Ohio State to a 21-7 triumph. A crowd of more than 82,000 were on hand at The Horseshoe.

1958: Clark played a crucial role again as the fifth-ranked Buckeyes grabbed a 19-13 win at Memorial Stadium.

1960: Ohio State's 34-7 trouncing of Illinois included Bill Wentz's 100-yard kick-off return for a touchdown (the longest ever against the Illini) and Tom Matte's 129 yards rushing.

1961: Bob Ferguson scored four times to help No. 7 Ohio State to an easy 44-0 decision at home.

1962: Mike Taliaferro and Mike Yavorski hooked up on a 90-yard scoring pass, the longest in Illinois history, but the Buckeyes did all of the celebrating with a 51-15 win. John Mummey of OSU rushed for 114 yards.

1963: The teams skirmished to a 20-all tie, which was good enough to give the Illini the conference title with a 5-1-1 record. All-America linebacker Dick Butkus was in on 23 tackles and made a diving interception to set up one touchdown as the Illini finished No. 3 in the Associated Press poll.

1964: Fourth-ranked Ohio State trounced the No. 2 Illini, 26-0, in the second weekend of Big Ten action in front of a homecoming crowd of more than 71,000 in Champaign.

1965: Fred Custardo gained 100 yards, but Ohio State doubled up on the Illini, 28-14, behind Thomas Barrington's 179 rushing yards.

1966: Illinois downed Ohio State, 10-9, defeating a Woody Hayes-coached Buckeyes team for only the third time. The Illini used a 74-yard drive during the final six minutes to score the deciding points. It overshadowed Gary Cairns' 55-yard field goal for the Buckeyes.

1967: John Wright Sr. had 112 yards receiving as Illinois won, 17-13. Dave Brungard gained 163 yards rushing for the host Buckeyes.

1968: Ohio State, en route to the national title, won, 31-24, in Champaign. The Illini rallied from a 24-0 halftime deficit to tie the game, but sophomore quarterback Ron Maciejowski led the winning march after replacing the injured Rex Kern.

1969: Jim Otis battered Illinois for 167 yards to key No. 1 Ohio State's 41-0 victory in front of more than 86,000 in Columbus.

1970: Darrell Robinson ripped the Buckeyes for 187 yards rushing, but it wasn't nearly enough as Ohio State rolled, 48-29. Buckeyes quarterback Kern added a 76-yard touchdown romp.

1971: Richard Galbos gained 112 yards during No. 15 Ohio State's 24-10 road victory.

1974: Archie Griffin gained 144 yards and quarterback Cornelius Greene chipped in 127 during Ohio State's 49-7 triumph. It was the 200th win of Hayes' coaching career.

1975: Tom Skladany connected on a 59-yard field goal, and Griffin had 127 yards rushing during Ohio State's 40-3 drubbing of the Illini.

1977: John Sullivan was all over the place, finishing with 25 tackles, including 10 solo stops, but Illinois needed several more like him in dropping a 35-0 decision. Sullivan had finished with 23 tackles in the teams' meeting two years earlier. Ron Springs accumulated 132 yards rushing for OSU.

1978: The Buckeyes gave Hayes his final victory at Ohio Stadium, a 45-7 decision with almost 88,000 fans in attendance.

1981: Tony Eason riddled the Buckeyes for 368 yards passing. But Ohio State pulled out a 34-27 decision as Tim Spencer rushed for 131 yards and Jimmy Gayle chipped in another 119.

1982: A crowd of 73,488, the largest at Memorial Stadium in 36 years, looked on as 15th-ranked Illinois lost a heartbreaking 26-21 decision despite Eason's 284 yards and Mike Martin's 12 catches for 177 yards. Spencer carried Ohio State with

152 yards rushing, and Cedric Anderson had 108 yards receiving.

1988–89: Illinois recorded its first back-to-back wins in the series since 1966–67. The first contest was a 31-12 decision for John Mackovic's first conference victory as Illinois coach. The Illini had not won at Ohio State since 1967. It occurred on Mackovic's 45th birthday as Jeff George passed for 224 yards (108 to Mike Bellamy), and the Illini defense limited the Buckeyes to 38 yards rushing.

In 1989, Jason Verduzco came off the bench for an injured George to help Illinois capture a 34-14 decision. It featured a 10-play, 99-yard scoring drive; 117 yards rushing from Howard Griffith; and 10 catches by Bellamy for 152 yards.

1990: Jeff Kinney replaced Verduzco to lead another Illini win, this one a 31-20 verdict. Shawn Wax finished with 159 yards receiving for Illinois. Raymont Harris gained 118 yards rushing in a losing cause, and Ohio State's Greg Frey was picked off four times.

1994: Dana Howard guaranteed an Illinois victory, and the Illini backed up his words with a 24-10 triumph in Columbus as Eddie George gained 124 yards for the hosts.

1995: Ohio State whipped the Illini, 41-3, behind a school-record 314 yards from George, who went on to win the Heisman Trophy after the season.

1996: No. 2 Ohio State waltzed to a 48-0 verdict on the road behind Pepe Pearson's 165 yards rushing.

1997: The fourth-ranked Buckeyes dominated Illinois, 41-6, despite allowing 143 yards rushing from Robert Holcombe. Ahmed Plummer raced 83 yards for a score with an interception, and Dee Miller finished with 103 receiving yards for the winners in scarlet and gray.

1998: Joe Germaine led the No. 1 and visiting Buckeyes' 41-0 spanking of Illinois with 307 yards on 17-of-28 passing.

1999: Steve Havard led the Illinois ground game with 104 yards as it won going away, 46-20. Kurt Kittner tossed four touchdown passes for the victors, while Jameel Cook had 100 yards in receptions. Kicker Neil Rackers booted four field goals, including a 50-yarder, to help offset Michael Wiley's 128 yards rushing.

2000: Ohio State safety Mike Doss drilled Kittner at the 2-yard line as the latter was starting his slide, giving Kittner a concussion that knocked him out of the game and ended his season. The No. 13 Buckeyes escaped with a 24-21 road win as Jonathan Wells rushed for 131 yards and Steve Bellisari passed for 251 yards.

2006: Top-ranked Ohio State grabbed a 17-0 halftime lead but got a major scare, holding off the pesky Illini, 17-10. The visiting Buckeyes had defeated their first nine foes by at least 17 points; nevertheless, Illinois managed to regroup and scored with 1:40 remaining. Ohio State recovered an onside kick and ran off all but a few seconds of the clock before punting, leaving Illinois only one play to go 98 yards. The Illini stymied the Buckeyes' running game, holding Troy Smith (soon to win the Heisman Trophy) to 37 yards on 11 carries. Smith completed 13-of-23 passes and was sacked three times.

Heisman Trophy winner Troy Smith drops back to pass as he leads
Ohio State to a 17-10 victory over the Illini in 2006.

ALL-TIME SERIES RESULTS

OHIO STATE LEADS, 60-29-4

November 15, 1902—Illinois 0, Ohio State 0 (T)

November 5, 1904—Illinois 46, Ohio State 0

October 17, 1914—Illinois 37, Ohio State 0

October 16, 1915—Illinois 3, Ohio State 3 (T)

October 21, 1916—Ohio State 7, Illinois 6

November 17, 1917—Ohio State 13, Illinois 0

November 16, 1918—Illinois 13, Ohio State 0

November 22, 1919—Illinois 9, Ohio State 7

November 20, 1920—Ohio State 7, Illinois 0

November 19, 1921—Illinois 7, Ohio State 0

November 25, 1922—Ohio State 6, Illinois 3

November 24, 1923—Illinois 9, Ohio State 0

November 22, 1924—Illinois 7, Ohio State 0

November 21, 1925—Illinois 14, Ohio State 9

November 20, 1926—Ohio State 7, Illinois 6

November 19, 1927—Illinois 13, Ohio State 0

November 24, 1928—Illinois 8, Ohio State 0

November 23, 1929—Illinois 27, Ohio State 0

November 22, 1930—Ohio State 12, Illinois 9

November 21, 1931—Ohio State 40, Illinois 0

November 19, 1932—Ohio State 3, Illinois 0

November 25, 1933—Ohio State 7, Illinois 6

October 13, 1934—Illinois 14, Ohio State 13

November 16, 1935—Ohio State 6, Illinois 0

November 14, 1936—Ohio State 13, Illinois 0

November 13, 1937—Ohio State 19, Illinois 0

November 12, 1938—Ohio State 32, Illinois 14

November 18, 1939—Ohio State 21, Illinois 0

November 16, 1940—Ohio State 14, Illinois 6

November 15, 1941—Ohio State 12, Illinois 7

November 14, 1942—Ohio State 44, Illinois 20

November 13, 1943—Ohio State 29, Illinois 26

November 18, 1944—Ohio State 26, Illinois 12

November 17, 1945—Ohio State 27, Illinois 2

November 16, 1946—Illinois 16, Ohio State 7

November 15, 1947—Illinois 28, Ohio State 7

November 13, 1948—Ohio State 34, Illinois 7

November 12, 1949—Ohio State 30, Illinois 17

November 18, 1950—Illinois 14, Ohio State 7

November 17, 1951—Illinois 0, Ohio State 0 (T)

November 15, 1952—Ohio State 27, Illinois 7

October 10, 1953—Illinois 41, Ohio State 20

October 9, 1954—Ohio State 40, Illinois 7

October 8, 1955—Ohio State 27, Illinois 12

October 13, 1956—Ohio State 26, Illinois 6

October 12, 1957—Ohio State 21, Illinois 7

October 11, 1958—Ohio State 19, Illinois 13

October 10, 1959—Illinois 9, Ohio State 0

October 8, 1960—Ohio State 34, Illinois 7

October 14, 1961—Ohio State 44, Illinois 0

October 13, 1962—Ohio State 51, Illinois 15

October 12, 1963—Illinois 20, Ohio State 20 (T)

October 10, 1964—Ohio State 26, Illinois 0

October 9, 1965—Ohio State 28, Illinois 14

October 8, 1966—Illinois 10, Ohio State 9

October 28, 1967—Illinois 17, Ohio State 13

October 26, 1968—Ohio State 31, Illinois 24

October 25, 1969—Ohio State 41, Illinois 0

October 24, 1970—Ohio State 48, Illinois 29

October 9, 1971—Ohio State 24, Illinois 10

October 14, 1972—Ohio State 26, Illinois 7

November 3, 1973—Ohio State 30, Illinois 0

November 2, 1974—Ohio State 49, Illinois 7

November 8, 1975—Ohio State 40, Illinois 3

November 6, 1976—Ohio State 42, Illinois 10

November 5, 1977—Ohio State 35, Illinois 0

November 11, 1978—Ohio State 45, Illinois 7

November 3, 1979—Ohio State 44, Illinois 7

November 8, 1980—Ohio State 49, Illinois 42

October 17, 1981—Ohio State 34, Illinois 27

October 16, 1982—Ohio State 26, Illinois 21

October 15, 1983—Illinois 17, Ohio State 13

October 13, 1984—Ohio State 45, Illinois 38

October 5, 1985—Illinois 31, Ohio State 28

October 4, 1986—Ohio State 14, Illinois 0

October 3, 1987—Ohio State 10, Illinois 6

October 1, 1988—Illinois 31, Ohio State 12

October 7, 1989—Illinois 34, Ohio State 14

October 6, 1990—Illinois 31, Ohio State 20

October 12, 1991—Illinois 10, Ohio State 7

October 10, 1992—Illinois 18, Ohio State 16

October 9, 1993—Ohio State 20, Illinois 12

October 8, 1994—Illinois 24, Ohio State 10

November 11, 1995—Ohio State 41, Illinois 3

November 9, 1996—Ohio State 48, Illinois 0

November 15, 1997—Ohio State 41, Illinois 6

October 10, 1998—Ohio State 41, Illinois 0

November 13, 1999—Illinois 46, Ohio State 20

November 11, 2000—Ohio State 24, Illinois 21

November 17, 2001—Illinois 34, Ohio State 22

November 16, 2002—Ohio State 23, Illinois 16

November 5, 2005—Ohio State 40, Illinois 2

November 4, 2006—Ohio State 17, Illinois 10

Bob Griese passed for 285 yards in Purdue's 1965 win over the Irish.

WRESTLING FOR THE CLUB:
PURDUE vs. NOTRE DAME

Notre Dame played its first football game ever in 1887, and it was against Michigan. Ever since, the Irish have enjoyed a severely competitive but tight relationship with members of the Big Ten, a conference that it has almost joined several times since the 1920s. Notre Dame took its most serious look in 1999, but the Board of Trustees voted against joining the league after alumni and students rallied against the proposal.

Made famous by such legendary figures as The Four Horsemen, Knute Rockne, Paul Hornung, and Joe Montana, this Catholic institution has maintained its prominent position as a national independent program. However, the Irish square off against at least three Big Ten schools every season and mirror those foes in many ways, including high academic performance and rich football traditions.

Notre Dame first met Indiana, Illinois, and Michigan State in the 1890s and Wisconsin in 1900. The Irish have played Ohio State only four times and haven't faced Minnesota since 1938.

But Notre Dame's No. 1 Big Ten adversary always has been Purdue. So, coincidence or not, Purdue has provided a measuring stick for the Notre Dame football program since World War II. Irish teams that defeated the Boilermakers have averaged more than eight victories per year; those that fell to Purdue won fewer than six contests each season.

The teams first met in 1896 and have hooked up every autumn since 1946. Notre Dame has won more than twice as often as Purdue, but 23 of the 78 showdowns between the two teams have been decided by seven points or less. More importantly, the Boilermakers have been the team that put a stop to several long Notre Dame unbeaten streaks. Purdue also has recorded more victories against the Irish than any other team except for USC, and its 51-19 triumph in 1960 forced Notre Dame to give up more points than it ever had before.

In fact, during the heyday of this nonconference rivalry, 1965–69, neither team entered the match up ranked lower than 16th. Purdue finished 4-1 during that span, beating Notre Dame even when the Irish were ranked No. 1 in 1965 and '67. The '68 game, in which eventual Heisman Trophy runner-up Leroy Keyes ran for two touchdowns and threw for a third, pitted the nation's No. 1 and No. 2 teams.

Notre Dame entered the 1965 contest at West Lafayette ranked No. 1 after pasting California, 48-6, in its opener while Purdue was sitting at No. 6. Boilermakers quarterback Bob Griese riddled the Irish secondary, completing 19 of 22 passes for 285 yards and three scores. The future Miami Dolphin great tossed the winning touchdown in a 25-21 Purdue triumph that featured five lead changes. Griese completed 86% of his passes that day, second best in school history.

The Boilermakers initially held an 18-10 advantage despite missing an extra point and two 2-point tries. Notre Dame soon rebounded, as Bill Wolski's 56-yard run and Tom Talaga's great catch on the conversion knotted things at 18-all. Ken Ivan's 24-yard field goal gave the Irish a 21-18 lead. Griese passed for 67 yards on three plays, and Gordon Teter blasted for the final three yards and the deciding score, a drive that lasted only 1:40. At least Purdue's Bob Hadrick didn't make it easy on the Irish defense, catching eight passes for 113 yards.

The next year, Notre Dame's Jim Seymour hauled in a team-record 13 passes for another Irish mark of 276 yards, scoring three times in a 26-14 victory. Irish signal-caller Terry Hanratty finished 16-of-24 for 304 yards in the season opener. Notre Dame entered the game No. 6, while the Boilermakers were ranked eighth.

Purdue's Keyes blazed 95 yards with a fumble return to help put Purdue up 7-0, but Nick Eddy returned the ensuing kickoff 96 yards for the equalizer that gave the hosts the momentum in front of 59,075 at Notre Dame Stadium. Hanratty and Seymour combined for scores of 84, 39, and 7 yards. The 84-yarder gave Notre Dame the lead for good, and the 39-yarder made it 20-7. Purdue closed to within 20-14 and was driving again until Alan Page sacked Griese to help set up the Irish offense for the third Hanratty-Seymour scoring play to clinch the win.

The Irish finished with a poll-topping 9-0-1 record in a season that featured the famous 10-all deadlock at Michigan State. Purdue finished 9-2 overall and went 6-1 in the Big Ten, one game behind the Spartans. But the Boilermakers qualified for the Rose Bowl because of the no-repeat rule; they downed Southern Cal, 14-13, and finished ranked sixth and seventh in the wire service polls.

Seymour said that the 1966 showdown against the Boilermakers was a classic example of what the series meant. Notre Dame eventually outscored its opponents that year by an amazing 362-38 margin, registering six shutouts along the way.

"Purdue was always big because it was normally the first or second game of the year and gave us a good idea where we stood," the Detroit native said from his Chicago office. "They had great talent and provided a good test. That '66 meeting was my first college game as a sophomore, so it was great because we were happy to be facing somebody other than our defense. That's not to take anything away from Purdue, but we thought it would be a little easier than going against the top defense in the nation. As for the three touchdowns, I got lucky."

Seymour said that as freshmen he and Notre Dame's excellent recruiting class were confident that they would put up good numbers.

"They took all of us down to the Purdue game in West Lafayette in '65 so we could experience the travel and everything, and we got to sit on the bench," Seymour said. "We watched Bob Griese march up and down the field, which was fun for the Purdue fans. But we went to the bus saying that we couldn't wait for the next year and that this wouldn't happen again. We knew we'd have a good team and felt that we could throw the ball against them."

That's exactly what they did during Seymour's record-setting afternoon. In 1967, Hanratty set a school record with 63 pass attempts, completing 29 and tying for the third-highest number of completions in Notre Dame history. He passed for 366 yards and finished with 420 yards total, but 10th-ranked Purdue grabbed a 28-21 victory over the top-ranked Irish.

Mike Phipps completed just 13-of-35 passing, but the Purdue sophomore finished with 238 yards, 166 of them coming when he converted six of eight third-down aerials. The teams combined for 834 yards, 485 from Notre Dame, which got eight catches and 114 yards from Seymour. Keyes caught nine passes for 108 yards for Purdue.

Notre Dame wound up 8-2 and ranked fourth and fifth; Purdue compiled the same overall record, sharing first in the Big Ten at 6-1 to grab ninth in both wire service polls.

Purdue was ranked No. 1 in the Associated Press poll when the teams tangled in 1968. After blasting fifth-ranked Oklahoma in its opener, Notre Dame sat atop the UPI rankings and was No. 2 according to AP. Purdue clobbered the Irish, 37-22, as Phipps completed 16-of-24 passes for 194 yards and was perfect on five third-down tosses. Bob Dillingham hauled in 11 passes for 147 yards and two scores for Purdue. Keyes ran for two scores and heaved a 17-yard touchdown pass to Dillingham that gave the Boilermakers a 23-7 cushion late in the first half. Notre Dame lost six fumbles, helping Purdue to a 479-454 margin in total yards.

Purdue finished 8-2 and shared third place at 5-2 in the Big Ten, falling 13-0 to eventual national champion Ohio State two weeks after downing the Irish. The Boilermakers took 10th in the final AP charts, while Notre Dame ended 7-2-1 and was fifth by AP and eighth in UPI voting.

Phipps became the first quarterback ever to beat Notre Dame three times as he led Purdue to a 28-14 win in front of 68,179 fans at Ross-Ade Stadium in 1969. The 16th-ranked hosts converted 12-of-19 third-down situations for 183 yards; Phipps finished 12-of-20 for 213 yards. Irish signal-caller Joe Theismann completed 14-of-26 for 153 yards, but eight of those completions came in the last six minutes of the game.

Notre Dame captured fifth and eighth in the polls and finished 8-2-1 after a 21-17 loss to top-ranked Texas in the Cotton Bowl. Purdue went 8-2 in Jack Mollenkopf's last season as head coach, and didn't make the final top 10.

Jack Calcaterra and the Boilermakers lost two of three outings to Notre Dame during the years he lettered (1964–66), but he loved every minute of facing the Irish.

"Watching the movie *Rudy* brings me back every time," Calcaterra said of the 1993 film. "It was awesome playing against them, especially in South Bend. Being in that locker room and going onto the field. We played them pretty tough. I remember the coaches telling us that Notre Dame always came out of the dressing rooms first and that we shouldn't look up because they'd be warming up in that end zone. We had to run right through them, and it caused some fights."

Mike McCoy was a star defensive tackle at Notre Dame from 1967 to 1969 before being chosen by Green Bay as the number two pick overall in the 1970 NFL draft.

"We beat Purdue my freshman year, but I, of course, wasn't eligible," McCoy said. "Then we lost to them three times in a row. They had guys like Bob Griese, Leroy Keyes, and Mike Phipps during those years. We were ranked No. 1 my sophomore year and they beat us, and the next year we were second and they were first. It killed me, because they'd beat us and then went on to lose to somebody like Wake Forest or Colgate."

No other period in the Notre Dame-Purdue series has approached that five-year span for combined importance and competitiveness, and this tussle for the Shillelagh (pronounced shuh-LAY-lee), a Gaelic war club, hasn't rivaled the national significance as much as Notre Dame's series against Southern Cal for the Jeweled Shillelagh (the latter trophy adorned with rubies and emeralds). The intrastate meetings are nonetheless important.

The late Joe McLaughlin, a merchant seaman and a Notre Dame fan from Ireland, donated the first gnarled piece of wood in 1957, and the foes have fought for the Club since 1958. The winner receives a miniature football, with the school's initials and the final score, which is attached to the base of the Shillelagh's stand.

Ross Fichtner was around for the birth of the Shillelagh. Fichtner lettered three years as a quarterback and safety for the Boilermakers from 1957 to 1959 before embarking on a nine-year NFL career with Cleveland and coaching stints with Chicago, Minnesota, and Green Bay. His son, Randy, lettered at Purdue from 1982 to 1983, and his youngest boy, Rusty, played at Michigan in 1988 and 1989.

"I remember the game my senior year when we had them down, 28-0, at halftime," said Fichtner. "I had a couple of touchdown passes and had rushed for 100-plus yards. Then on the third play of the second half, I got hit by Myron Pottios and broke my shoulder. They put me in one of those goofy body casts where your arm sticks out from your side, but I was back on the sidelines in three weeks and played four weeks after getting hurt."

Bronko Nagurski Jr. played offensive and defensive tackle during the final three seasons of Terry Brennan's five-year run as Notre Dame's coach, 1956–58. His legendary father starred at Minnesota from 1927 to 1929 and then for George Halas' Chicago Bears in the 1930s, and is enshrined in both the college and pro football halls of fame.

The younger Nagurski said it took a lot of soul searching before he decided to join the Irish over his father's Gophers and other schools such as Michigan, Oklahoma, Southern Cal, and Army. He never regretted the decision; after all, he still got to play against several Big Ten schools every year, including Purdue and other highly touted programs around the country. Bronko Jr. later played eight seasons in the Canadian Football League before settling down in his hometown of International Falls, Minnesota.

"That was a transition time after the Frank Leahy years, especially my soph-omore year when we won only two games," said Nagurski. "We started nine sophomores in '56 and played a difficult schedule. That was tough football in those days when you consider an 18- or 19-year-old kid like me has to face an all-American like Iowa's Alex Karras. I got a lesson in life that afternoon. So after that season, Purdue and every team was a rival because everybody was gunning for us and wanted to beat us. USC was probably our biggest rival at that time.

"I was a small-town kid, and the only football we ever got was listening to the University of Minnesota on the radio," Nagurski said. "So, I didn't have a big appreciation of what it was all about, and then you go play at Michigan with 100,000 fans. But there was nothing like football on the Notre Dame campus, with the band and pep rally. And then running out of that tunnel onto the field was an awesome feeling."

Notre Dame supporter Wayne Pflugmacher knows all about the luck of the

Irish, having witnessed a shining example on September 24, 1977, in West Lafayette.

"My mom was born in Germantown, Illinois, in an all-Catholic family, so I grew up following Notre Dame," Pflugmacher said. "I got to go to games during the eight years that my company had season tickets, and the one I remember was when Notre Dame beat Purdue. The Irish were down two or three touchdowns in the second half, and a substitute quarterback named Joe Montana came in and rallied Notre Dame to victory. And the rest is history."

Notre Dame scored with 1:39 remaining as Montana, who started the game as the third-stringer, ignited the Irish from a 24-14 deficit entering the fourth quarter for a 31-24 win to stun a crowd of 68,96620.

Freshman Mark Herrmann passed for three touchdowns and 351 yards for Purdue, but the Montana mystique began with this comeback. Rusty Lisch started behind center but was relieved by Gary Forstek, who broke his collarbone. This forced coach Dan Devine to bring in Montana, who had separated his shoulder in the 1976 opener and sat on the bench all of his sophomore year.

Montana and key targets Kris Haines and Ken MacAfee spearheaded two scoring drives. Luther Bradley's interception set up a Montana-to-MacAfee TD and a 24-all tie. Then Purdue's punt traveled only 19 yards, putting the Irish at their 42 with less than three minutes left. Three Montana completions covered 48 yards, and two runs got the visitors into the end zone.

Notre Dame finished 10-1 and won the national crown after trouncing top-ranked Texas, 38-10, in the Cotton Bowl.

Ken Loushin started at defensive tackle for Purdue as a sophomore in 1976 and again from 1978 to 1979 after missing most of '77 because of an injury. He lost his first two times against the Irish, but as a senior he and the Boilers got revenge against No. 5 Notre Dame with a 28-22 home victory.

"It was a big rivalry, and we looked forward to playing them because they were always one of the top teams in the country," Loushin said. Loushin only played in three games in '77, but one of them was Joe Montana's famous comeback for Notre Dame. "Then my last year, we beat them in front of the biggest crowd ever at Purdue to that point. They had won the national championship a couple years before, so to beat them in that atmosphere was great," he said.

Purdue pulled off another shocker in 1950. Notre Dame started the season ranked first after winning national titles three of the past four seasons. Although both squads faltered after this meeting, the Boilermakers win was a huge upset at the time and contributed to the first non-winning campaign for the Irish since 1933.

Notre Dame entered the game with a streak of 39 games without a defeat (there were two ties), but the Irish crashed to the tune of 28-14. In the process, Purdue ended the Irish's 28-game winning string at Notre Dame Stadium, handing the Irish their first home loss since Michigan's 32-20 win back in 1942.

Purdue's 18-year-old quarterback, Dale Samuels, tossed three touchdown passes as the Boilermakers dominated the 1950 meeting and could have won by more had two scores not been called back because of penalties. John Kerestes scored visiting Purdue's first two TDs and Samuels hooked up with Neil Schmidt for a 30-yard score for a 21-0 halftime advantage. Notre Dame climbed to within 21-14 on the first play of the fourth quarter, but Samuels hit Mike Maccioli with a 56-yard bomb for the deciding tally.

Purdue backup quarterback Dick Schnaible, a Lafayette native, said afterward: "I've hated Notre Dame for 21 years. I've waited four years to beat them."

The Irish hadn't lost since the 1945 finale against Great Lakes. Notre Dame finished 4-4-1 and, amazingly, Purdue won only one more game to finish 2-7.

Jim Mutscheller played end for the Irish from 1949 to 1951, and was captain his senior season. He served two years in the Marines and then played in the NFL, most notably for eight seasons with the Baltimore Colts.

PURDUE SPORTS

Quarterback Dale Samuels helped Purdue prevail in 1950.

Notre Dame whipped unranked Purdue during Mutscheller's sophomore and senior seasons; the 1950 Irish squad never recovered and finished 0-3-1 vs. Big Ten schools that year, falling to Indiana two weeks after the Purdue debacle.

"We lost to Indiana that season for the first time in quite a few years [since 1906, in fact], but Purdue was always the bigger rivalry," Mutscheller said. "In that 1950 game against the Boilermakers, what I remember is Dale Samuels throwing the ball all over the place."

Purdue fan Charles Cameron, now in his 80s, has followed the team for almost 40 years. "Indiana and Purdue have been playing for a long time, and the fans really get into it," Cameron said. "It makes the season for whichever team wins that game. But you can buy tickets for that game on the street. At Notre Dame, you have to know somebody to get into that stadium. Purdue and Notre Dame have quite a rivalry."

Joe McConnell was the assistant sports information director at Purdue in the mid-1960s. He has been a broadcaster ever since, covering everything from the NFL, NBA, major league baseball, college basketball, and, of course, NCAA football, including the favorite team of his childhood, the Boilermakers.

"The first memory I have of Purdue football was from third grade, in 1950, when I bet my dad's uncle 25 cents that Purdue would beat Notre Dame," McConnell said. "He just laughed at me. But Dale Samuels led Purdue to that win at South Bend and snapped Notre Dame's 39-game streak.

"I also remember working the game from the press box as assistant SID when Terry Hanratty and Jim Seymour went wild for Notre Dame," McConnell said of the 1966 encounter. "Seymour was a tall, angular receiver who could out-jump defenders. But the 1960s under Jack Mollenkopf was Purdue's golden era, and they owned the Irish at that time. One game that sticks out is when Bob Griese was nearly perfect and hit Jim Beirne for a score at Ross-Ade Stadium [in 1965]. Beirne made one of the greatest catches I've seen, laying out horizontally at the goal line between two Irish defenders to haul it in. And the Boilermakers had Leroy Keyes, who was and still is the best football player to have played there. He did everything but lace up the footballs."

Former Purdue standout Harry Szulborski recalled some of the legendary Irish players he squared off against right after World War II.

"I remember playing against guys like Johnny Lujack and Leon Hart, who both won the Heisman," Szulborski said. "They beat us every year, but we always played tough. They beat us, 28-27, in '48. It was great playing in those games. During all of my years of coaching after college, the only two games I wanted tickets for were Purdue-Notre Dame and Purdue-Indiana."

Those sentiments haven't changed much across the Hoosier state during the past 60 years. Former Irish linebacker Kory Minor enjoyed a 3-1 record against Purdue from 1995 to 1998, two years under Lou Holtz and two under Bob Davie.

"Purdue was always important and reminded me of a backyard brawl because of the in-state rivalry aspect," Minor said. "We had great rivalries against all of our Big Ten opponents."

San Francisco drafted Minor in the seventh round, but he was released and played five seasons with Carolina before retiring from pro ball. He said that contests against Purdue were among the highlights of his college career, including an interception against Drew Brees, now a star with the New Orleans Saints.

Irish linebacker Kory Minor participated in three Purdue defeats.

"We played over there when I was a freshman, and I remember how I wanted to be a force and didn't want to make a mistake," Minor said of the eventual 35-28 Irish win. "But Purdue was driving in the fourth quarter, and it was third and long and I got called for roughing the quarterback. Coach Holtz was livid. I was so scared to go to the sidelines and figured I better pack my bags, but our defense stepped up and stopped them. Coach called me later in my dorm room and apologized for yelling at me, and I told him I understood why he was upset. That's why I had so much respect for Coach Holtz."

Brees, Holtz, and Minor—just three of the more recent names to adorn this storied series. Notre Dame played only Michigan (1887) and Northwestern (1889) before meeting the Boilers for the first time in 1896. And the foes, separated by about 100 miles, have tangled every fall since 1946, which equals the Irish's other "club" rivalry, Southern Cal, as the second-longest continuous series in Notre Dame history.

MORE SERIES HIGHLIGHTS

1896: Alpha Jamison scored four touchdowns and added four extra points for 20 points in Purdue's 28-22 victory in the teams' first meeting. Touchdowns were worth four points at the time.

1905: Purdue claimed a 32-0 decision, but it would wait 28 years for its next shutout in the series, suffering eight straight losses in the interim.

1906: The Irish had four touchdowns called back on penalties and settled for a 2-0 victory on a blocked punt that went out of the end zone. Notre Dame finished 6-1, while Purdue ended up 0-5, its only points all season coming in a 29-5 loss to Wisconsin.

1918–1932: Notre Dame under Knute Rockne won all six meetings by an average score of 29-6 after the teams didn't play each other from 1908 to 1917.

1921: Notre Dame won easily, 33-0, but the Irish's Paul Castner still punted 12 times. However, he set a school single-game record by averaging 44.8 yards for those who've punted at least 10 times.

1933: Duane Purvis, who was treated for an infected knee the Wednesday before the game, scored on a 50-yard pass from Paul Pardonner to highlight Purdue's 19-0 win. This increased the Boilers' unbeaten string to 20 contests.

1934: Fred Carideo returned an interception 72 yards for a score during Notre Dame's 18-7 win in South Bend, where a crowd of more than 34,000 showed up.

1948: Notre Dame held on to win, 28-27. Purdue scored on the final play of the game, but the Irish had sealed the victory with about three minutes left when Steve Oracko nailed a 25-yard field goal after missing three of them earlier. John Panelli returned a blocked kick for a score and Al Zmijewski did the same with an interception for the Irish in this season opener.

1949: Purdue limited the Irish to 1-of-4 passing for 14 yards, and Norbert Adams racked up 104 yards rushing, but the Boilers still lost, 35-12.

1952: Notre Dame fumbled 10 times but recovered seven; in the meantime, the Irish took advantage of Purdue's miscues, which included losing eight of 11 fumbles. Notre Dame also threw four interceptions but prevailed, 26-14. Bernie Flowers caught four balls for 108 yards for the Boilermakers.

1954: Notre Dame started the season ranked second and whipped Texas, 21-0, to gain the top spot in the polls. However, Purdue quarterback Len Dawson passed for four scores as the Boilermakers claimed a 27-14 decision. Dawson completed only 7-of-12 attempts, but they covered 216 yards. The future Dallas Texans/Kansas City Chiefs star booted three extra points and set up a score with an interception, while his 73-yard connection with big Lamar Lundy broke a 14-all tie. This proved to be Notre Dame's only loss in 10 outings, while the Boilermakers finished 5-3-1.

1956: Jack Mollenkopf took over as Purdue coach, beginning his successful run against Notre Dame with a 28-14 triumph. Mel Dillard scored twice and rushed for 142 yards as the Boilermakers outgained the Irish, 370-129.

1957: Notre Dame claimed a 12-0 victory in the first Shillelagh trophy encounter. Purdue punted the ball 11 times and turned it over three times in 14 possessions. Notre Dame finished 7-3, including the huge 7-0 win that ended Oklahoma's record 47-game winning streak.

1958: No. 15 Purdue outlasted No. 11 Notre Dame, 29-22, after leading, 26-7, in the final quarter in front of 59,563 fans. George Izo tossed touchdown passes of 29 and 43 yards to Monty Stickles, but the Boilermakers stopped the Irish on a fourth-and-2 play from the Purdue 27 with 1:21 left. Bob Jarus scored three times for the victors, who notched three touchdowns in the first eight minutes of the third period.

1959: The Boilermakers hadn't beaten Notre Dame at home since moving from Stuart Field to Ross-Ade Stadium in 1924. In fact, their 28-7 verdict was their first win against the Irish in West Lafayette since 1905.

1960: Purdue registered 31 points during a 10:52 span of the second quarter en route to a 51-19 thrashing, the most points it had ever scored against the Irish and its second-largest victory margin. Purdue led only 14-13 after the first quarter, but the second-quarter outburst was the biggest that Notre Dame had ever allowed in a single period.

1961: Notre Dame bounced back for a 22-20 win as sophomore kicker Joe Perkowski nailed a 28-yard field goal in the fourth quarter after missing two field goals and an extra point. Skip Ohl of Purdue missed a potential game-winning 36-yard try with just over three minutes remaining. The Boilermakers led, 17-7, before the Irish rallied to narrow the lead to 20-19 after a two-point conversion failed.

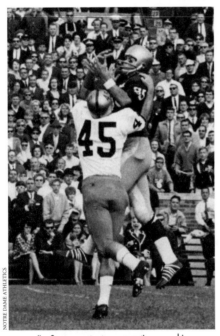

Jim Seymour set a team reception record in Notre Dame's 1966 victory.

1963: Quarterback John Huarte, who doubled as Notre Dame's kicker, reinjured his bum ankle on a 41-yard touchdown pass to Jim Kelly. The Irish went for two and failed, leaving them with a 6-0 second-quarter cushion. However, Ron DiGravio hooked up with Bob Hadrick for a 7-yard score with 9:15 left. Gary Hogan tacked on the all-important extra point for a 7-6 win. Purdue, which had blown two good scoring opportunities in the second quarter, then held off the Irish. Henry Dudgeon blocked Huarte's 28-yard field-goal attempt with 2:10 showing, and Gordon Teter swatted away Huarte's pass for Jack Snow at the Boilers' 8 as the gun sounded.

1964: Ara Parseghian took over the Irish head coaching job and watched Notre Dame's stars take over Purdue during a 34-15 victory. Kevin Hardy blocked a punt that Alan Page rumbled 57 yards with to give the home team a 21-7 lead.

1970: The Irish's Tom Gatewood caught 12 passes for 192 yards and three scores as Joe Theismann's leading target. The latter finished 17-of-25 for 304 yards to give Notre Dame a 48-0 win in a laughable, rain-soaked affair. The Irish defense throttled Purdue's passing game, which was limited to 48 yards on a woeful

7-of-32 effort. Notre Dame outgained the Boilermakers, 329-96, and forced nine turnovers.

1971: Gary Danielson's 26-yard pitch to Otis Armstrong gave Purdue a 7-0 half-time lead, which held up until 1:58 remained. That's when Bob Hoidahl's snap bounced back to punter Scott Lougheed, whose end-zone kick was blocked by Walt Patulski and Clarence Ellis. Fred Swendsen blanketed the loose pigskin to make it 7-6, and Notre Dame won it when quarterback Pat Steenberge, who was only 6-of-25, tossed a two-point conversion to Mike Creaney.

1974: Purdue upset 30-point favorite Notre Dame, 31-20, making it the fourth time that the Boilermakers had ended an Irish unbeaten streak of at least 12 games. Purdue bolted to a 21-0 cushion in the first eight minutes and led 24-0 after the first quarter. The Irish's first three drives ended in two turnovers and a punt, and Purdue took advantage quickly, scoring three times in 11 plays.

1975: Luther Bradley set a team record for interception return yardage in a game with 103 on two pickoffs, including a 99-yarder, to ignite Notre Dame's 17-0 victory in Dan Devine's first year coaching the Irish in this series. Bradley's long gainer made it 9-0 after he pilfered Purdue running back Scott Dierking's attempted pass back to quarterback Craig Nagel.

1979: Mark Herrmann rallied the Boilermakers from a 20-7 deficit to a 28-22 triumph, helping them eventually grab 10th in both wire service polls. It was the first time since the rankings were established in 1936 that Purdue finished in the top 10 and Notre Dame didn't.

1981: Purdue won at home, 15-14. Boilermakers quarterback Scott Campbell led the final 80-yard touchdown drive. Campbell connected with Steve Bryant on a fourth-and-goal play from the 7 to make it 14-13. With 19 seconds left, he then lofted another toss to Bryant in the opposite corner of the end zone for a two-point conversion and the stunning victory.

Phil Carter's 30-yard burst with 2:57 remaining had given the Irish a 14-7 lead, but the Boilermakers survived a fourth-and-1 play from their own 29 to start the decisive possession. Campbell and Bryant combined on a 56-yard play to the Irish 1 that set up their heroic finish.

1985: Purdue won, 35-17, behind Jim Everett's 368 yards on 27-of-49 passing in front of a capacity throng of more than 69,000 at West Lafayette.

1990: Top-ranked Notre Dame throttled Purdue, 37-11, despite Eric Hunter's 354 yards passing and Ernest Calloway's three catches for 114 yards, to send a partisan crowd of 59,075 home happy.

1991: Notre Dame quarterback Rick Mirer hit on 12-of-14 passes, an 86% completion rate that shares second place in school history, as the eighth-ranked Irish won handily, 45-20.

1992: Sixth-ranked Notre Dame crushed the visiting Boilermakers, 48-0, the first time the Irish had shut out Purdue since back-to-back contests in 1975–76.

1995: Ron Powlus threw four touchdown passes as Notre Dame earned a 35-28 road victory. Mike Alstott gained 115 yards on 21 carries for the Boilermakers.

1996: Notre Dame's Allen Rossum returned a kickoff 99 yards for a score to highlight the ninth-ranked Irish's 35-0 rout.

1997: Powlus completed 31 passes (two behind Theismann's school mark) in 43 attempts. However, Purdue, under first-year coach Joe Tiller, stunned the 12th-ranked Irish, 28-17, to end the longest winning streak in the series: Notre Dame's 11-game run. Billy Dicken completed 26-of-38 aerials for 352 yards, including eight to Vinny Sutherland for 100 yards. Notre Dame didn't bring the Shillelagh, so Purdue had to call and get it.

1998: The No. 23 Irish scored with 57 seconds left on Jim Sanson's 17-yard field goal to stun Purdue, 31-30, in front of more than 80,000 at Notre Dame Stadium, the largest crowd to witness a game in the series up to that point. Tony Driver's interception set up the deciding score and his second theft with 39 seconds left prevented any last-minute Purdue heroics. Autry Denson rushed for 143 yards for Notre Dame.

1999: No. 20 Purdue earned a 28-23 decision over No. 16 Notre Dame behind 317 passing yards from Drew Brees. Chris Daniels caught 13 for 123 yards and Randall Lane had 11 more for 121 yards.

2000: Notre Dame, ranked No. 21, returned two fumbles for scores to pull out a 23-21 decision, which offset Sutherland's 112 yards on four receptions for No. 16 Purdue.

2001: Vontez Duff's 96-yard kickoff return for a touchdown proved crucial in

Notre Dame's 24-18 triumph. Travis Dorsch tied a Purdue mark with four field goals, including a 50-yarder, while John Standeford caught 10 passes for 118 yards.

2002: Joey Harris rushed for 109 yards on 25 carries and Anthony Chambers returned a punt 76 yards, but the host Irish prevailed, 24-17.

2003: Brady Quinn completed 29-of-59 attempts, including an 85-yard touchdown to Maurice Stovall, but Purdue controlled the contest, 23-10. Quinn was intercepted four times. Stovall finished with nine catches for 171 yards, while Standeford topped Purdue with five catches for 110 yards.

2004: Quinn registered 432 yards passing on 26-of-46 attempts without an interception. Theismann's 526 yards against Southern California in 1970 was the only other 400-yard game in team history to that point. Purdue's Jerome Brooks had a 100-yard kickoff return. His teammate Kyle Orton threw for 385 yards and five touchdown passes in the Boilermakers' 41-16 triumph, which also featured seven catches and 181 yards receiving from Taylor Stubblefield, including a 97-yarder.

2005: The Irish reclaimed the Shillelagh for the 31st time in 49 tries with a 49-28 win in front of a sellout crowd of 65,491 in West Lafayette. Notre Dame rolled to a 28-0 halftime advantage and accumulated 621 total yards overall. Brady Quinn completed 29-of-36 passes for 440 yards and three scores, and became the fourth Irish player to surpass 6,000 career yards in the air. Jeff Samardzija had seven catches for 153 yards and two scores. The Irish took control early, marching 90 and 98 yards for touchdowns in the first quarter. The last time Notre Dame had two marches of 90 or more yards in a game was in 1996 against the Boilermakers.

2006: Quinn, Darius Walker, and Notre Dame's offense lit up Purdue again, racing to a 21-point halftime lead en route to a 35-21 victory. Quinn riddled the Boilermakers' defense, hitting 24 of his first 28 pass attempts for the 12th-ranked Irish. Quinn finished 29-for-38 for 316 yards, and Walker carried 36 times for 146 yards. Curtis Painter finished 23-for-46 for 398 yards for the Boilers, and Selwyn Lymon had eight catches for 238 yards, the second most by a Purdue receiver and the most by an Irish opponent.

ALL-TIME SERIES RESULTS

NOTRE DAME LEADS, 51-25-2

November 14, 1896—Purdue 28, Notre Dame 22

November 18, 1899—Notre Dame 10, Purdue 10 (T)

November 9, 1901—Notre Dame 12, Purdue 6

November 27, 1902—Notre Dame 6, Purdue 6 (T)

November 24, 1904—Purdue 36, Notre Dame 0

November 24, 1905—Purdue 32, Notre Dame 0

November 3, 1906—Notre Dame 2, Purdue 0
November 23, 1907—Notre Dame 17, Purdue 0
November 23, 1918—Notre Dame 26, Purdue 6
November 22, 1919—Notre Dame 33, Purdue 13
November 6, 1920—Notre Dame 28, Purdue 0
October 15, 1921—Notre Dame 33, Purdue 0
October 14, 1922—Notre Dame 20, Purdue 0
November 3, 1923—Notre Dame 34, Purdue 7
November 11, 1933—Purdue 19, Notre Dame 0
October 13, 1934—Notre Dame 18, Purdue 7
September 30, 1939—Notre Dame 3, Purdue 0
October 12, 1946—Notre Dame 49, Purdue 6
October 11, 1947—Notre Dame 22, Purdue 7
September 25, 1948—Notre Dame 28, Purdue 27
October 8, 1949—Notre Dame 35, Purdue 12
October 7, 1950—Purdue 28, Notre Dame 14
October 27, 1951—Notre Dame 30, Purdue 9
October 18, 1952—Notre Dame 26, Purdue 14
October 3, 1953—Notre Dame 37, Purdue 7
October 2, 1954—Purdue 27, Notre Dame 14
October 22, 1955—Notre Dame 22, Purdue 7
October 13, 1956—Purdue 28, Notre Dame 14
September 28, 1957—Notre Dame 12, Purdue 0
October 25, 1958—Purdue 29, Notre Dame 22
October 3, 1959—Purdue 28, Notre Dame 7
October 1, 1960—Purdue 51, Notre Dame 19
October 7, 1961—Notre Dame 22, Purdue 20
October 6, 1962—Purdue 24, Notre Dame 6
October 5, 1963—Purdue 7, Notre Dame 6
October 3, 1964—Notre Dame 34, Purdue 15
September 25, 1965—Purdue 25, Notre Dame 21
September 24, 1966—Notre Dame 26, Purdue 14
September 30, 1967—Purdue 28, Notre Dame 21
September 28, 1968—Purdue 37, Notre Dame 22
September 27, 1969—Purdue 28, Notre Dame 14
September 26, 1970—Notre Dame 48, Purdue 0

September 25, 1971—Notre Dame 8, Purdue 7
September 30, 1972—Notre Dame 35, Purdue 14
September 29, 1973—Notre Dame 20, Purdue 7
September 28, 1974—Purdue 31, Notre Dame 20
September 20, 1975—Notre Dame 17, Purdue 0
September 18, 1976—Notre Dame 23, Purdue 0
September 24, 1977—Notre Dame 31, Purdue 24
September 30, 1978—Notre Dame 10, Purdue 6
September 22, 1979—Purdue 28, Notre Dame 22
September 6, 1980—Notre Dame 31, Purdue 10
September 26, 1981—Purdue 15, Notre Dame 14
September 25, 1982—Notre Dame 28, Purdue 14
September 10, 1983—Notre Dame 52, Purdue 6
September 8, 1984—Purdue 23, Notre Dame 21
September 28, 1985—Purdue 35, Notre Dame 17
September 27, 1986—Notre Dame 41, Purdue 9
September 26, 1987—Notre Dame 44, Purdue 20
September 24, 1988—Notre Dame 52, Purdue 7
September 30, 1989—Notre Dame 40, Purdue 7
September 29, 1990—Notre Dame 37, Purdue 11
September 28, 1991—Notre Dame 45, Purdue 20
September 26, 1992—Notre Dame 48, Purdue 0
September 25, 1993—Notre Dame 17, Purdue 0
September 24, 1994—Notre Dame 39, Purdue 21
September 9, 1995—Notre Dame 35, Purdue 28
September 14, 1996—Notre Dame 35, Purdue 0
September 13, 1997—Purdue 28, Notre Dame 17
September 26, 1998—Notre Dame 31, Purdue 30
September 11, 1999—Purdue 28, Notre Dame 23
September 16, 2000—Notre Dame 23, Purdue 21
December 1, 2001—Notre Dame 24, Purdue 18
September 7, 2002—Notre Dame 24, Purdue 17
September 27, 2003—Purdue 23, Notre Dame 10
October 2, 2004—Purdue 41, Notre Dame 16
October 1, 2005—Notre Dame 49, Purdue 28
September 30, 2006—Notre Dame 35, Purdue 21

BIBLIOGRAPHY

BOOKS

Arnold, Robert D. *Hoosier Autumn: The Remarkable Story of Indiana University's 1945 Football Championship Team.* Indianapolis: Guild Press of Indiana, 1996.

Arnold, Robert D. *The Rivalry: Indiana and Purdue and the History of Their Old Oaken Bucket Battles 1924-2002.* Bloomington, Ind.: Author House, 2004.

Borton, John, and Paul Dodd. *Wolverines Handbook: Stories, Stats and Stuff About Michigan Football.* Wichita, Kan.: Wichita Eagle and Beacon, 1996.

Brandstatter, Jim. *Tales From Michigan Stadium: Volume II.* Champaign, Ill.: Sports Publishing LLC, 2005.

Butler, Tom. *The Badger Game: Mickey McGuire to Al Toon.* Madison, Wis.: William C. Robbins, 1991.

Christensen, Ray. *Gopher Tales: Stories From All 11 University of Minnesota's Men's Sports.* Champaign, Ill.: Sports Publishing LLC, 2002.

Cohane, Tim. *Great College Football Coaches of the 1920s and '30s.* New Rochelle, N.Y.: Arlington House, 1973.

Colletti, Ned. *Golden Glory: Notre Dame vs. Purdue.* New York: Leisure Press, 1983.

Delsohn, Steve. *Talking Irish: The Oral History of Notre Dame Football.* New York: Avon Books, 1998.

Emmanuel, Greg. *The 100-Yard War: Inside the 100-Year-Old Michigan-Ohio State Football Rivalry.* Hoboken, N.J.: John Wiley & Sons, 2004

Eubanks, Lou. *The Fighting Illini: A Story of Illinois Football.* Huntsville, Ala.: Strode Publishers, 1976.

Grady, Al. *25 Years With the Fighting Hawkeyes: Fourth Quarter 1964-1988.* Iowa City, Iowa: University of Iowa Athletic Department, 1989.

Hoffman, Ken, and Larry Bielat. *Spartan Football: 100 Seasons of Gridiron Glory.* Champaign, Ill.: Sagamore Publishing, 1996.

Lamb, Dick, and Bert McGrane. *75 Years With the Fighting Hawkeyes.* Iowa City, Iowa: University of Iowa Athletic Department, 1964.

McCallum, John D. *Big Ten Football Since 1895.* Radnor, Pa.: Chilton Book Co., 1976.

Menzer, Joe. *Buckeye Madness: The Glorious, Tumultuous, Behind-the-Scenes Story of Ohio State Football.* New York: Simon & Schuster, 2005.

Schoor, Gene. *100 Years of Notre Dame Football: A Century Celebration of the Fighting Irish Tradition.* New York: William Morrow and Co., 1987.

Sharpe, Wilton. *Buckeye Madness: Great Eras in Ohio State Football.* Nashville, Tenn.: Cumberland House, 2005.

Sweeney, Vince. *Always a Badger: The Pat Richter Story.* Black Earth, Wis.: Trails Books, 2005.

Turnbull, Buck. *Stadium Stories: Iowa Hawkeyes.* Guilford, Conn.: Globe Pequot, 2005.

Wilson, Kenneth L., and Jerry Brondfield. *The Big Ten.* Englewood Cliffs, N.J.: Prentice-Hall, 1967.

Wood, Bob. *Big Ten Country: A Journey Through One Football Season.* New York: William Morrow and Co., 1989.

Young, Linda. *Hail to the Orange and Blue! 100 Years of Illinois Football Tradition.* Champaign, Ill.: Sagamore Publishing, 1990.

BIBLIOGRAPHY

NEWSPAPERS/WIRE SERVICES

Ann Arbor News

Arizona Daily Star

The Associated Press

Austin (Texas) American-Statesman

Bloomington (Illinois) Pantagraph

Buckeye Buzz

Champaign News-Gazette

Charleston (South Carolina) Post
   and Courier

Chicago Sun-Times

Chicago Tribune

Cleveland Plain Dealer

Columbus Dispatch

Daily Northwestern

Dayton Daily News

Detroit Free Press

Detroit News

Dubuque Telegraph-Herald

Evansville Courier & Press

Florida Times Union

Fort Lauderdale Sun Sentinel

Fort Wayne Journal-Gazette

Fort Wayne News-Sentinel

Gannett News Service

Gary Post-Tribune

Grand Rapids Press

Hartford Courant

Houston Chronicle

Janesville Gazette

Knight-Ridder Tribune

Los Angeles Times

Madison Capital-Times

Milwaukee Journal Sentinel

Minneapolis Star-Tribune

Omaha World-Herald

Orange County Register

Peoria Journal-Star

Pittsburgh Post-Gazette

St. Louis Post-Dispatch

St. Paul Pioneer Press

St. Petersburg Times

San Antonio Express-News

Seattle Times

South Bend Tribune

USA Today

Washington Post

Wisconsin State Journal

OTHER SOURCES

University media guides and Web sites

www.espn.com

BuckeyeXtra.com

INDEX

INDEX

MORE GREAT
SPORT TITLES FROM
TRAILS BOOKS

After They Were Packers, *Jerry Poling*

Always a Badger: The Pat Richter Story, *Vince Sweeney*

Baseball in Beertown: America's Pastime in Milwaukee, *Todd Mishler*

Badger Sports Trivia Teasers, *Jerry Minnich*

Before They Were the Packers: Green Bay's Town Team Days,
Denis J. Gullickson and Carl Hanson

Boston Red Sox Trivia Teasers, *Richard Pennington*

Chicago Bears Trivia Teasers, *Steve Johnson*

Cold Wars: 40+ Years of Packer-Viking Rivalry, *Todd Mishler*

Denver Broncos Trivia Teasers, *Richard Pennington*

Detroit Red Wings Trivia Teasers, *Richard Pennington*

Green Bay Packers Titletown Trivia Teasers, *Don Davenport*

Mudbaths and Bloodbaths: The Inside Story of the Bears-Packers Rivalry,
Gary D 'Amato and Cliff Christl

New York Yankees Trivia Teasers, *Richard Pennington*

No Bed of Roses: My Sideline View of the Badgers' Return to Greatness,
Chris Kennedy

Packers By the Numbers: Jersey Numbers and the Players Who Wore Them,
John Maxymuk

Vagabond Halfback: The Life and Times of Johnny Blood McNally,
Denis J. Gullickson

For a free catalog, phone, write, or visit us online.

Trails Books
A Division of Big Earth Publishing
923 Williamson Street, Madison, WI 53703
800.258.5830 · www.trailsbooks.com

$$
\begin{array}{r}
8 \\
60\overline{)520.0} \\
48 \\
\overline{00}
\end{array}
$$